Jules William Press JWP

This Book

Old Norse – Old Icelandic: A Concise Introduction is a modern "primer" for learning to read the Icelandic sagas in their original language. This straightforward, easy-to-use primer requires no previous language knowledge. It is designed for self-learning, in-class use, and distance or remote learning. Starting with the first page, students read Old Norse passages from Icelandic sagas as well as episodes from Scandinavian myth and medieval sources. The language and thought of the Viking Age come alive in these critical, Old Norse reading segments. For a free Answer Key to the exercises, visit our website: www.oldnorse.org.

About the Authors

JESSE BYOCK is distinguished research professor of Old Norse and Medieval Scandinavian at UCLA. He specializes in the Viking World: its sagas, history, and archaeology. He earned his Ph.D. from Harvard University and is professor at the UCLA Cotsen Institute of Archaeology. In Iceland, he directs the Mosfell Archaeological Project (MAP) and teaches at the University of Iceland (Háskóli Íslands) in the Department of History and the programs of Medieval Icelandic and Viking Studies.

RANDALL GORDON is a specialist in historical linguistics of Celtic and Germanic Languages, with concentrations on the development and grammar of Old Norse and Old Irish. He received his Ph.D. in Indo-European Studies from UCLA.

www.juleswilliampress.com & www.oldnorse.org

Jules William Press publishes a range of books about the Viking Age. Its series of Old Norse primers, grammars, texts, studies, and audio pronunciation albums answer the needs of the modern student, instructor, and self-learner. The books and materials are purposely affordable and conceived with distance learning in mind. JWP also publishes a series of novels and eBooks as well as archaeological reports about the Viking period.

Old Norse – Old Icelandic
Concise Introduction to the Language of the Sagas

by

Jesse Byock and Randall Gordon

Volume 1 in the Old Norse Icelandic Series

Jules William Press JWP

www.juleswilliampress.com
www.oldnorse.org

Jules William Press

www.Juleswilliampress.com
www.oldnorse.org

Old Norse – Old Icelandic: Concise Introduction to the Language of the Sagas, Volume 1 in the Old Norse Icelandic Series

Paperback ISBN: 978-0-9881764-4-7

eBook ISBN: 978-0-9881764-3-0

Cover design by Basil Arnould Price
Printed in Cambria font

Keywords: Old Norse, Old Icelandic; Icelandic saga, Learn Old Norse, how to learn Old Norse, Icelandic, Norse, Viking, Scandinavia, Germanic languages, Germanic, textbook, Old Norse primer, grammar, language, saga, Altnordisch

About This Old Norse – Old Icelandic "Primer"

This new book answers the need for a concise primer for learning Old Icelandic. It requires no previous foreign language knowledge, and in a straightforward, incremental way, it teaches how to read Icelandic sagas and Old Norse texts in the original. The lessons supply all necessary information (grammar, vocabulary, and exercises) and are designed for in-class teaching, self-instruction, and distance or remote learning. It is a resource for today's students and instructors.

Free Answer Key on www.oldnorse.org

For a free downloadable Answer Key to the exercises in the lessons of this Old Norse–Old Icelandic primer, visit our webpage: www.oldnorse.org.

Arrangement of the Book

Old Norse – Old Icelandic is divided into 17 short lessons. Each lesson opens with a passage in Old Icelandic drawn from sagas or mythological sources. Lessons focus on the grammar and vocabulary necessary to master the reading(s). In this way, original texts determine the instruction, and students master grammatical elements as they are needed. To speed the learning, each lesson contains a short vocabulary of new words and phrases, as well as practice exercises, reinforcing the grammatical explanations. Reading passages are drawn from the following Old Icelandic texts.

Egils saga Skalla-Grímssonar (*The Saga of Egil Skalla-Grimsson*)
Fóstbrœðra saga (*The Saga of the Foster-Brothers*)
Gísla saga Súrssonar (*The Saga of Gisli Sursson*)
Gunnlaugs saga ormstungu (*The Saga of Gunnlaug Serpent-Tongue*)
Hávarðar saga (*The Saga of Havard*)
Heimskringla (*The History of the Kings of Norway*)
Hrafnkels saga Freysgoða (*The Saga of Hrafnkell the Priest of Frey*)
Landnámabók (*Sturlubók*) (*The Book of Settlements* [*Sturla's Book*])
Magnúss saga Erlingssonar (*The Saga of Magnus Erlingsson*)
Njáls saga (*Njal's Saga*)
Óláfs saga Tryggvasonar (*The Saga of Olaf Tryggvason*)
Ragnars saga loðbrókar (*The Saga of Ragnar Lodbrok*)
Snorra Edda (*Snorri's Edda* [*The Prose Edda*])
Vápnfirðinga saga (*The Saga of the Families of Weapon's Fjord*)
Ynglinga saga (*The Saga of the Ynglings*)
Þorsteins þáttr stangarhǫggs (*The Tale of Thorstein Staff-Struck*)

Appendices

The rear of the book contains several helpful appendices:

- a Pronunciation Guide to Old Icelandic (with a discussion of Modern Icelandic pronunciation)
- an extensive Reference Grammar of Old Norse – Old Icelandic
- a full Vocabulary of all Words and Phrases.

Additional Resources

This introductory primer, *Old Norse – Old Icelandic* is complemented by a series of additional texts:

eBook version of the *Old Norse – Old Icelandic: Concise Introduction to the Language of the Sagas* (the primer).

Supplementary Exercises for Old Norse–Old Icelandic. This stand-alone volume of additional exercises augments the exercises found in each lesson of the *Old Norse – Old Icelandic* primer. *Supplementary Exercises* also includes two long mythological tales from *The Prose Edda.* These additional practice readings first recount a strange journey of the gods. Then they tell of events involving Sigurd the Volsung, slayer of the dragon Fafnir. *Supplementary Exercises* features a complete vocabulary with all words and phrases found in the exercises and readings. It is a book useful for anyone learning Old Norse.

***Saga of the Families of Weapon's Fjord* (*Vápnfirðinga saga*)** is a classic Icelandic prose tale of blood feud in Viking Age Iceland. Issues of vengeance, honor, and survival dominate as two rival chieftain families struggle for power in Iceland's East Fjords. This saga edition offers a new translation and includes the original Old Norse text presented in a way that teaches how to read a complete saga in both English and Old Icelandic. The edition contains extensive notes, maps, vocabulary, and cultural explanations. The student has everything necessary to master a saga of feud, violence, and the claims of honor.

The Tale of Thorstein Staff-Struck (***Þorsteins þáttr stangarhǫggs***). This short and not-so-sweet Icelandic *þáttr* ('tale', in this instance a short saga) weighs the role of violence, while exploring insult and the duty of vengeance. *Þorsteins þáttr* captures the essence of the Icelandic sagas but with an unusual twist. This edition offers a new English translation along with the original Old Norse text, extensive vocabulary, detailed notes, and grammar explanations. Here is a compact volume that teaches how to read sagas and to evaluate how these medieval narratives are constructed.

For More Comprehensive Old Norse Textbooks, Including Runes, Sagas, Eddas, and History

Viking Language 1: Learn Old Norse, Runes, and Icelandic Sagas (2nd Edition). *Viking Language 1* is for those who want a more thorough and broad-based volume about the Old Norse language. It includes introductions to the literature, history, and geography of Viking Age Scandinavia (Denmark, Iceland, Norway, and Sweden). *Viking Language 1* also includes a wealth of grammar exercises and reading passages about the different kinds of sagas and core myths. A feature of the *Viking Language* Series (*VL1* and the accompanying *VL2*) is an extensive introduction to Viking Age runes.

Ancient Norwegian Wood Carving, thought to be Óðinn, the one-eyed god.

Viking Language 2: The Old Norse Reader is a broad collection of longer Old Norse readings, including complete sagas, myths, and runic inscriptions. This volume significantly deepens the learning by providing copious examples and explanations of eddic and skaldic verse. We suggest turning to the readings of *Viking Language 2* upon completing Lesson 8 of the *Old Norse –Old Icelandic* primer and lesson 7 of *Viking Language 1*.

Books Co-authored by Jesse Byock & Randall Gordon

Old Norse – Old Icelandic: Concise Introduction to the Language of the sagas. Jules William Press (JWP)

Supplementary Exercises for Old Norse – Old Icelandic. JWP

The Tale of Thorstein Staff-Struck (*Þorsteins saga stangarhǫggs*). JWP

Saga of the Families of Weapon's Fjord (*Vápnfirðinga saga*). JWP

Books by Jesse Byock

Viking Age Iceland. Penguin Books

L'Islande des Vikings. Flammarion, Editions Aubier (France)

La Stirpe di Odino: La Civiltà Vichinga in Islanda. Oscar Mondadori (Italy)

Исландия эпохи викингов. Corpus Books (Russia)

Feud in the Icelandic Saga. University of California Press (UC Press)

ｻｶﾞ ﾉ ｼｬｶｲｶｲｼ ﾁｭｰｾｲｱｲｽﾗﾝﾄﾞ ﾉ ｼｭｳｺｯｶ. Tokai University Press (Japan)

Medieval Iceland: Society, Sagas, and Power. UC Press

Island i sagatiden: Samfund, magt og fejde. C.A. Reitzel (Denmark)

ｱｲｽﾗﾝﾄﾞ ｻｶ Tokai University Press (Japan)

Viking Archaeology in Iceland: Mosfell Archaeological Project. Editors Davide Zori and Jesse Byock. Brepols Publisher, Cursor Mundi

Grettir's Saga. Oxford University Press

The Prose Edda: Norse Mythology. Penguin Books

The Saga of the Volsungs: The Norse Epic of Sigurd the Dragon Slayer. Penguin Books

The Saga of King Hrolf Kraki. Penguin Books

The Viking Language Series (JWP)

Viking Language 1: Learn Old Norse, Runes, and Icelandic Sagas (2nd Edition)

Viking Language 2: The Old Norse Reader

Viking Language 1 Audio Lessons 1-8: Pronounce Old Norse

Viking Language 1 Audio Lessons 9-15: Pronounce Old Norse

Altnordisch 1: Die Sprache der Wikinger, Runen, und isländischen Sagas (*Altnordisch 1*, *Viking Language 2*, and the pronunciation MP3 downloads available on Amazon.de)

Table of Contents
for *Old Norse – Old Icelandic:* *Concise Introduction to the Language of the Sagas*

---

[1] Original reading passages from sagas and myths are indicated by bold type. The Old Norse word ***ór*** (modern Icelandic *úr*) means 'from'.

DEDICATION

This book is dedicated to Kenneth Chapman, whose ideas, examples, and approach to teaching Old Icelandic were the inspiration for this work. Ken was a brilliant linguist, a wonderful friend, and a generous teacher who thoroughly enjoyed sharing his great knowledge and helping students and colleagues. Ken passed away as we were beginning the project, and we greatly miss him.

ACKNOWLEDGEMENTS

We thank Basil A. Price, Chad Laidlow, Kevin Elliott, Ágúst Guðmundsson, Cassandra Ruiz, Jack Hartley, Gunnar Karlsson, Meg Morrow, Helgi Þorláksson, and Ilya Sverdlov. In one way or another, they assisted us with the completion of this book.

The Old Icelandic Alphabet, Spelling, and Vowels

a, á, b, d, ð, e, é, f, g, h, i, í, j, k, l, m, n, o, ó, p, r, s, t, u, ú, v, x, y, ý, z, þ, æ, œ, ǫ(ö), ø

The Latin alphabet adopted by the Icelanders in the 11th century was probably modeled on Anglo-Saxon writing brought to the northern lands by English missionaries and clerics during the Viking Age. From this source, Icelanders may have learned the use of ink and parchment. By the 12th century, Icelandic writers were utilizing the newly acquired Latin alphabet and writing vernacular texts in considerable numbers, However, they did not follow a standardized spelling.

The variety of spellings in the manuscripts greatly complicated the task of making Old Icelandic/Old Norse vocabularies and dictionaries when the sagas and Old Norse were rediscovered by European and British scholars in the late 1700s. Scholars, in the early 1800s, addressed this issue by adopting a normalized Old Icelandic spelling and alphabetic order. The reading passages and vocabularies in this current book follow the normalized spelling as found in the standard Icelandic *Íslenzk fornrit* saga editions. This spelling convention, which is found in most of today's saga editions and dictionaries, maintains the medieval distinction between the vowels *æ* and *œ*, and *ǫ* and *ø*.

In the Old Norse/Icelandic alphabet, long vowels are distinguished from short vowels by an acute accent (for ex., long *é* and short *e*). The long vowels *æ*, *œ*, *ø*, and *ǫ* (umlauted *a,* which becomes modern *ö*) are listed at the end of the Icelandic alphabet. The letters *c*, *q*, and *w* are occasionally found in manuscripts, but these foreign letters have not been adopted into the standardized alphabet.

Abbreviations

acc.	accusative	num.	numeral
adj.	adjective	obj.	object
adv.	adverb	OI	Old Icelandic
art.	article	ON	Old Norse
comp.	comparative	ord.	ordinal
conj.	Conjunction	part.	participle
Dan.	Danish	pers.	personal
dat.	dative	pl.	plural
def.	definite	poet.	poetical usage
dem.	demonstrative	poss.	possessive
dir. obj.	direct object	ppart.	past participle
f.ex.	for example	pref.	prefix
fem., f.	feminine	prep.	preposition
gen.	genitive	pres.	present
i.e.	that is	pret.	preterite
impers.	impersonal	pron.	pronoun
ind. obj.	indirect object	refl.	reflexive
indef.	indefinite	rel.	relative
indic.	indicative	R.S.	reading selection
inf.	infinitive	sing., sg.	singular
int.	interrogative	subj.	subject
intrans.	intransitive	subjunct.	subjunctive
lit.	literally	superl.	superlative
masc., m.	masculine	Swed.	Swedish
NB	Nota Bene	trans.	transitive
neut., n.	neuter	var.	variant
nom.	nominative	vb.	verb
Norw.	Norwegian	w.	with
MI.	Modern Icelandic		

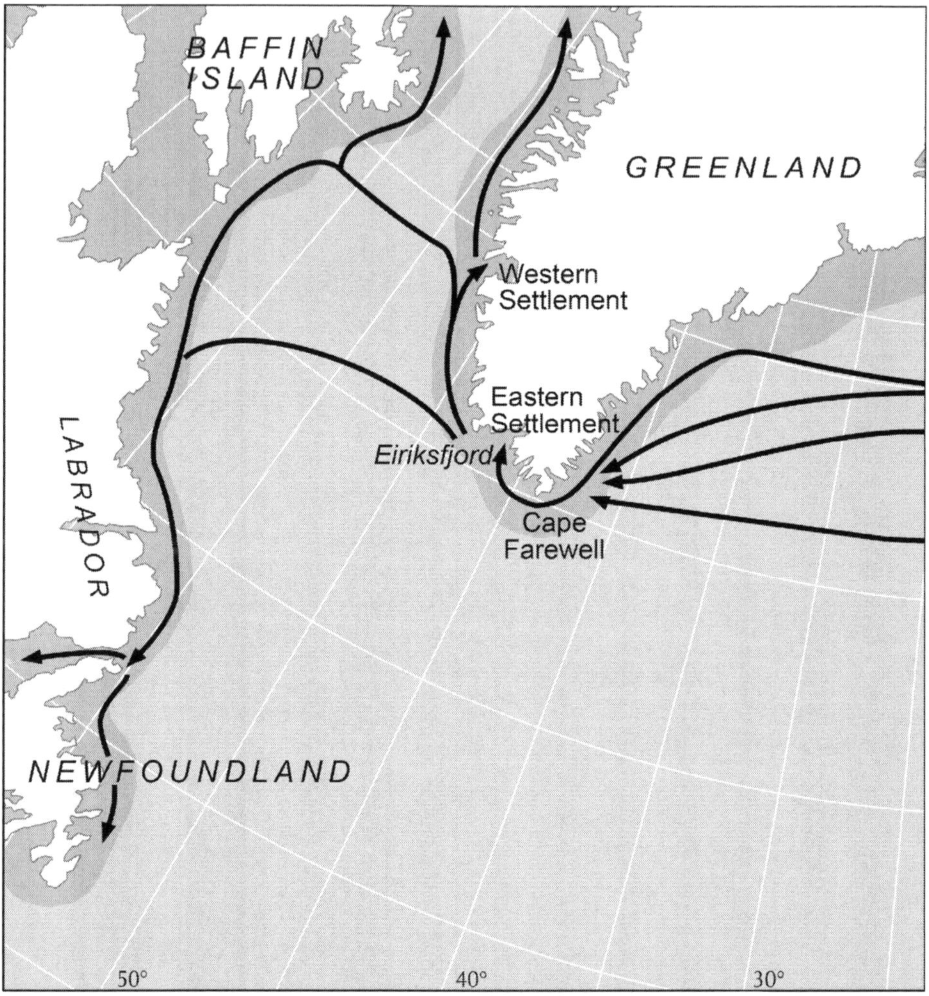

The Norse Settlement (*Landnám*) of the North Atlantic and the Spread of Old Norse Across the Atlantic. The islands of Shetland, Orkney, and the Faroes were known to Norse seamen by the 8th century. Iceland was discovered and first settled in the 9th century during the Viking Age (ca. 780–1100 CE). Most settlers, who were called *landnámsmenn*, a term that includes women, came from Norway, but some arrived from other regions of mainland Scandinavia, as well as from the Viking colonies in Ireland, Scotland, Shetland, Orkney and the Hebrides. The settlers were mostly Old Norse speakers, but there were also Celts among them, especially women.

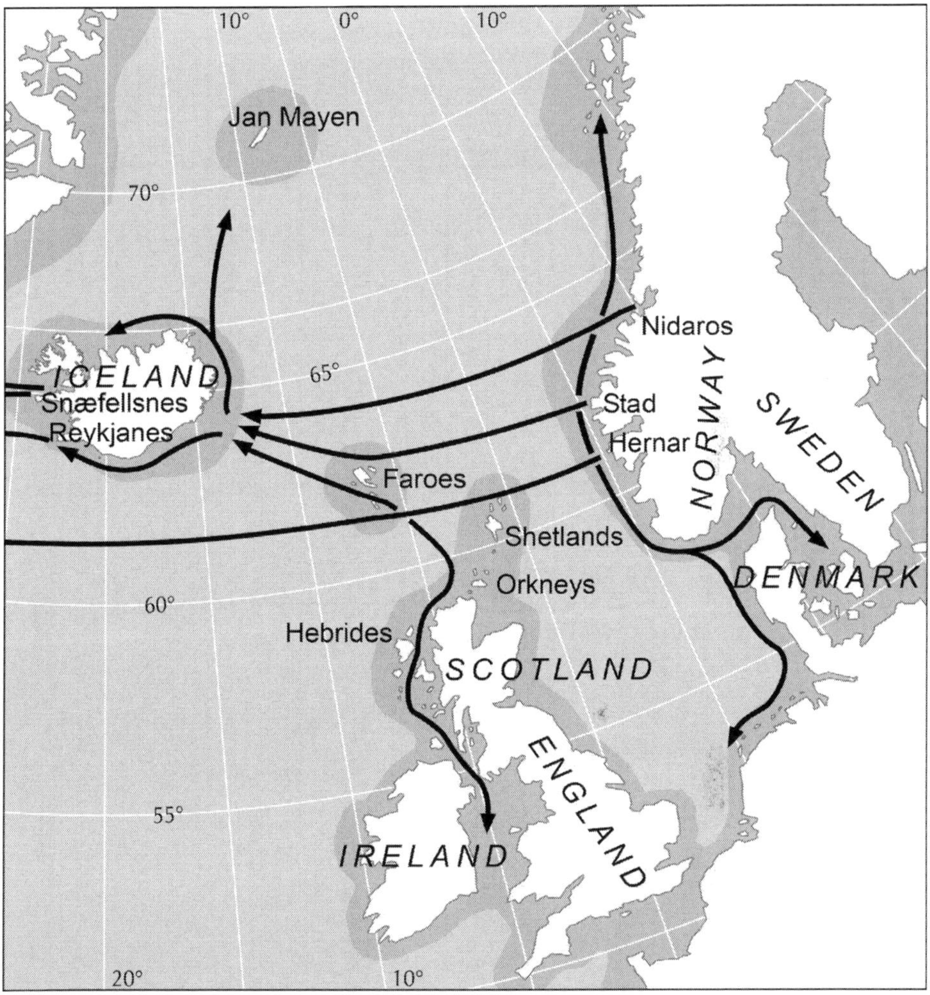

From Iceland, the Old Norse language was carried over seas by explorers and settlers to Greenland and Vínland (North America). The map shows the major sailing routes across the North Atlantic, connecting the large geographical region where Old Norse was spoken. Old Icelandic, the language of the sagas, is the dialect that developed in Iceland from the variants of Old Norse brought to the island by the Viking Age settlers.

LESSON 1

Ór *Gunnlaugs sǫgu ormstungu* (1. kap.)

(From the *Saga of Gunnlaug Serpent-Tongue*, Chap. 1)

Þorsteinn hét maðr; hann var Egilsson, Skalla-Grímssonar, Kveld-Úlfssonar, hersis ór Nóregi; en Ásgerðr hét móðir Þorsteins ok var Bjarnardóttir. Þorsteinn bjó at Borg í Borgarfirði; hann var auðigr at fé ok hǫfðingi mikill, vitr maðr ok hógværr ok hófsmaðr um alla hluti.

A man was named Thorstein; he was the son of Egil, the son of Skalla-Grim, son of Kveld-Ulf, a chieftain from Norway; and Thorstein's mother was named Asgerd and was the daughter of Bjorn. Thorstein lived at Borg in Borgarfjord; he was wealthy and a great leader, a wise man and gentle and a man of moderation in all respects.

1.1. Stems and endings.

	root (+ suffix)	
word =	stem	+ ending

Most words in Old Norse are composed of two primary parts, a **stem** and an **ending**. The stem can also have two parts, a **root** and a **suffix**. The root is the most basic part of the word. If no suffix is attached to the root, then the stem is the same as the root.

1.2. Cases of Old Icelandic.

Cases play a large role in Old Icelandic. An easy way to understand cases is to consider English pronouns. Today's English inherited its pronouns from Old English (Anglo-Saxon), which was closely related to Old Norse.[2] Take for example English 'I' and 'me'. Both refer to the **first person**, that is the person who is currently speaking or writing, but they cannot be used in the same contexts. You say '**I** hit the ball' but not '**Me** hit the ball', and you say 'John saw **me**', but not 'John saw **I**'.

'I' can only be used as the subject of a sentence, and 'me' can only be used as an object. 'I' and 'me' show different cases of the same word: 'I' is in the **subject case** and 'me' is in the **object case**. Other subject-object pronoun pairs are 'he/him', 'she/her', 'we/us', and 'they/them'.

In addition to subject and object cases, English pronouns have a **possessive** case, which indicates belonging.[3] Hence, the possessive

---

[2] Medieval speakers of these two languages could, with some effort, understand each other.

[3] The term "possessive" does not necessarily indicate literal ownership, but some sort of special association. For example, when you say "**my** clothes", you

pronoun 'my' corresponds to the first person 'I/me', and likewise the other possessive pronouns 'his', her', 'our', and 'their'.

These series of subject, object, and possessive pronouns ('I/me/my', 'he/him/his', etc.) illustrate the case system of modern English. Nouns in English also have cases. Nouns do not show any difference in form between subjects and objects, but have a distinct possessive form spelled with -'s: f.ex., 'ship**'s**', 'Thorstein**'s**'.

In Old Icelandic, every pronoun, noun, and adjective must be in one of four cases: nominative (nom.), accusative (acc.), dative (dat.), or genitive (gen.). Principal uses of the four Old Icelandic or Old Norse cases are the following:

- **Nominative case** is used for the **subject** of a sentence. For example, in the sentence ***Þórólfr*** *sýndi Eiríki skip* '**Thorolf** showed (to) Eirik a ship', *Þórólfr* is the subject and in the nominative case.
- **Accusative case** distinguishes the **direct object** of a verb. In the sentence *Þórólfr sýndi Eiríki* ***skip*** 'Thorolf showed (to) Eirik a **ship'**, *skip* is the direct object of the action of the verb *sýndi* 'showed' and is in the accusative case.
- **Dative case** designates the **indirect object** of a verb. For example, in *Þórólfr sýndi* ***Eiríki*** *skip* 'Thorolf showed (to) **Eirik** a ship', *Eiríki* '(to) Eirik' is the indirect object of the verb *sýndi* 'showed' and is in the dative case. As this example implies, the preposition 'to' or 'for' sometimes accompanies the indirect object in English, but not in Old Icelandic.
- **Genitive case** signals belonging. For example, if the ship belongs to Thorstein, it would be ***Þorsteins*** *skip* '**Thorstein's** ship'. The Icelandic genitive *Þorstein**s*** corresponds to the English possessive 'Thorstein**'s**'. Both Icelandic -*s* and English -'s are the same ending in origin. They are inherited from their common ancestor, Northwest Germanic.[4] (The apostrophe in English is merely a spelling convention to distinguish the possessive from the plural in writing.)

As a rule, whenever you see a noun, pronoun or adjective in Old Icelandic, it is best to determine its case in order to understand its role in the sentence. For example, consider the sentence *Í þann tíma réð fyrir Danmǫrku Sigurðr hringr.*

---

may mean that you "own" your clothes, but when you say "**my** boss", you do not mean you "own" your boss.

[4] The separation between the western group of Northwest Germanic dialects, from which Old English arose, and the northern group, from which Old Icelandic arose, began to be distinguishable around the year 200 CE. The separation was complete by around 500 CE.

Even if you do not understand the meaning, you can quickly determine that the phrase *Sigurðr hringr* (Sigurd Ring) is the subject of the sentence (in spite of the fact that it is placed at the end). This is because *Sigurðr* and *hringr* are both in the nominative case. The sentence means 'At that time Sigurd Ring ruled over Denmark.'

The chart below gives the singular declension of the masculine noun *hestr* 'horse' and the masculine forms of the adjective *góðr* 'good'.

	hestr (masc. noun)	**góðr (adj. in masc.)**
***Sg** nom*	hestr	góðr
acc	hest	góðan
dat	hesti	góðum
gen	hests	góðs

Such charts illustrate the pattern, or **paradigm** (from a Greek word for 'model'), that these words follow in forming their cases. The paradigm of *hestr* is typical of many masculine nouns such as *hringr* 'ring' and *úlfr* 'wolf', and the paradigm of *góðr* is typical of adjectives such as *ágætr* 'excellent' and *hvítr* 'white'.

1.3. No indefinite article.

There is no indefinite article in Icelandic. When translating into English, the indefinite article, if it is necessary, must be supplied. For example, the sentence *Hann var hǫfðingi mikill ok vitr maðr* is translated 'He was **a** great leader and **a** wise man.'

1.4. Strong nouns and adjectives: Masculine nominative singular.

The nominative singular of one group of masculine nouns and adjectives (traditionally called **strong** masculine nouns and adjectives) is formed with the ending *-r*. This ending is added directly to the stem of the noun or adjective: hence *auðig-**r***.

Some masculine nouns such as *Þorstei**nn*** and *Egi**ll*** double the final stem consonant instead of adding *-r*. This doubling is the result of predictable rules discussed in section 2.1.

1.5. Strong nouns: Masculine genitive singular.

The genitive singular of strong masculine nouns is formed with either the ending *-s* (as mentioned earlier) or the ending *-ar*. The ending *-s* is by far the more common of the two. As in the case of the nominative ending, the genitive endings are added directly to the stem: *Gunnlaug-**s**, Egil-**s**, Þorstein-**s**, son-**ar**, Bjarn-**ar***.

The genitive can be expressed in two different ways in English, by adding the ending -'s or by using the preposition 'of': For example, *Gunnlaugs saga* means both 'Gunnlaug's saga' and 'the saga of Gunnlaug'. Old Icelandic, however, has only one way to make a genitive, always adding a genitive ending like *-s* and *-ar* in the singular and *-a* in the plural: *Gunnlaug**s** saga* 'Gunnlaug's Saga', *Hávarð**ar** saga* 'Havard's Saga', *Fóstbræð**ra** saga* 'Saga of the Foster-Brothers'.

1.6. Strong adjectives: Genitive singular masculine.

Adjectives describe people and things. As descriptive words, Old Norse adjectives themselves do not belong to a specific gender class, but decline to match the noun they modify. The details of adjective declensions will be described in the coming lessons. In the case of masculine strong adjectives, *-s* is the only possible genitive singular ending, f.ex., *gǫfug**s*** and *ágæt**s*** in the following passage:

Ór *Fóstbrœðra sǫgu* (2. kap.)

(From the *Saga of the Foster-Brothers*, Chap. 2)

Hon var dóttir Álfs, **gǫfugs** manns ok **ágæts**.	She was the daughter of Álf, a **noble** and **excellent** man.

1.7. Agreement of adjectives with nouns; noun apposition.

Adjectives agree (meaning they match) in case, number, and gender with the noun they modify. For example, in the phrase *Álfs, gǫfugs manns ok ágæts*, the two adjectives (*gǫfugs, ágæts*) and the noun *manns* are all in the genitive case. They are in agreement with the personal name *Álfs* (nom. *Álfr*), which is in the genitive because of its relationship to the noun *dóttir* (Alf's daughter).

Apposition. The first Reading Selection (R.S.) includes the sentence: *hann var Egilsson, Skalla-Grímssonar, Kveld-Úlfssonar hersis.* Such sentences, which are very common in Old Norse, illustrate what is known as **apposition**. Apposition involves pairs of nouns (or noun phrases) in which the second noun more fully identifies the first noun. An important observation is that both nouns are always in the same case. The sentence above offers three such noun pairs:

- *Skalla-Grímsson**ar*** (gen.) is in the same case as *Egil**s*** (gen.);
- *Kveld-Úlfsson**ar*** (gen.) is in the same case as *Skalla-Grím**s*** (gen.);
- *hersi**s*** (gen.) is in the same case as *Kveld-Úlf**s*** (gen.).

As mentioned in 1.5, *-ar* and *-s* are the two possible endings of masculine genitive singular nouns.

1.8. Review paradigms: Nom. and gen. sing. of strong masc. nouns and adjectives.

	Noun	Adjective
nom	-r (for modifications see 2.1)	-r (for modifications see 2.1)
gen	-s, -ar	-s

1.9. Prepositions: A first look.

Prepositions are small words such as 'to', 'from', 'with', 'of', etc. that precede a noun or pronoun and show how the noun or pronoun is related to the rest of the sentence. A preposition and its object (the noun or pronoun that follows) form a prepositional phrase. The preposition requires its object to be in a particular case: f.ex., *um* ('about') takes the accusative case, and *ór* ('from') takes the dative.

In the title to the R.S., the preposition *ór* changes the form of the noun from ***saga*** (nominative) to ***sǫgu*** (dative): ***ór*** *Gunnlaugs* ***sǫgu*** 'from the Saga of Gunnlaug'. Prepositions are found throughout the language and are discussed in later lessons.

Exercises

1. Identify the stem and ending of each of the following adjectives, nouns, and personal names.

Ex.: ágætr:	stem *ágæt-*	ending *-r*
ágæts:	stem ______	ending ____
Gunnlaugr:	stem ______	ending ____
Gunnlaugs:	stem ______	ending ____
hersir:	stem ______	ending ____
hersis:	stem ______	ending ____
hógværr:	stem ______	ending ____
hógværs:	stem ______	ending ____
sonr:	stem ______	ending ____
sonar:	stem ______	ending ____

2. Identify the case (nom. or gen.) of the adjectives, nouns, and personal names indicated in bold type.

Sigurðr (____) hét **maðr** (____); hann var Bjarnarson, **Þorsteinssonar** (____), **hersis** (____) ór Nóregi, en Ásgerðr hét móðir **Sigurðar** (____). Hann var **ágætr** (____) maðr og **hógværr** (____).

3. Decline the masc. nouns *hringr* 'ring' and *úlfr* 'wolf' in the sing., and the adjectives *ágætr* 'excellent' and *hvítr* 'white' in the masc. sing., following the paradigms of *hestr* and *góðr* given in 1.2.

	Masc. nouns		Masc. adjectives	
nom	*hringr*	*úlfr*	*ágætr*	*hvítr*
acc	______	______	______	______
dat	______	______	______	______
gen	______	______	______	______

4. Vocabulary training.

Across
3 lived, dwelt
4 rich, wealthy
6 excellent
7 local chieftain
8 wise

Down
1 daughter
2 noble
3 brother
5 great
7 was named

Supplementary Exercises for Old Norse – Old Icelandic

For those who want to sharpen their skills, we have assembled a workbook entitled *Supplementary Exercises for Old Norse – Old Icelandic.* This second volume in the Old Norse Icelandic Series offers a wealth of additional exercises along with an answer key and full vocabulary. There are also Old Norse readings drawn from the *Saga of Ragnar Lodbrok*, recounting Ragnar's attack on England and his death in the snake pit, as well as passages from *The Prose Edda*, telling of the Norse gods and the legendary hero Sigurd the Volsung, slayer of the dragon Fafnir.

Vocabulary

alla *acc pl masc of* **allr**
allr *adj* all
at *prep* [*w dat*] at; with respect to
auðigr *adj* rich, wealthy
ágætr *adj* excellent
Álfr *m* Alf ('Elf') (*personal name*)
Ásgerðr *f* Asgerd (*personal name*)
Bjarnardóttir *f* daughter of Bjorn
bjó (*inf* **búa**) *vb* lived, dwelt
Bjǫrn (*gen* Bjarnar) *m* Bjorn ('Bear') (*personal name*)
Borg *f* Borg (*place name*)
Borgarfjǫrðr *m* 'Borg's Fjord', a fjord in Western Iceland (*place name*)
bróðir *m* brother
búa (*past* bjó) *vb* live (in a place),

dwell
Danmǫrk (*dat* Danmǫrku) *f* Denmark
dóttir *f* daughter
Egill (*gen* Egils) *m* Egil (*personal name*)
Egilsson *m* son of Egil
Eiríkr *m* Eirik (*personal name*)
en *conj* but; and (on the other hand)
fé *n* property, wealth; cattle
fóstbróðir *m* foster-brother
fóstbrœðra *gen pl* (*see* **fóstbróðir**) of the foster-brothers
góðr *adj* good
Gunnlaugr *m* Gunnlaug (*personal name*)
gǫfugr *adj* noble
hann *pron* he
heita (*past* hét) *vb* be named, called
hersir (*gen* -is) *m* local chieftain
hestr *m* horse
hét (*inf* **heita**) *vb* was named, called
hlutr (*acc pl* hluti) *m* part
hon *pron* she
hófsmaðr *m* man of moderation and restraint
hógværr *adj* gentle
hringr *m* ring
hvítr *adj* white
hǫfðingi *m* leader
í *prep* [*w dat*] in
kveld *n* evening
Kveld-Úlfr (*gen* Kveld-Úlfs) *m* Kveld-Ulf ('Evening-Wolf') (*personal name*)
Kveld-Úlfssonnar *gen* of the son of Kveld-Ulf
maðr (*gen* manns) *m* man; person
mikill *adj* great
móðir *f* mother
Nóregr *m* Norway
ok *conj* and (in addition)
ormr *m* serpent, snake
ormstunga *f* 'Serpent's Tongue' (*nick-name*)
ór *prep* [*w dat*] out of, from
saga *f* story
sǫgu *dat sg of* **saga**
Sigurðr (*gen* -ar) *m* Sigurd (*personal name*)
Skalla-Grímr (*gen* Skalla-Gríms) *m* Skalla-Grim (*personal name*)
Skalla-Grímssonar *gen* of the son of Skalla-Grim
skip *n* ship
son(r) (*gen* sonar) *m* son
sýna (-d-) *vb* show
sýndi (*inf* **sýna**) *vb* showed
tunga *f* tongue
um *prep* [*w acc*] about, in regard to
úlfr *m* wolf
var (*inf* **vera**) *vb* was
vera (*past* var) *vb* be
vitr (*gen* vitrs) *adj* wise
Þorsteinn (*gen* Þorsteins) *m* Thorstein (*personal name*)
Þórólfr *m* Thorolf (*personal name*)

PHRASES

auðigr at fé wealthy
ór Nóregi from Norway
um alla hluti in all respects
í [__]firði in [__]fjord (f.ex., *í **Borgar**firði* 'in Borgar Fjord')
ór [__] sǫgu from the saga of [__], from [__]'s saga (f.ex., *ór **Gunnlaugs** sǫgu* 'from the saga of Gunnlaug' or 'from Gunnlaug's saga')
[__]son the son of [__] (f.ex., ***Egils**son* 'the son of Egil')
[__]dóttir the daughter of [__] (f.ex., ***Bjarnar**dóttir* 'the daughter of Bjorn')

LESSON 2

Ór *Hrafnkels sǫgu Freysgoða* (2. kap.)

(From the *Saga of Hrafnkell the Priest of Frey*, Chap. 2)

En þá er Hrafnkell hafði land numit á Aðalbóli, þá efldi hann blót mikil. Hrafnkell lét gera hof mikit. Hrafnkell elskaði eigi annat goð meir en Frey. Hrafnkell bygði allan dalinn ok gaf mǫnnum land, en vildi þó vera yfirmaðr þeira ok tók goðorð yfir þeim. Við þetta var lengt nafn hans ok kallaðr Freysgoði, ok var ójafnaðarmaðr mikill.	And when Hrafnkell had taken land at Adalbol, then he performed great sacrifices. Hrafnkell had a large temple built. Hrafnkell loved no other god more than Frey. Hrafnkell occupied the whole valley and gave land to people, and wanted though to be their leader and became a *goði* over them. With this his name was lengthened and [he was] called the *goði* of Frey, and [he] was a very unjust man.

2.1. Special stem rules.

Two special stem rules affect the specific form of the nominative ending -*r* of strong masculine nouns and pronouns. These rules reflect the natural patterns of speech that occurred especially when people spoke rapidly. The patterns simplify difficult sequences of sound by smoothing out the articulation. The changes depend on the length of the vowel (whether short or long) that appears in the stem to which the ending is added and whether the vowel is stressed.

Short		Long
i	—	í
y	—	ý
e	—	é
ø	—	œ
–		æ
a	—	á
ǫ		–
o	—	ó
u	—	ú

The table at right shows the short and long vowels of Old Icelandic. The long vowel is simply a longer version of the short vowel.[5] The short vowels are represented each by a single, simple letter, while each long vowel either has an acute accent (´) or is a combination of two letters, called a **ligature** (*æ* and *œ*).[6] There is no short equivalent of *æ* and no long equivalent of *ǫ*.

---

[5] Vowels in Modern Icelandic have changed somewhat; f.ex., ***á*** is no longer simply a lengthened version of ***a*** as it was in the medieval period, but now sounds similar to **ou** in English '**ou**t'. Consonants have scarcely changed from the medieval to the Modern Icelandic. Overall the changes in pronunciation from Old to Modern Icelandic are relatively small for such a long period of time. (For more information, see Appendix 1. Pronunciation Guide to Old Icelandic (With a Discussion of Modern Icelandic Pronunciation).

[6] These ligatures were originally pronounced as single long vowels. In modern Icelandic they have merged into a vowel sound similar to the **ai** of English

Stress is much simpler in Icelandic than in English. In English, the stressed syllable (i.e., the most forcefully pronounced syllable) may be any syllable of a word; compare the words '**ta**-ble', 're-**spect**', '**au**-to-mo-bile', 'a-**part**-ment', 'o-ver-**whelm**'. In Icelandic, the stress almost always falls on the first syllable of the word stem: ***her**-sir*, ***mó**-ðir*, ***hǫf**-ðing-i*, ***hófs**-mað-r*, etc. A vowel will therefore generally be stressed if it is in the first syllable of the word, and unstressed if it is not. For example, the vowel *-i-* is stressed in ***vin**-r*, but unstressed in ***E**-gill*.

Now we can explain the two special stem rules that affect the nominative singular ending of strong masculine nouns and adjectives ending originally in *-r*.

Special Stem Rules:

1. If the stem ends in *-l-*, *-n-* or *-s-* preceded by a long vowel (or diphthong) or an unstressed short vowel, this final stem consonant is doubled, the second consonant taking the place of the ending *-r*: *ljós-**s*** (adj. 'light'), *væn-**n*** (adj. 'handsome'), *Þorstein-**n***, *mikil-**l***, *Egil-**l***. We say that the ending *-r* **assimilates** to the final consonant of the stem.

The *-r* does not change in the following situations:

- If *-l-*, *-n-* or *-s-* is preceded by a stressed short vowel, the ending *-r* is added as usual: *dal-**r*** 'valley,' *vin-**r*** 'friend.'
- If the stem ends in *-r-* preceded by a vowel, the ending *-r* is added as usual: *hógvær-**r***.

2. If the stem ends in *-r-* preceded by a consonant, the ending *-r* is not added. For example, the final *-r* of the adjective *vit**r*** 'wise' belongs to the stem, and is not the nominative singular masculine ending (which is dropped). That the *–r* belongs to the stem is illustrated by the genitive singular *vitr-**s***, which adds the genitive –s. Another example is the adjective *fag**r*** 'fair, beautiful' (with genitive singular *fagr-**s***). This rule simplifies consonant clusters (like *-trr* and *-grr*) that would be hard to pronounce.

2.2. Other uses of the genitive.

In addition to denoting possession or belonging (1.2), the genitive case in Old Icelandic has two other very important uses:

- Certain prepositions require that their object (the noun or pronoun that follows it) take the genitive case. Two such prepositions are *til* 'to' and *milli* 'between'. (The first of these is by far the more important.) If we wish to say 'to Thorstein' in Old Icelandic, we must use the genitive form of *Þorsteinn*: hence *til Þorstein**s***.

'**ai**sle'. This is a sequence of two vowel sounds, a short **a** (as in 'b**a**r') which glides to a short **i** (as in 'b**i**d'), but it functions as a single vowel. Such vowel combinations are called **diphthongs**, and count the same as long vowels for the sake of these rules. Other examples of diphthongs in Old Icelandic are *au*, *ei*, *ey*.

- Certain verbs require that their direct objects take the genitive case instead of the accusative. For instance, the verb *þurfa* 'to need' takes the genitive: *þeir þurfa hersis* 'they need a chieftain'. The direct object *hersis* 'chieftain' must appear in the genitive, not the accusative. It is helpful to think of the meaning as 'have need of'.

It is important to know that verbs of asking require that the thing asked for must take the genitive, as in a marriage proposal, one person asking for the other. *Ásgerðr biðr Þorsteins* 'Asgerd asks for Thorstein'. This verb appears in a reading selection in Lesson 9.

2.3. Strong nouns: Masculine accusative and dative singular.

- The accusative singular of strong masculine nouns has no ending: *konung* 'king' (nom. *konungr*), *dal* 'valley, dale' (nom. *dalr*).
- The dative ending is usually *-i*: *konung**i***; we have already encountered two datives in R.S. 1, *Nóreg**i*** and *firð**i***. In some instances, there is no ending in the dative: *bekk* 'bench', *dal* 'valley, dale' (the acc. and dat. are the same).

2.4. Strong adjectives: Accusative and dative singular masculine.

- The accusative singular masculine ending of strong adjectives is *-an*: *ágæt**an***, *góð**an***.
- The dative is *-um*: *ágæt**um***, *góð**um***.

2.5. Review paradigms: Endings of masc. sing. strong nouns and adjectives (see 1.8).

	Noun	Adjective
nom	-r (see 2.1)	-r (see 2.1)
acc	–	-an
dat	-i, –	-um
gen	-s, -ar	-s

2.6. The noun *maðr*.

The noun *maðr* is irregular in that its stem *mann-* changes to *mað-* in the nominative singular. This noun is also irregular in other cases. Since it is one of the most frequent nouns in Old Icelandic, its different forms are best learned early. Here is a complete paradigm in the singular and plural.

	Sg	Pl
nom	maðr	menn
acc	mann	menn
dat	manni	mǫnnum
gen	manns	manna

Exercises

1. Fill in the appropriate endings.

Grím__ var mikil__ mað__. Hann var Þorstein__son, Egil__son___.

2. Repeat the sentence from exercise **1**, with the following changes.

a. Make Grim the son of Egil and Egil the son of Thorstein.

____

b. Change the sentence to be about Egil, and make Egil the son of Grim and Grim the son of Thorstein.

____

c. Change the sentence to be about Thorstein, and make Thorstein the son of Egil and Egil the son of Grim.

____

3. Fill in the appropriate endings.

Ásgerðr var dóttir Úlf___, mikil___ mann___ ok auðig___.

Hann var hersi___, ágæt___ mað___ ok gǫfug___.

4. Repeat the first sentence of exercise **3**, with the following changes.

a. Replace *mikill* with *hógværr* and *auðigr* with *vitr*.

____

b. Replace *mikill* with *ríkr* 'powerful' and *auðigr* with *vænn* 'handsome'.

____

5. Vocabulary training.

Across

1 took, seized
3 wished, wanted
4 inhabit, dwell
8 fair, beautiful
10 make, build
11 name
12 valley, dale

Down

2 call, name
5 give
6 land
7 they
9 man, person

Vocabulary

Aðalból *n* Adalbol (*place name*)
allan *acc sg masc of* **allr**
allr *adj* all
annarr (*n* annat) *adj* other, another
á *prep* [*w dat*] on; at
blót (*pl* blót) *n* sacrifice
bygði (*inf* **byggja**) *vb* inhabited
byggja (*past* bygði) *vb* inhabit, dwell
dalr *m* valley, dale
dalinn = **dal** (*acc sg of* **dalr**) + **-inn** (*art*) the valley
efla (*past* efldi) *vb* make, perform
efldi (*inf* **efla**) *vb* made, performed
eigi *adv* not; no
elska (-að-) *vb* love; be fond of
elskaði (*inf* **elska**) *vb* loved
en *conj* but; and (on the other hand); *w comp* than
er *conj* when
fagr (*gen* fagrs) *adj* fair, beautiful
Freyr *m* Frey (*mythological name*, one of the Vanir)
Freysgoði *m* 'Frey's Chief' (*nickname*)
gaf (*inf* **gefa**) *vb* gave
gefa (*past* gaf) *vb* give
gera *vb* make, build
goð *n* god, one of the pagan gods
goði *m* chief (and priest)
goðorð *n* chieftainship, rank and authority of a **goði**
hafa (*past* hafði) *vb* have
hafði (*inf* **hafa**) *vb* had
hans *poss pron* his
hof *n* temple
Hrafnkell *m* Hrafnkel (*personal name*)
-inn *art* the (*suffixed to noun*)
kalla (-að-) *vb* call, name
kallaðr (*inf* **kalla**) *ppart* called (*nom sg masc*)
land *n* land
láta (*past* lét) *vb* let, allow; [*w inf*] have something done
lengja (*ppart* -dr) *vb* lengthen
lengt (*inf* **lengja**) *ppart* lengthened (*nom/acc sg neut*)
lét (*inf* **láta**) *vb* let, allowed; caused to be done
ljóss *adj* light
maðr (*gen* manns) *m* man; person, human being
meir *comp adv* (*see* **mjǫk**) more
mikill (*n sg* mikit; *n pl* mikil) *adj* big, great
milli *prep* [*w gen*] between
mjǫk (*comp* meir[r]) *adv* much
mǫnnum *dat sg and pl of* **maðr**
nafn *n* name
nema (*ppart* numit) *vb* take
numit (*inf* **nema**) *ppart* taken (*nom/acc sg neut*)
ok *conj* and (in addition)
ójafnaðarmaðr *m* unjust man, quarrelsome and overbearing, difficult to deal with
ríkr *adj* powerful, mighty
taka (*past* tók) *vb* take, seize
til *prep* [*w gen*] to
tók (*inf* **taka**) *vb* took, seized
var (*inf* **vera**) *vb* was
vera (*past* var) *vb* be
við *prep* [*w acc*] with, according to
vildi (*inf* **vilja**) *vb* wished, wanted
vilja (*past* vildi) *vb* wish, want
vinr (*gen* vinar) *m* friend
vænn *adj* fine, handsome, beautiful
yfir *prep* [*w acc/dat*] over, above
yfirmaðr *m* leader, chieftain
þá *adv* then
þeim *dat pl pron* (*see* **þeir**) them
þeir (*dat* þeim) *m pl pron* they
þeira *poss pron* their
þetta *dem pron* this (*nom/acc sg neut*)
þurfa *vb* [*w gen*] need, have need of
þó *adv* yet, though, nevertheless

Phrases

lét gera had built
þá er *conj* when

LESSON 3

Ór *Egils sǫgu Skalla-Grímssonar* (50. kap.)

(From the *Saga of Egil Skalla-Grimsson*, Chap. 50)

Elfráðr inn ríki réð fyrir Englandi; hann var fyrstr einvaldskonungr yfir Englandi; þat var á dǫgum Haralds ins hárfagra, Nóregs konungs. Eptir hann var konungr í Englandi sonr hans Játvarðr; hann var faðir Aðalsteins ins sigrsæla, fóstra Hákonar ins góða.	Alfred the powerful ruled over England; he was the first sole ruler (monarch) over (all of) England; that was in the days of Harald the fair-haired, king of Norway. After him his son Edward was king of England; he was the father of Athelstane the victorious, foster-father of Hakon the good.

3.1. Definite article: Singular masculine.

The chart at right declines the def. art. in the sing. masc. The nom. and gen. sing., *inn* and *ins*, correspond to strong nouns and adjectives ending in *-nn* (f.ex., *Þorsteinn*, *vænn*). The acc. and dat., however, are different from the acc. and dat. of strong nouns and adjectives: the acc. is *inn* (identical to the nom.) and the dat. is *inum*.

nom	inn
acc	inn
dat	inum
gen	ins

3.2. Weak adjectives: Singular masculine.

When an adj. is preceded by the def. art. or another limiting word (a demonstrative pronoun or possessive adj.), it is traditionally called **weak**. The endings of weak adjectives differ from those of strong adjectives. They are *-i* for the nom. sing. masc. and *-a* for the other sing. masc. cases: nom. *inn rík**i***, acc. *inn ágæt**a***, dat. *inum fagr**a***, gen. *ins góð**a***.

nom	-i
acc	-a
dat	-a
gen	-a

3.3. Weak nouns: Masculine singular.

Corresponding to the weak declension of adjectives is a weak noun declension: nom. *hǫfðing**i*** (R.S. 1), *goð**i*** (R.S. 2), gen. *fóstr**a***. All three of these nouns are masc. Many masc. names belong to the weak declension: *Helg**i***, *Gísl**i***, *Ing**i*** – acc./dat./gen. *Helg**a***, *Gísl**a***, *Ing**a***. Note that the sing. endings of weak masc. nouns are identical with the corresponding endings of weak adjectives.

nom	-i
acc	-a
dat	-a
gen	-a

Whereas adjectives vary between strong and weak forms depending on whether or not they are paired with an article or other determiner (3.2), nouns are either weak or strong by nature and do not alternate.

3.4. The noun *sonr* (*-son*).

The nom. sing. of the word for 'son' is irregular. When it occurs attached to the gen. form of a name (*Egils**son***, etc.), it does not use the normal nominative singular masculine ending ***-r***. When it occurs independently (as in R.S. 3), it usually has the ending *-r*. The gen. sing. is always *son**ar***.

3.5. Disyllabic adjectives and nouns.

When a disyllabic adj. takes an ending that contains a vowel, the vowel of the second syllable is lost. For example, the nom. sing. masc. weak form of *mikill* is *mik**li***. This is true for all adjectives except those of participial form with the second syllable *-að-* (see 5.3.1, 8.7, 10.3.1). Disyllabic nouns also behave this way: f.ex., the dat. sing. of the neut. noun *sumar* 'summer' is *su**mr**i* (R.S. 9).

3.6. Personal pronouns: First and second persons.

Examples of the 1st person sing. pron. *ek* 'I' and the 2nd person sing. *þú* 'you' and *þér* '(to) you' will appear in R.S. 4. The full declensions are as follows.

	1st		**2nd**	
Sg *nom*	ek	'I'	þú	'you'
acc	mik	'me'	þik	'you'
dat	mér	'(to) me'	þér	'(to) you'
gen	mín	'of me'	þín	'of you'
Pl *nom*	vér	'we'	þér/ér	'you'
acc	oss	'us'	yðr	'you'
dat	oss	'(to) us'	yðr	'(to) you'
gen	vár	'of us'	yð(v)ar	'of you'

3.7. Preview of the verb: The infinitive.

Almost all Icelandic verbs form the infinitive by adding *-a* to the verb stem (i.e., the basic verb minus any endings): *gef**a*** 'give', *þiggj**a*** 'accept'. The infinitve is used after modal auxiliary verbs:[7] *ek vil gefa* 'I will (= wish to) give', *ek vil þiggja* 'I will (= wish to) accept'. You will see these forms in R.S. 4.

---

[7] Modal auxiliary verbs, also called helping verbs, add qualities of meaning to the main verb to make it something other than a simple statement of fact. They express characteristics such as ability, possibility, necessity, intention, etc. Examples in English include 'can', 'could', 'may', 'might', 'must', 'shall', 'should', 'will', 'would', etc.

3.8. Infinitive marker *at*.

When an infinitive appears in its own phrase (f.ex., *at segja* in *ok er frá honum gott* ***at segja*** 'and about him there is good **to tell**', R.S. 7), the infinitive is preceded by the particle *at*, which correspondes to English 'to'. Note that it is identical in form with the prep. *at* and the conj. *at*.

3.9. Additional Reading.

The following passage from the beginning of *Þorsteins þáttr Stangarhǫggs* (*Tale of Thorstein Staff-Struck*) is a typical opening to an Icelandic saga. The characters who appear at the start of the saga are introduced with a terse description of their background, where they lived, and a glimpse of their personal character.

Ór *Þorsteins þætti stangarhǫggs* (1. kap.)

(From the *Tale of Thorstein Staff-Struck*, Chap. 1)

Maðr hét Þórarinn, er bjó í Sunnudal, gamall maðr ok sjónlítill. Hann hafði verit rauðavíkingr í œsku sinni. Hann var eigi dældarmaðr, þótt hann væri gamall. Son átti sér einn, er Þorsteinn er nefndr. Hann var mikill maðr ok ǫflugr ok vel stilltr.

A man was named Thorarin, who lived in Sunnudal, an old man and of poor eyesight. He had been a red viking in his youth. He was not a gentle man, although he was old. He had one son, who is named Thorstein. He was a big man and strong and very calm.

Exercises

1. Fill in the appropriate endings.

a. Mað__ hét Helgi. Hann var Hákon___son, Nóreg__ konung__. Helgi var væn__ mað__ ok vitr.

b. Móðir Helg__ hét Ásgerðr, dóttir Þorstein__ in__ auðg__, rík__ mann__ ok góð__.

c. Aðalstein__ var son__ Harald__ in__ góð__, hersi__ rík__ í Nóreg__.

d. Játvarð__ in__ góð__ var góð__ konung__ ok sigrsæl__. Hann réð fyrir England__ á dǫgum Harald__ in__ hárfagr__.

e. Egil__ in__ mikl__ hét hersi__, son__ Þorstein__ in__ mikl__.

2. Supply suitable personal names, nouns, and adjectives.

a. __________i (name) inn __________i (adj.) hét __________r (noun). Hann var sonr __________s (name) ins __________a (adj.), __________s (adj.) __________s (noun) ok __________s (adj.).

b. Repeat exercise **a**, interchanging the two names and using different adjectives.

____

____

____

3. Match the Old Norse infinitives with their English meanings by drawing a line between the two.

at búa	to love
at elska	to dwell
at gefa	to be named
at gera	to give
at hafa	to rule
at heita	to have
at kalla	to let
at láta	to be
at ráða	to make
at taka	to want
at vilja	to call
at vera	to take

4. Supply the Icelandic pronouns.

	1st	2nd
Sg *nom*	__________ 'I'	__________ 'you'
acc	__________ 'me'	__________ 'you'
dat	__________ '(to) me'	__________ '(to) you'
gen	__________ 'of me'	__________ 'of you'
Pl *nom*	__________ 'we'	__________ 'you'
acc	__________ 'us'	__________ 'you'
dat	__________ '(to) us'	__________ '(to) you'
gen	__________ 'of us'	__________ 'of you'

VOCABULARY

Aðalsteinn *m* Athelstane (*personal name*)
at *inf marker* to
á *prep* [*w dat*] on, at, in (*location*)
Ásvaldr *m* Asvald (*personal name*)
dagr (*pl dat* dǫgum) *m* day
dalr (*dat* dal(i)) *m* valley, dale
dældarmaðr *m* gentle, easy man
dǫgum *dat pl of* **dagr**
eigi *adv* not
einn *num* one
einvaldskonungr *m* sole ruler

Elfráðr *m* Alfred (*personal name*)
England *n* England
eptir *prep* [*w acc*] after (*in time*)
er *rel pron* who
er (*inf* **vera**) *vb* is
faðir *m* father
fóstri *m* foster-father
fyrir *prep* [*w dat*] before, at the head of (leading)
fyrstr *superl adj* first
gamall *adj* old
Gísli *m* Gisli (*personal name*)
góðr *adj* good
hafa (*past* hafði) *vb* have
hafði (*inf* **hafa**) *vb* had
hann *pron* (*nom*) he; (*acc*) him
hans *poss pron* his
Haraldr *m* Harald (*personal name*)
Hákon (*gen* Hákonar) *m* Hakon (*personal name*)
hárfagr *adj* fair-haired
heita (*past* hét) *vb* be named, be called
Helgi *m* Helgi ('Holy') (*personal name*)
hét (*inf* **heita**) *vb* was named, called
honum *pron* (to) him (*dat sg of* **hann**)
hǫgg *n* stroke, blow
Ingi *m* Ingi (*personal name*)
inn *art* the
í prep [*w dat*] in (*location*)
Játvarðr *m* Edward (*personal name*)
konungr *m* king
maðr *m* man; person, human being
mikill *adj* big, great
nefna *vb* name, call
nefndr (*inf* **nefna**) *ppart* named
Nóregr *m* Norway
rauðavíkingr *m* 'red' viking, a particularly fierce and violent viking
rauðr *adj* red
ráða (*past* réð) *vb* rule, govern
réð (*inf* **ráða**) *vb* ruled, governed
ríkr *adj* powerful, mighty
segja *vb* say, tell
sér *dat refl pron* (for) himself
sigrsæll *adj* victorious
sinn (*dat fem* sinni) *refl poss adj* his (own)
sjónlítill *adj* having poor eyesight
sonr (*gen* sonar) *m* son
stangarhǫgg *n* Staff-Struck (*nick-name*)
stilltr *adj* calm, composed
stǫng (*gen* stangar) *f* pole, staff
sunna *f* sun
Sunnudalr (*dat* Sunnudal(i)) *m* Sunnudal ('Sun Dale') (*place name*)
var (*inf* **vera**) *vb* was
vel *adv* well, very
vera (*past* var) *vb* be
verit (*inf* **vera**) *ppart* been
víkingr *m* a viking, sea-raider
væri (*inf* **vera**) *vb* was (*subjunct*)
yfir *prep* [*w acc/dat*] over, above
þat *dem pron* that
þáttr (*dat* þætti) *m* short story, tale
Þórarinn *m* Thorarin (*personal name*)
þótt = **þó at** *conj* [*w subjunct*] although, even though
þætti *dat sg of* **þáttr**
œska (*dat* œsku) *f* youth, childhood
ǫflugr *adj* strong, powerful

Phrases

á dǫgum in the days (of)
átti sér had for himself = had
í Englandi in England
konungr yfir king of
hann réð fyrir he ruled over

LESSON 4

Ór *Egils sǫgu Skalla-Grímssonar* (36. kap.)

(From the *Saga of Egil Skalla-Grimsson*, Chap. 36)

Þat var einn dag, er þeir Þórólfr ok Bjǫrn gengu ofan til skipsins; þeir sá, at Eiríkr konungsson var þar, gekk stundum á skipit út, en stundum á land upp, stóð þá ok horfði á skipit.

Þá mælti Þórólfr: "Vandliga hyggr þú at skipinu, konungsson; hversu lízk þér á?"

"Vel," segir hann, "it fegrsta er skipit," segir hann.

"Þá vil ek gefa þér," sagði Þórólfr, "skipit, ef þú vill þiggja."

"Þiggja vil ek," segir Eiríkr.

It was one day when (they) Thorolf and Bjorn went down to the ship; they saw that Prince Eirik was there, [that he] went at times out onto the ship, and at times up onto land, then stood and looked at the ship.

Then Thorolf spoke: "Carefully you consider the ship, prince; how do you like it?"

"Very much," he says, "the ship is the most beautiful," he says.

"Then I wish to give you," said Thorolf, "the ship, if you wish to accept."

"I wish to accept," says Eirik.

4.1. Strong nouns: Neuter singular.

The singular declension of a strong neut. noun can be illustrated by the word *skip*. Note:

nom	skip
acc	skip
dat	skipi
gen	skips

- There is no ending in the nom., differing in this respect from strong masc. nouns.
- The nom. and acc. are identical.
- The dat. ending is *-i*, in common with the majority of strong masc. nouns.
- The gen. ending is *-s*, as in the case of many masc. nouns.

4.2. Review paradigms: Masc. and neut. sing. strong noun endings (see 2.5).

	Masc	**Neut**
nom	-r (see 2.1)	–
acc	–	–
dat	-i, –	-i
gen	-s, -ar	-s

4.3. Definite article: Singular neuter.

The nom. form of the neut. sing. art. occurs in the R.S.: ***it** fegrsta* 'the fairest'. The complete paradigm is shown in the table at right. Note:

nom	it
acc	it
dat	inu
gen	ins

- The nom. and acc. forms are identical (this is a characteristic of the neut. declension in general).
- The gen. form *ins* is identical with the gen. sing. masc. (3.1).

4.4. Review paradigms: Masc. and neut. sing. forms of the article (see 3.1, 4.3).

	Masc	Neut
nom	inn	it
acc	inn	it
dat	inum	inu
gen	ins	ins

4.5. Strong and weak adjectives: Singular neuter.

The strong neut. declension of adjectives has the endings shown in the box at right. Note:

nom	-t
acc	-t
dat	-u
gen	-s

- The nom. and acc. are identical.
- The gen. ending is *-s*, in common with masc. strong adjectives.
- The endings match those of the article: ***it**, **it**, **inu**, **ins*** (4.3).

Weak neut. adjectives have the ending *-a* in all cases of the singular. The nom. sing. neut. weak adj. ending was seen in R.S. 4: *it fegrst**a***. The dat. sing. ***sama*** '[the] same' appears in the following reading example:

nom	-a
acc	-a
dat	-a
gen	-a

Ór *Magnúss sǫgu Erlingssonar* (16. kap.)

(From the *Saga of Magnus Erlingsson*, Chap. 16)

Eysteinn var vígðr á **sama** ári ok Ingi konungr fell.	Eystein was ordained in [the] same year that ('as') King Ingi fell.

4.6. Review paradigms: Sing. masc. and neut. of strong and weak adjectives (see 2.5, 3.2, 4.5).

	Strong		Weak	
	Masc	Neut	Masc	Neut
nom	-r (see 2.1)	-t	-i	-a
acc	-an	-t	-a	-a
dat	-um	-u	-a	-a
gen	-s	-s	-a	-a

4.7. Weak nouns: Neuter singular.

A weak neut. noun declension exists, but it has only a few members, none of which have occurred in the reading selections so far. Most of them refer to parts of the body; the main ones are: *auga* 'eye', *eyra* 'ear', *hjarta* 'heart', *lunga* 'lung'.

As with adjectives (4.5), neut. weak nouns end in *-a* in all cases of the singular.

4.8. Suffixed definite article.

The article is suffixed to the noun when the noun is not modified by an adj., as illustrated by the forms *skip**it*** (nom./acc.), *skip**inu*** (dat.), and *skips**ins*** (gen.) in the R.S.

	Strong		Weak	
	Masc	**Neut**	**Masc**	**Neut**
nom	konungr-inn	skip-it	goði-nn	auga-t
acc	konung-inn	skip-it	goða-nn	auga-t
dat	konungi-num	skipi-nu	goða-num	auga-nu
gen	konungs-ins	skips-ins	goða-ns	auga-ns

Note:

- The article is added after the appropriate case ending: *konungrinn = konung-r + -inn*; *konungsins = konung-s + -ins*; *skipsins = skip-s + -ins*.
- When the noun ends in a vowel, the initial *i-* of the article is dropped: strong dat. *konungi + -inum = konunginum*; *skipi + -inu = skipinu*; weak nom. *goði + -inn = goðinn*; *auga + -it = augat*; gen. *goða + -ins = goðans*; *auga + -ins = augans*.
- Although the masc. nom. and acc. forms of the article are identical, the two cases are distinguishable when the article is suffixed to the noun, because the forms of the noun differ: strong *konungrinn* (nom.), *konunginn* (acc.); weak *goðinn* (nom.), *goðann* (acc.).

4.9. More on the accusative and dative cases.

As explained in 1.2, the acc. is generally used for direct objects and the dat. for indirect objects. For example: *Þá vil ek gefa **þér*** (dat.) ***skipit*** (acc.). 'Then will I give (to) you the ship'.

It is not necessary for a sentence to contain both a direct object and an indirect object. Sometimes only the direct object appears: *Þeir sá **skipit*** (acc.) 'They saw the ship'.

Old Icelandic sentences can also contain only an indirect object: *Þá vil ek gefa **þér*** (dat.) 'Then will I give (to) you'. Here the direct object is understood, and not made explicit.

Like the gen., the dat. is also required by certain prepositions and verbs:

- The following **prepositions** require the noun that goes with them to take the dat. case: *af, at, frá, hjá, móti, nær, ór, undan*. For example, *ór **Nóregi*** (dat.) 'from Norway'.

- Certain **verbs** require that their direct objects take not the acc. case but the dat. These are usually verbs whose direct objects can be understood as "instruments" of the action. An instrument is, as you might imagine, an object used deliberately to cause some effect. *Halda* 'hold,' *kasta* 'throw' and *skjóta* 'shoot' take the dat. in this way. For example, *Hann kastar* ***sverði*** (dat.) 'He throws a sword'.

We can see here that the subject is really using the direct object (the sword) as an instrument to cause some effect, probably on another person or thing.

Most prepositions in Old Icelandic can take either the acc. or the dat., depending on their meaning. Examples are: *á, eptir, í, fyrir, með, of, um, undir, við, yfir*. In general, these prepositions take the dat. when they express a position in space or time (or refer to an "instrument"), and take the acc. when they express motion with respect to a place or duration of time. For example:

Hann gekk ***á skip*** (acc.) 'He went **onto a ship**'
Hann stóð ***á skipi*** (dat.) 'He stood **on a ship**'

In the first example, *á* means 'onto', implying motion with respect to the ship, and requires the noun that goes with it to take the acc.; in the second example, *á* means 'on', implying a stationary position with respect to the ship, and requires the dat.

Exercises

1. Fill in the appropriate endings.

a. Egil__ gekk til konung______. "Ek vil gef__ þér land____," sagði konung______. (all def.)

b. Kveld-Úlf__ gekk ofan til skip______ (def.).

c. Þorgerðr var dóttir Egils. Hon var stór__ barn ok fagr__. (*stórr* adj. 'big'; *barn* neut. 'child')

d. It stór__ sverð Egils var skarp__ ok lang__. (*skarpr* adj. 'sharp'; *langr* adj. 'long')

e. Helg__ in__ vitr hét konungsson__; hann gekk á skip___ (def.) út ok á land___ (def.) upp.

f. Konung___ stóð á inu fegrst__ skip__ ok horfð__ á land___.

2. Decline the independent def. art. in the masc. and neut. singular.

masc. nom.	_________	neut. nom.	_________
acc.	_________	acc.	_________
dat.	_________	dat.	_________
gen.	_________	gen.	_________

3. Decline the def. art. suffixed to the nouns *úlfr* 'wolf', *sverð* 'sword', *fóstri* 'foster-father', and *hjarta* 'heart'.

nom.	úlfr______	sverð______	fóstri______	hjarta______
acc.	úlf______	sverð______	fóstra______	hjarta______
dat.	úlfi______	sverði______	fóstra______	hjarta______
gen.	úlfs______	sverðs______	fóstra______	hjarta______

4. Vocabulary training.

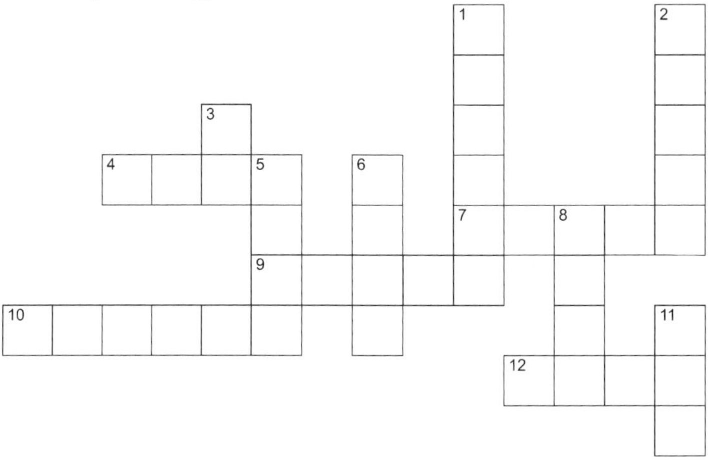

Across
4 be
7 said (*sg*)
9 went (*pl*)
10 accept
12 ship

Down
1 how
2 spoke (*sg*)
3 year
5 eye
6 one
8 went (*sg*)
11 up, upwards

VOCABULARY

at *conj* that
auga *n* eye
á *prep* [*w acc*] onto (motion), toward (*direction*); [*w dat*] on (*location*)
ár *n* year
barn *n* child
einn *num* (*m nom*) one
Eiríkr *m* Eirik (*personal name*)
ek *pron* I
ef *conj* if
er *conj* when
er (*inf* **vera**) *vb* is
Erlingr *m* Erling (*personal name*)
eyra *n* ear
Eysteinn *m* Eystein (*personal name*)
fagr *adj* fair, beautiful
falla (*past* fell) *vb* fall
fegrstr *superl adj* fairest, most beautiful (*see* **fagr**)
fell (*inf* **falla**) *vb* fell
ganga (*past* gekk, gengu) *vb* go, walk
gefa *vb* give
gekk (*inf* **ganga**) *vb* went (*sg*)
gengu (*inf* **ganga**) *vb* went (*pl*)
halda *vb* [*w dat*] hold
hjarta *n* heart
horfa (*past* -ði) *vb* (turn so as to) look on
horfði (*inf* **horfa**) *vb* looked on (*sg*)
hversu *int adv* how
hyggja (*pres* hyggr) *vb* think; give heed
kasta *vb* [*w dat*] throw
konungsson(r) *m* prince
land *n* land; estate

langr *adj* long
lunga *n* lung
Magnús *m* Magnus (*personal name*)
mæla (*past* -ti) *vb* say, speak
mælti (*inf* **mæla**) *vb* said, spoke (*sg*)
ofan *adv* down, downwards
ok *conj* as
sagði (*inf* **segja**) *vb* said (*sg*)
samr *adj* same
sá (*inf* **sjá**) *vb* saw
segir (*inf* **segja**) *vb* says
segja (*past* sagði) *vb* say
sjá (*past* sá) *vb* see
skarpr *adj* sharp
skip *n* ship
skjóta *vb* [*w dat*] shoot
standa (*past* stóð, stóðu) *vb* stand
stóð (*inf* **standa**) *vb* stood (*sg*)
stórr *adj* big
stund *f* length of time, a while
stundum *adv* sometimes, at times (*dat pl of* **stund**)
sverð *n* sword
til *prep* [*w gen*] to
upp *adv* up (*motion*), upwards
út *adv* out (*motion*), outwards
vel *adv* well, very much
vera (*pres* er) *vb* be
vil (*inf* **vilja**) *vb* (I) want, wish
vilja (*1sg pres* vil, *2/3sg pres* vill) *vb* wish, want
vill (*inf* **vilja**) *vb* (you *sg*) want, wish
vígðr (*inf* **vígja**) *ppart* ordained (*nom sg masc*)
vígja (*ppart* vígðr) *vb* ordain, consecrate
þar *adv* there
þat *pron* it
þá *adv* then
þeir *pron* they (*m*)
þér *pron* (*dat* of **þú**) you (*sg*)
þiggja *vb* accept
Þorgerðr *f* Thorgerd (*personal name*)
Þórólfr *m* Thorolf (*personal name*)
þú *pron* you (*sg*)

Phrases

einn dag one day (*definite time*)
horfa á look at
hversu lízk þér á how do you like, what do you think of
þú hyggr at you (*sg*) pay attention to, consider

> From this point on, only new words are given in the lesson vocabularies. The rear of the book contains a full vocabulary.

Notes

LESSON 5

Ór *Snorra Eddu, Gylfaginning* (6. kap.)

(From *Snorri's Edda* [*The Prose Edda*], *The Beguiling of Gylfi*, Chap. 6)

Þá mælti Gangleri: "Hvar bygði Ymir? eða við hvat lifði hann?"	Then said Gangleri: "Where did Ymir dwell? or on what did he live?"
Hár svarar: "Næst var þat, þá er hrímit draup, at þar varð af kýr sú er Auðhumla hét, en fjórar mjólkár runnu ór spenum hennar, ok fœddi hon Ymi."	Har answers: "Next it was, when the rime dripped, that there appeared the cow that was called Audhumla, and four milk-streams ran from her teats, and she fed Ymir."
Þá mælti Gangleri: "Við hvat fœddisk kýrin?"	Then said Gangleri: "With what did the cow feed herself?"
Hár segir: "Hon sleikti hrímsteina, er saltir váru, ok hinn fyrsta dag, er hon sleikti steina, kom ór steininum at kveldi manns hár, annan dag manns hǫfuð, þriðja dag var þar allr maðr. Sá er nefndr Buri."	Har says: "She licked [the] rime stones, which were salty; and the first day, when she licked [the] stones, came from the stone at evening the hair of a man, [the] second day a man's head, [the] third day [the] whole man was there. That one is named Buri."

5.1. Personal pronouns: 3rd person.

We have already encountered several 3rd person pronouns ('he/she/it/they') in the readings. The full declension is as follows.

	Masc		**Fem**		**Neut**	
Sg *nom*	hann	'he/it'	hon	'she/it'	þat	'it'
acc	hann	'him/it'	hana	'her/it'	þat	'it'
dat	honum	'him/it'	henni	'her/it'	því	'it'
gen	hans	'his/its'	hennar	'her(s)/its'	þess	'its'
Pl *nom*	þeir	'they'	þær	'they'	þau	'they'
acc	þá	'them'	þær	'them'	þau	'them'
dat	þeim	'them'	þeim	'them'	þeim	'them'
gen	þeir(r)a	'their(s)'	þeir(r)a	'their(s)'	þeir(r)a	'their(s)'

Points to note:

- Noun gender in Old Norse is largely arbitrary. Old Norse requires that a pronoun always reflect the noun's gender, whether masc., fem., or neut. For example, *fjǫrðr* 'fjord' is a masc. noun and is therefore referred to by the pronoun *hann* 'he', *mjólk* 'milk' (fem.) is referred to as *hon* 'she', and *skip* 'ship' (neut.) is referred to as *þat* 'it'. All these words are translated 'it' in English.

- In the plural, where English has 'they', Old Norse distinguishes all three genders: *þeir* (masc.), *þær* (fem.), and *þau* (neut.).

5.2. Verbs: Weak and strong verbs.

Some verbs (traditionally called **weak** verbs) form their past tense by adding a dental suffix (*-ð-* and its variants *-d-* and *-t-*, described below) to the verb stem (f.ex., *haf**ð**i* 'had', past tense of *hafa*). Another group (traditionally called **strong** verbs) form their past tense by changing the root vowel without the addition of a dental suffix (f.ex., *t**ó**k* 'took', past tense of *taka*).

The same distinction between weak and strong verbs exists in English. Weak verbs form their past tense by adding the dental suffix **-ed** ('walk/walk**ed**') or a variant ('hear/hear**d**', 'dwell/dwel**t**'). Strong verbs form their past tense by changing the root vowel without the addition of a dental suffix ('r**u**n/r**a**n', 's**i**ng/s**a**ng', 't**a**ke/t**oo**k').

This lesson presents the past-tense formation of weak verbs, and Lesson 6 presents the strong verbs.

5.3. Weak verbs: Formation of the past tense.

As noted, weak verbs form their past tense by adding a dental suffix (*-ð-* or a variant) to the verb stem.

1. Weak verbs with vocalic link -a-.

One large group of weak verbs is characterized by the presence of a vocalic link *-a-* suffixed to the verb root. These verbs form the largest group of weak verbs by far, and the conjugation is highly regular.

In this group of weak verbs, the vocalic link *-a-* forms part of the stem. (Recall from 1.1 that the stem of a word equals the root plus any suffixes that are added to it.) Additional suffixes, such as the past-tense dental suffix *-ð-*, are added after the vocalic link. Personal endings (f.ex., 3 sing. *-i*, 5.5) are added after the dental suffix. For example:

elsk- + *-a-* + *-ð-* + *-i* → *elskaði* '(he) loved'
kall- + *-a-* + *-ð-* + *-i* → *kallaði* '(he) called'

2. Weak verbs without vocalic link.

Weak verbs that do not have the vocalic link *-a-* described above attach the past-tense dental suffix *-ð-* directly to the root. For example:

horf- + *-ð-* + *-i* → *horfði* '(he) looked'
lif- + *-ð-* + *-i* → *lifði* '(he) lived'
sag- + *-ð-* + *-i* → *sagði* '(he) said'

5.4. Weak verbs: Variation in the dental suffix.

The dental suffix *-ð-* sometimes changes to *-t-*, *-d-*, or zero (i.e., it disappears), depending on the sound that immediately precedes it. Several rules help to explain when the changes occur.

1. Change of dental suffix: Predictable rules.

Following are three rules that are predicatable:

- When the root ends in *-t-* or *-s-*, *-ð-* becomes *-t-*.

  flut- + *-ð-* + *-i* → *flu**tt**i* '(he) conveyed'

- When the root itself ends in *-ð-*, the dental suffix *-ð-* becomes *-d-*, and the stem-final *-ð-* also becomes *-d-*.

  kvað- + *-ð-* + *-i* → *kva**dd**i* '(he) greeted'
  fœð- + *-ð-* + *-i* → *fœ**dd**i* '(he) fed'

- When the root ends in *-d-* or *-t-* preceded by another consonant, *-ð-* becomes zero, i.e., disappears.

  skipt- + *-ð-* + *-i* → *ski**pt**i* '(he) divided'
  send- + *-ð-* + *-i* → *se**nd**i* '(he) sent'

2. Change of dental suffix: Less predictable rules.

In other environments, the patterns are less predicable, and there is considerable variation in the manuscripts. The following guidelines help to recognize the variations.

- When the root ends in *-f-*, the suffix *-ð-* usually remains unchanged:

  horf- + *-ð-* + *-i* → *horf**ð**i* '(he) looked'
  lif- + *-ð-* + *-i* → *lif**ð**i* '(he) lived'

  More rarely, *-ð-* changes to *-t-*:

  þurf- + *-ð-* + *-i* → *þurf**t**i* '(he) needed'

- When the root ends in *-p-* or *-k-*, the suffix *-ð-* often becomes *-t-*.

  vak- + *-ð-* + *-i* → *vak**t**i* '(he) woke'
  sleik- + *-ð-* + *-i* → *sleik**t**i* '(he) licked'
  keyp- + *-ð-* + *-i* → *keyp**t**i* '(he) bought'

  In other instances *-ð-* remains unchanged:

  þak- + *-ð-* + *-i* → *þak**ð**i* '(he) thatched'
  glap- + *-ð-* + *-i* → *glap**ð**i* '(he) confused'

- When the root ends in *-n-* or *-m-* (**nasal** sounds), *-ð-* generally becomes *-d-*.

  mun- + *-ð-* + *-i* → *mun**d**i* '(he) remembered'
  nefn- + *-ð-* + *-i* → *nefn**d**i* '(he) named'
  tam- + *-ð-* + *-i* → *tam**d**i* '(he) tamed'

  But *-ð-* may also remain unchanged:

  van- + *-ð-* + *-i* → *van**ð**i* or *van**d**i* '(he) trained'

- When the root ends in *-l-*, the suffix *-ð-* sometimes becomes *-t-*, sometimes becomes *-d-*, and sometimes does not change.

  mæl- + *-ð-* + *-i* → *mæl**t**i* '(he) spoke'
  mul- + *-ð-* + *-i* → *mul**d**i* '(he) crushed'
  val- + *-ð-* + *-i* → *val**ð**i* '(he) chose'

5.5. Weak Verbs: 3rd person past-tense endings.

The 3rd person sing. ending of weak verbs in the past tense is *-i* (compare the examples given in 5.3). The 3rd person pl. ending is *-u*. Personal endings are added after the dental suffix; f.ex.:

horfð- + *-i* → *horfði* '(he) looked'
horfð- + *-u* → *horfðu* '(they) looked'
lifð- + *-i* → *lifði* '(he) lived'
lifð- + *-u* → *lifðu* '(they) lived'

5.6. Weak Verbs: Vowel alternation in short roots with *j*-suffix.

Some weak verbs that add the dental suffix directly to the stem (5.3.2) have a different root vowel in the pres. tense.[8] The verbs of this group all have a **short** root followed by a *-j-* suffix in the infinitive: *kve**ðj**a*, *ve**kj**a*, *fly**tj**a*, and *spy**rj**a*. A short root is one that contains a short vowel (see 2.1) followed by a single consonant; f.ex., the roots of the above verbs are *kvað-*, *vak-*, *flut-*, and *spur-*. These verbs are explained in greater detail in 14.2.

The following two changes are the most important:

- If *a* in the past, then *e* in the pres.; f.ex.:
  *kv**a**ddi* 'greeted' – *kv**e**ðja* 'greet'
  *v**a**kti* 'woke' – *v**e**kja* 'wake'
- If *u* in the past, then *y* in the pres.; f.ex.:
  *fl**u**tti* 'conveyed' – *fl**y**tja* 'convey'
  *sp**u**rði* 'asked' – *sp**y**rja* 'ask'

Here are further examples:

*s**a**gði* 'said' – *s**e**gja* (root *sag-*) 'say'
*m**u**ldi* 'crushed' – *m**y**lja* (root *mul-*) 'crush'

Note the *-j-* before the infinitive ending *-a*. The stem-vowel changes are the result of an **umlaut**[9] process caused by the influence of this *-j-* in the pres. forms. This will be explained in 11.2.1.

Exercises

1. Fill in the appropriate endings. (NB: All verbs are weak verbs in the past tense.)

a. Þeir Þorstein__ ok Grím__ horf____ á land____ (def.).

b. Hrafnkel__ elsk_____ goð_____ (def.) Frey ok efl___ blót mikit.

---

[8] Modern English verbs such as 's**e**ll/s**o**ld', 't**e**ll/t**o**ld', 's**ee**k/s**ou**ght', and 't**ea**ch/t**au**ght', show a similar type of sound change inherited from Old English.

[9] Umlaut, a term borrowed from German, refers to the change in pronunciation that some vowels undergo due to the influence of other vowels or vowel-like sounds in the following syllable. Umlaut originally arose in rapid speech as speakers, anticipating the next syllable, would slightly alter the vowel to bring it closer in pronunciation to the upcoming sound.

c. Gangleri mæl___: "Við hvat lif___ Ymi___?"

d. Hár sag___: "Auðhumla sleik___ steininn, ok kom ór stein______ (def.) at kveld__ mann__ hár."

2. Supply the Icelandic pronouns.

	Masc		Fem		Neut	
Sg *nom*	________	'he'	________	'she'	________	'it'
acc	________	'him'	________	'her'	________	'it'
dat	________	'(to) him'	________	'(to) her'	________	'(to) it'
gen	________	'his'	________	'her(s)'	________	'its'
Pl *nom*	________	'they'	________	'they'	________	'they'
acc	________	'them'	________	'them'	________	'them'
dat	________	'(to) them'	________	'(to) them'	________	'(to) them'
gen	________	'their(s)'	________	'their(s)'	________	'their(s)'

3. Give the 3 sing. past form of the following verbs.

a. Weak verbs with vocalic link -*a*-:

Ex.: at kalla (*past* -að-): hann kallaði

at elska (*past* -að-): hon ____________

at kasta (*past* -að-): þat ____________

b. Weak verbs without vocalic link:

Ex.: at mæla (*past* -t-): hon mælti

at fœða (*past* -dd-): þat ____________

at lifa (*past* -ð-): hann ____________

at sýna (*past* -d-): hon ____________

c. Weak verbs with vowel alternation (see 5.6):

Ex.: at flytja (*past* flutt-): þat flutti

at kveðja (*past* kvadd-): hann ____________

at segja (*past* sagð-): hon ____________

at spyrja (*past* spurð-): þat ____________

4. The following 3 sing. past-tense weak verbs appeared in R.S. 5. Supply the 3 pl. past-tense form of each.

bygði: þeir ____________ fœddi: þær ____________

lifði: þau ____________ mælti: þeir ____________

sleikti: þær ____________

Vocabulary

af *adv* off, away
allr *adj* all, whole
annan *acc sg masc of* **annarr**
annarr (*acc m* annan) *adj* other, another; second
Auðhumla *f* Audhumla (*mythological name*, the primeval cow)
á (*pl* ár) *f* river
Buri *m* Buri (*personal name*)
draup (*inf* **drjúpa**) *vb* dripped
drjúpa (*past* draup, drupu) *vb* drip
eða *conj* or
efla (*past* -d-) *vb* make, perform
elska (*past* -að-) *vb* love; be fond of
fjórar *fem of* **fjórir**
fjórir *num* four
flutti (*inf* **flytja**) *vb* conveyed
flytja (*past* flutt-) *vb* convey
fyrstr *superl adj* first
fœða (*past* -ddi) *vb* feed
fœddi (*inf* **fœða**) *vb* fed
fœddisk (*inf* **fœða-sk**) *vb* fed itself, was fed
Gangleri *m* Gangleri (*personal name*)
glepja (*past* glapð-) *vb* confuse
hár *n* hair
Hár *m* Har ('High') (*mythological name*, pseudonym of Odin)
hennar *poss pron* her
hinn *var of art* **inn**
hrím *n* hoar-frost, rime
hrímsteinn *m* rime-stone
hvar *int adv* where
hvat *int pron* what
hǫfuð *n* head
kaupa (*past* keypt-) *vb* buy
kom (*inf* **koma**) *vb* came (*sg*)
koma (*past* kom, kómu) *vb* come
kvaddi (*inf* **kveðja**) *vb* greeted (*sg*)
kveðja (*past* kvadd-) *vb* greet
kveld *n* evening
kýr *f* cow
kýrin = **kýr** + **-in** (*art*) the cow
lifa (*past* -ð-) *vb* live
lifði (*inf* **lifa**) *vb* lived
mjólk *f* milk
mjólk-á *f* milk-stream, river of milk
muldi (*inf* **mylja**) *vb* crushed
mylja (*past* muld-) *vb* crush
muna (*past* -d-) *vb* remember
næst *adv* next (following)
renna (*past* rann, runnu) *vb* run
runnu (*inf* **renna**) *vb* ran (*pl*)
saltir *nom pl masc of* **saltr**
saltr *adj* salt(y)
sá (*f* sú) *dem pron* that (one)
senda (*past* -nd-) *vb* send
skipta (*past* -pt-) *vb* divide
sleikja (*past* -t-) *vb* lick
sleikti (*inf* **sleikja**) *vb* licked
Snorri *m* Snorri (*personal name*); Snorri Sturluson, author of *The Prose Edda*
speni *m* teat
spenum *dat pl of* **speni**
spurði (*inf* **spyrja**) *vb* asked
spyrja (*past* spurð-) *vb* ask
steina *acc pl of* steinn
steinn *m* stone
sú *dem pron* that (one) (*fem of* **sá**)
vakti (*inf* **vekja**) *vb* woke
valði (*inf* **velja**) *vb* chose
varð (*inf* **verða**) *vb* became
váru (*inf* **vera**) *vb* were
vekja (*past* vakt-) *vb* wake
velja (*past* valð-) *vb* choose
vera (*past* var, váru) *vb* be
verða (*past sg* varð) *vb* become; come to pass
við *prep* [*w acc*] with, by
Ymir *m* Ymir (*mythological name*, the first giant)
þekja (*past* þakð-) *vb* cover, thatch
þriði *ord num* third
þriðja *acc sg masc of* **þriði**
þurfa (*past* þurft-) *vb* [*w gen*] need, have need of

Phrases

hinn fyrsta dag ... annar dag ... þriðja dag (*acc*) on the first day ... on the second day ... on the third day
lifa við [*w acc*] live on, feed on
verða af come about, appear

LESSON 6

Ór *Ragnars sǫgu loðbrókar* (3. kap.)

(From the *Saga of Ragnar Lodbrok*, Chap. 3)

that time Denmark Ring
Í þann tíma réð fyrir Danmǫrku Sigurðr hringr. Hann var ríkr konungr
('is famous become')
has become famous from that battle which fought
ok er frægr orðinn[10] af þeiri orrostu, er hann barðisk við Harald
Wartooth Bravoll fell as known
hilditǫnn á Brávelli,[11] ok fyrir honum féll Haraldr, sem kunnigt
('is')
[it] has become over all northern region of the world had who
er orðit[9] of alla norðrálfu heimsins. Sigurðr átti einn son, er
in size of appearance intelligent
Ragnarr hét; hann var mikill vexti, vænn yfirlits ok vel viti borinn,
magnanimous his fierce to his enemies
stórlyndr við sína menn, en grimmr sínum óvinum.

6.1. Strong verbs: Formation of the past tense.

Strong verbs form their past tense without a dental suffix (*-ð/d/t-*). Instead, they change the root vowel (sometimes with accompanying change in consonant structure of the stem). The R.S. above has four past-tense strong verbs: *réð* 'ruled', *hét* 'was named', *féll* 'fell', and *var* 'was'. In addition to these, the following strong verb forms have occurred in other Reading Selections:

*h**é**t* (R.S. 1, 3.9, 5) from *h**ei**ta*
*l**é**t* (R.S. 2) from *l**á**ta*
*t**ó**k* (R.S. 2) from *t**a**ka*
*r**é**ð* (R.S. 3) from *r**á**ða*
*g**e**kk* and *g**e**ngu* (R.S. 4) from *g**a**nga*
*s**á*** (R.S. 4) from *sj**á***
*st**ó**ð* (R.S. 4) from *st**a**nda*
*dr**au**p* (R.S. 5) from *drj**ú**pa*
*r**u**nnu* (R.S. 5) from *r**e**nna*.

---

[10] *Hann er orðinn* 'he has become', (*þat*) *er orðit* '(it) has become': lit., 'is become'. Past participles such as *orðinn/orðit* 'become' are verbal adjectives and agree in gender, number, and case with the noun they modify. See 8.7, 10.3.

[11] The legendary Battle of Bravoll is described in several sagas and in the Danish history *Gesta Danorum*. In this battle, Sigurd Hring, king of Sweden, defeated Harald Wartooth, king of Denmark, on the plain of Brávǫllr (modern Bråvalla) in Sweden.

var (R.S. 1, 1.6, 2, 3, 3.9, 4, 4.5, 5) and *váru* (R.S. 5) from *vera*
varð (R.S. 5) from *verða*

Many Old Icelandic strong verbs have corresponding strong verbs in English. For example, English equivalents of some of the verbs listed above are 'f**a**ll' – 'f**e**ll', 'r**u**n' – 'r**a**n', 's**ee**' – 's**aw**', 'st**a**nd' – 'st**oo**d', 't**a**ke' – 't**oo**k'.

6.2. Verbs: 3rd person past-tense endings.

Strong verbs regularly have no ending in the 3rd person sing. past. As in the case of weak verbs, the ending is *-u* in the 3rd person pl. The ending *-u,* however, is not added when the past-tense verb stem ends in *-á* or *-ó*, f.ex., *þeir **sá**.*

6.3. Review paradigms: 3rd person past-tense endings of the verb.

	Weak	Strong
3sg	(-a)-ð/d/t-i	–
3pl	(-a)-ð/d/t-u	-u

6.4. Strong verbs: Singular and plural past-tense stems (see 6.1).

Many strong verbs have different stems in the sing. and pl. of the past tense:

*hann **var** – þeir **váru*** (R.S. 5)
*hon **kom** – þær **kóm**u*
*hon **rann** – þær **runn**u* (R.S. 5)
*hann **skaut** – þeir **skut**u*
*hon **bjó** – þær **bjogg**u*
*hann **gekk** – þeir **geng**u* (see R.S. 4)

In some instances, the vowel in the past pl. stem is the long variant of the vowel in the past sing.: *hann v**a**r – þeir v**á**ru* (from *vera*); *hann k**o**m – þeir k**ó**mu* (from *koma*). More often, however, the sing. and pl. of strong verbs have radically different vowels: *hann r**a**nn – þeir r**u**nnu* (from *renna*); *hann sk**au**t – þeir sk**u**tu* (from *skjóta*). Some verbs have different consonant structures in the past sing. and pl. stems: *hann g**ekk** – þeir g**eng**u* (from *ganga*); *hann bj**ó** – þeir bj**ogg**u* (from *búa*).

Not all strong verbs show such alternation in the past stems, however. Some have the same vowel in both past sing. and pl.: *hann h**é**t – þeir h**é**tu* (from *heita*); *taka – hann t**ó**k – þeir t**ó**ku* (from *taka*).

6.5. The verbs *vera* and *hafa*.

Two of the most common verbs are *vera* 'be' and *hafa* 'have'. They are conjugated as follows:

***vera* 'be'**

	Pres.			Past		
1sg	ek	em	'I am'	ek	var	'I was'
2sg	þú	ert	'you are'	þú	vart	'you were'
3sg	hann / hon / þat	er	'he/she/it is'	hann / hon / þat	var	'he/she/it was'
1pl	vér	erum	'we are'	vér	várum	'we were'
2pl	þér	eruð	'you are'	þér	váruð	'you were'
3pl	þeir / þær / þau	eru	'they are'	þeir / þær / þau	váru	'they were'

***hafa* 'have'**

	Pres.			Past		
1sg	ek	hef(i)	'I have'	ek	hafða	'I had'
2sg	þú	hef(i)r	'you have'	þú	hafðir	'you had'
3sg	hann / hon / þat	hef(i)r	'he/she/it has'	hann / hon / þat	hafði	'he/she/it had'
1pl	vér	hǫfum	'we have'	vér	hǫfðum	'we had'
2pl	þér	hafið	'you have'	þér	hǫfðuð	'you had'
3pl	þeir / þær / þau	hafa	'they have'	þeir / þær / þau	hǫfðu	'they had'

6.6. Additional Reading.

The following passage is from the opening of *Vápnfirðinga saga* ('Saga of the Families of Weapon's Fjord'). In common with many sagas, the story begins with genealogical details, telling of family history and placing the family in geographical settings.

Ór *Vápnfirðinga sǫgu* (1. kap.)

(From the *Saga of the Families of Weapon's Fjord*, Chap. 1)

begin we this tale where Hof Weapon's Fjord who

Þar hefjum vér þenna þátt, er sá maðr bjó at Hofi í Vápnafirði,[12] er

Helgi hét. Hann var sonr Þorgils Þorsteinssonar, Ǫlvis sonar, Ásvalds

landed man in [the] days

sonar, Øxna-Þóris sonar. Ǫlvir var lendr maðr[13] í Nóregi um daga

---

[12] *Vápnafjǫrðr* (modern Icelandic *Vopnafjörður*) is a fjord in northeastern Iceland, named after one of its first settlers, Eyvindr Vápni (Eyvind the Weapon). Hence the name means 'Vápni's (or Weapon's) Fjord'.

[13] *Lendr maðr* 'landed man' is the Old Icelandic form of Norw. *lendmann*, the title of a medieval Norwegian nobleman whose lands and income were granted by the king in return for enforcement of the king's will. A *lendr maðr* (or

earl
Hákonar jarls Grjótgarðssonar.

[the] white Iceland of those forefathers
Þorsteinn hvíti kom fyrst út til Íslands þeira langfeðga ok bjó

Toptavoll out beyond
at Toptavelli fyrir útan Síreksstaði. En Steinbjǫrn bjó at Hofi, sonr

red when his wealth was squandered because of open-handedness
Refs ins rauða. Ok er honum eyddisk fé fyrir þegnskapar sakar,

bought the Hof estate sixty (of) winters
þá keypti Þorsteinn Hofsland ok bjó þar sex tigu vetra. Hann

was married to white
átti Ingibjǫrgu Hróðgeirsdóttur ins hvíta.

6.7. Additional Adjectives.

Adjectives are indispensable for describing people and things, and at this point in the lessons, it would be helpful to introduce a few more. Below are some of the most common adjectives found in the sagas.

	Strong			**Weak**		
	Masc	**Fem**	**Neut**	**Masc**	**Fem**	**Neut**
nom	stór-r	stór	stór-t	stór-i	stór-a	stór-a
acc	stór-an	stór-a	stór-t	stór-a	stór-u	stór-a
dat	stór-um	stór-ri	stór-u	stór-a	stór-u	stór-a
gen	stór-s	stór-rar	stór-s	stór-a	stór-u	stór-a

The following adjectives decline according to the paradigm above. The example sentences below are taken from various sagas:

fullr 'full' — ***fullr*** *af silfri* 'full of silver'
illr 'bad, evil': *til góðs ok* ***ills*** 'for good and **bad'**
kyrr 'still, quiet': *er nú* ***kyrt*** *þar* 'it is now **quiet** there'
sterkr 'strong': } *hann smíðaði honum boga* ***stóran*** *ok* ***sterkan***
stórr 'big': } 'he made for him a bow **big** and **strong'**
ungr 'young': *menn á* ***ungum*** *aldri* 'men of a young age'

When the stem ends in a dental (*-t-*, *-d-*, *-ð-*), this dental assimilates with the ending *-t* in the neut. nom./acc. sing. (see 7.3).

	Strong			**Weak**		
	Masc	**Fem**	**Neut**	**Masc**	**Fem**	**Neut**
nom	dauð-r	dauð	dau**t-t**	dauð-i	dauð-a	dauð-a
acc	dauð-an	dauð-a	dau**t-t**	dauð-a	dauð-u	dauð-a
dat	dauð-um	dauð-ri	dauð-u	dauð-a	dauð-u	dauð-a
gen	dauð-s	dauð-rar	dauð-s	dauð-a	dauð-u	dauð-a

The following adjectives follow this pattern.

dauðr 'dead' (neut. nom./acc. *dau**tt***): *eftir þat mun dýrit* ***dautt*** *upp koma* 'after that the beast will come up **dead'**

---

lendmann) was roughly equivalent to an English baron, with a rank below *jarl* (earl) but above the *hǫldr* (Norw. *hauldr*), a free farmer holding ancestral land.

fríðr 'beautiful, fine' (neut. nom./acc. *frí**tt***): *hann var mikill vexti ok **fríðr** sýnum* 'he was great in stature and **fine** in appearance'
reiðr 'angry' (neut. nom/acc. sing. *rei**tt***): *í **reiðum** hug* 'in an **angry** mood'
vándr 'bad, wretched' (neut. nom./acc. *ván**t***): *ór húsi litlu ok **vándu*** 'from a little and **wretched** house'

The paradigm of *heill* 'healthy, well; whole' shows assimilation of *-r-* to stem-final *-l-* according to the Special Stem Rule (2.1.1): *er Eymundr var **heill** orðinn* 'when Eymund had become **well**'.

	Strong			Weak		
	Masc	**Fem**	**Neut**	**Masc**	**Fem**	**Neut**
nom	heil-**l**	heil	heil-t	heil-i	heil-a	heil-a
acc	heil-an	heil-a	heil-t	heil-a	heil-u	heil-a
dat	heil-um	heil-**l**i	heil-u	heil-a	heil-u	heil-a
gen	heil-s	heil-**l**ar	heil-s	heil-a	heil-u	heil-a

Vinsæll 'popular' follows the same pattern: *han var vitr og **vinsæll*** 'he was wise and **popular**'.

The paradigm of *lítill* 'little' is similar in many ways to *mikill* 'great', with assimilation of *-r-* (*mikil**l***, 2.1.1), nom./acc. neut. ending in *-it* (*miki**t***, R.S. 2), and loss of the second syllable when the ending contains a vowel (*mik**l**i*, 3.5): *ór húsi **litlu** ok vándu* 'from a house **little** and wretched'. (NB: The the long *-í-* of *lítill* is shortened when the second syllable is dropped.)

	Strong			Weak		
	Masc	**Fem**	**Neut**	**Masc**	**Fem**	**Neut**
nom	lítil-**l**	lítil	líti-**t**	**litl**-i	**litl**-a	**litl**-a
acc	**litl**-an	**litl**-a	líti-**t**	**litl**-a	**litl**-u	**litl**-a
dat	**litl**-um	lítil-**l**i	**litl**-u	**litl**-a	**litl**-u	**litl**-a
gen	lítil-s	lítil-**l**ar	lítil-s	**litl**-a	**litl**-u	**litl**-a

Exercises

1. Fill in the appropriate endings.

a. Harald__ hersi__ stóð ok horf____ á skip____ (def.).

b. Bjǫrn ok Þórólfr geng__ á skip____ (def.) út. Þeir stóð__ þá þar.

c. Þeir hét__ Þórólfr ok Egill.

d. Þeir Harald__ ok Álf__ réð__ fyrir Vínland__.

2. Give the 3 sing. and 3 pl. past forms of the following strong verbs:

Ex.: at vera: hon _var_______ þær _váru_______

at bera: hann __________ þeir __________

(NB: *bera* follows the pattern of *vera* in the past tense.)

at ganga: hann __________ þeir __________

at heita:	hon ___________	þær ___________
at koma:	þat ___________	þau ___________
at renna:	hann ___________	þeir ___________
at taka:	þat ___________	þau ___________

3. Translate the following phrases.

***vera* 'be'**

I am ___________	I was ___________
you (sing.) are ___________	you (sing.) were ___________
he is ___________	she was ___________
we are ___________	we were ___________
you (pl.) are ___________	you (pl.) were ___________
they (neut.) are ___________	they (fem.) were ___________

***hafa* 'have'**

I have ___________	I had ___________
you (sing.) have ___________	you (sing.) had ___________
it has ___________	he had ___________
we have ___________	we had ___________
you (pl.) have ___________	you (pl.) had ___________
they (masc.) have ___________	they (neut.) had ___________

4. The noun-adjective phrases *boga stóran ok sterkan* and *húsi litlu ok vándu* appeared in the examples in 6.7. Based on the noun and adj. declensions that you have learned (see especially 3.3, 4.2, and 4.6), answer the following:

a. What is the gender of *boga*? ___________

b. What is the gender of *húsi*? ___________

c. Complete the charts below:

nom.	___________
acc.	boga stóran ok sterkan
dat.	___________
gen.	___________

d.

nom.	___________
acc.	___________
dat.	húsi litlu ok vándu
gen.	___________

5. Vocabulary training.

Across
1 begin
4 size, stature
5 known
7 bear, carry
8 day
9 enemy
11 time

Down
2 earl
3 had, was married to
4 become
6 north (adv.)
10 winter

VOCABULARY

af *prep* [*w dat*] out of, from; of
aldr *m* age
alla *acc sg fem of* **allr**
allr *adj* all
átti (*inf* **eiga**) *vb* had; was married to
barðisk (*inf* **berjask**, *see* **berja**) *refl vb* fought (*sg*)
bera (*past* bar, báru; *ppart* borinn) *vb* carry, bear
berja (*past* barð-) *vb* beat, strike, smite; *refl* **berjask** fight
bogi *m* bow
borinn (*inf* **bera**) *ppart* borne; endowed
Brávǫllr (*dat* Brávelli) *m* Bravoll, a plain in Sweden (*place name*)
brók (*gen* -ar) *f* pants-leg; breeches
dagr (*pl acc* daga) *m* day
Danmǫrk (*dat* Danmǫrku) *f* Denmark
dauðr (*n* dautt) *adj* dead
dýr *n* animal, beast
eiga (*past* átti) *vb* own, have; be married to
er *rel pron* who, which, that
er *conj* when; where
eyða (*past* -dd-) *vb* lay waste; spend up, squander; *refl* **eyðask** (*past* eyddisk) be squandered, come to naught
eyddisk (*inf* **eyðask**, *see* **eyða**) *refl vb* was squandered
Eymundr *m* Eymund (*personal name*)
falla (*past* fell/féll, fellu/féllu) *vb* fall
féll (*inf* **falla**) *vb* fell
frægr *adj* famous
fríðr (*n* frítt) *adj* beautiful, handsome, fine
fullr *adj* full
fyrir *prep* [*w acc*] for, because of; [*w dat*] before, in front of
fyrst *superl adv* first
ganga (*past* gekk, gengu) *vb* go, walk
grimmr *adj* grim, fierce, savage
Grjótgarðr *m* Grjotgard ('Stone-

Fence') (*personal name*)
hálfa *f* region, part
hefja (*1pl* hefjum) *vb* begin
heill *adj* healthy, well, 'hale'; whole
heimr *m* world; land, region of the world
heita (*past* hét, hétu) *vb* be named, be called
hilditǫnn *f* 'War Tooth' (*nickname*)
hildr *f* battle, war (*poetic*)
Hof *n* Hof ('Temple') (*place name*)
Hofsland *n* the Hof estate
hringr *m* ring
Hróðgeirr *m* Hrodgeir (*personal name*)
hugr (*dat* hug(i), *gen* -ar) *m* mind; mood
hús *n* house
hvítr *adj* white
illr *adj* bad, evil, 'ill'
Ingibjǫrg *f* Ingibjorg (*personal name*)
Ísland *n* Iceland
jarl *m* earl
kaupa (*past* keypt-) *vb* buy
keypti (*inf* **kaupa**) *vb* bought
koma (*past* kom, kómu) *vb* come
kunnigr *adj* known
kyrr *adj* still, quiet
langfeðgar *m pl* forefathers, ancestors (through the father's line)
lendr *adj* 'landed', having lands
lítill (*n* lítit) *adj* little, small
loðbrók (*gen* -ar) *f* 'Hairy Breeches' (*nickname*)
munu (*pres* mun) *vb* will, shall
norðr *adv* north
norðrálfa = **norðrhálfa** (*acc* norðr(h)álfu) *f* northern region
nú *adv* now
of *prep* [*w acc/dat*] over
orðinn (*inf* **verða**) *ppart* become
orrosta (*dat* orrostu) *f* battle
óvinr (*gen* -ar) *m* enemy
óvinum *dat pl of* **óvinr**
Ragnarr *m* Ragnar (*personal name*)
Refr *m* Ref ('Fox') (*personal name*)
reiðr (*n* reitt) *adj* angry, wrathful
renna (*past* rann, runnu) *vb* run
sakar *acc pl of* **sǫk**
sem *conj* as
sex *num* six; **sex tigir** *num* [*w gen*] sixty
silfr *n* silver
sinn *refl poss adj* his (own)
sína *acc pl of* **sinn**
sínum *dat pl of* **sinn**
Síreksstaðir *m pl* Sireksstadir ('Sirek's Farmstead') (*place name*)
smíða (*past* -að-) *vb* work in wood or metals, make, build
staðr (*pl* staðir) *m* stead, parcel of land
Steinbjǫrn *m* Steinbjorn ('Stone-Bear') (*personal name*)
sterkr *adj* strong
stórlyndr *adj* magnanimous
stórr *adj* big
sýn *f* sight, appearance
sǫk (*pl acc* sakar) *f* cause, reason, sake
taka (*past* tók, tóku) *vb* take
tigr (*pl nom* tigir, *acc* tigu) *m* [*w gen*] ten, a group of ten
tími *m* time
topt *n* toft, site of a house; foundation or bare walls, ruins of a house
Toptavǫllr (*dat* Toptavelli) *m* Toptavoll ('Field of Ruined Walls') (*place name*)
um *prep* [*w acc*] during, in (*time*)
ungr *adj* young
útan *adv* from without, from outside
vándr (*n* vánt) *adj* bad, wretched
Vápnafjǫrðr (*dat* -firði) *m* Vápnafjord ('Weapon's Fjord') (*place name*)
verða (*ppart* orðinn) *vb* become
vetr (*pl gen* vetra) *m* winter; year (*in reckoning time*)
vinsæll *adj* popular
vit *n* good sense, wit, intelligence
vǫllr *m* field
vexti *dat of* **vǫxtr**
vér *pron* we
vǫxtr (*dat* vexti) *m* size, stature
yfirlit *n* look, personal appearance
þann *acc sg masc of* **sá**
þegnskapr (*gen* -ar) *m* generosity, open-handedness
þeira *gen pl of* **sá** (of) those
þeiri *dat sg fem of* **sá**
þenna *acc sg masc of* **þessi**
þessi *dem pron* this, these
Þorgils *m* Thorgils (*personal name*)
Ǫlvir (*gen* Ǫlvis) *m* Olvir (*personal name*)

Øxna-Þórir *m* Thorir 'of the Oxen' (*personal name*)

Phrases

er frægr orðinn has become famous
fríðr sýnum handsome, fine in appearance
fyrir ... sakar on account of, because of
fyrir útan [*w acc*] outside; out beyond
í þann tima at that time, then
koma út til Íslands come out to Iceland (usually from Norway)
lendr maðr 'landed man' (= Norw. *lendmann*), a Norwegian nobleman whose lands and income were granted by the king
mikill vexti big, great in stature
sex tigu vetra for sixty years (lit. winters)
vel viti borinn intelligent, endowed with good sense

Hundreds of Medieval Icelandic Manuscripts have survived, preserving a range of Old Norse texts including sagas, laws, histories, church documents, and European literature, such as French romances, translated into Old Icelandic. The manuscripts come in a variety of sizes and states of preservation. The covers of some were made of wood while others were encased in calfskin. Some have only written text while others are illustrated. Many today are remnants; that is, pages or sections of what were once full books. (Photo Courtesy of Árni Magnússon Manuscript Institute, Reykjavík.)

LESSON 7

Ór *Snorra Eddu, Gylfaginning* (22. kap.)

(From *Snorri's Edda* [*The Prose Edda*], *The Beguiling of Gylfi*, Chap. 22)

[there] is about good
Annarr sonr Óðins er Baldr, ok er frá honum gott at segja. Hann
best praise all so handsome radiant so
er beztr, ok hann lofa allir. Hann er svá fagr álitum ok bjartr, svá at
[it] shines one herb so white likened [it] is eyelash
lýsir af honum, ok eitt gras er svá hvítt, at jafnat er til Baldrs brár.
that of all herbs [the] whitest accordingly can infer beauty
Þat er allra grasa hvítast, ok þar eptir mátt þú marka fegrð hans,
('fairest spoken')
both of hair of body wisest of the gods most eloquent
bæði á hár ok á líki. Hann er vitrastr ásanna ok fegrst talaðr ok
most gracious lives in the place that is called that heaven
líknsamastr. Hann býr þar, sem heitir Breiðablik. Þat er á himni.

7.1. Nouns and adjectives: Genitive plural.

The gen. pl. of all nouns ends in *-a*: *gras**a*** from *gras* (neut.) and *ás**anna*** (= *ás**a*** + *inna* with the loss of the initial *i-* of the article *inna* after a vowel) from *áss* (masc.).

The gen. pl. of all strong adjectives ends in *-ra*: *all**ra** grasa;* similarly *all**ra** ása, góð**ra** ása,* etc. This ending is added to the stem of the adj. according to the same rules that apply to the nom. sing. masc. ending *-r* (see 2.1, Special Stem Rules): *mikil**la** ása, væn**na** ása, fag**ra** grasa*, etc.

7.2. Definite article: Genitive plural.

The following passage illustrates the detached gen. pl. art. *inna* (the same for all genders). *Inna* offers another example of the assimilation of *-r* to stem-final *-n-* (2.1): *in-* + *-ra* = *in**na***.

Ór *Egils sǫgu Skalla-Grímssonar* (20. kap.)

(From the *Saga of Egil Skalla-Grimsson*, Chap. 20)

of the
Maðr hét Yngvarr, ríkr ok auðigr; hann hafði verit lendr maðr **inna**
former
fyrri konunga.

7.3. Strong adjectives: Nominative/accusative singular neuter stem rules (see 4.5).

As explained in 4.5, the basic ending of nom./acc. sing. neut. strong adjectives is *-t*, added directly to the stem of the adj.: masc. *hvít-r* – neut. *hvít-**t***. Two special stem rules affect this ending.

Special Stem Rules:

1. If the stem ends in *-ð-*, it is changed to *-t-*: *gó**ð**-r – go**t**-**t***.
2. If the stem ends in *-t-* preceded by another consonant, a second *-t* is not added: *hvíta**st**-r – hvíta**st**, be**zt**-r – be**zt**, bja**rt**-r – bja**rt***.

7.4. Superlative adjective formation.

Superlative adjectives are formed by adding either *-ast-* or *-st-* to the stem of the basic adj. In the latter instance, the root vowel is often changed: ***fa**gr* – ***fe**grstr*. (The retention of the final *-r* of *fagr* in the superl. *feg**r**-str* shows that this final *-r* is not the nom. sing. masc. ending, but belongs to the stem [see 2.1.2]. Similarly, *vitr* – *vit**r**-astr*, but *hvít-r* – *hvít-astr*.)

7.5. Adverb formation.

Adverbs comprise a broad class of descriptive words that express manner (how), time (when), place (where), and degree (how much): f.ex., 'carefully', 'today', 'here', 'greatly'. Many adverbs are directly related to a corresponding adj., but whereas adjectives describe nouns, adverbs describe verbs, adjectives and other adverbs. Examples of adj./adv. pairs are 'good/well', 'careful/carefully', 'great/greatly'. As the last two examples show, adverbs are frequently formed in English by adding the suffix '-ly' to an adj.

In Old Icelandic, adverbial forms of adjectives are identical with the nom. sing. neut. form: f.ex., *fegrst* 'most beautifully' in the phrase *fegrst talaðr*, lit. 'most beautifully spoken.' Adverbs are also formed from adjectives by means of suffixes: f.ex., *vand-**liga*** 'careful-**ly**' from *vandr* 'careful'.

7.6. Verbs: 3rd person singular present-tense endings.

The 3 sing. pres. of most verbs ends in *-r*, sometimes preceded by the vowel *-a-* or *-i-*. The following guidelines will help you determine when the 3 sing. pres. ending is *-ar*, *-ir*, or *-r*.

- Section 5.3.1 described weak verbs that employ the vocalic link *-a-* before the dental suffix of the past tense. These verbs also insert *-a-* before the 3 sing. pres. ending *-r*: *kall-**ar*** 'calls', from *kalla* (3 sing. past *kall-aði*).
- Section 5.3.2 described weak verbs that form their past by adding the dental suffix directly to the root of the verb. The majority of these verbs insert *-i-* before the 3 sing. pres. ending *-r*: *lýs-**ir*** 'shines' (R.S. 7), from *lýsa* (3 sing. past *lýs-ti*).
- Section 5.6 described weak verbs with vowel alternation between the present and the past. These verbs usually do not insert *-i-*; instead they add the 3 sing. pres. ending *-r* directly to the stem: *spyr-**r*** 'asks' (R.S. 8), from *spyrja* (3 sing. past *spur-ði*).

- Strong verbs regularly add the 3 sing. pres. ending *-r* directly to the verb stem: *bið-**r*** 'asks, bids' and *get-**r*** 'gets' (R.S. 9.3), from *biðja* and *geta* (3 sing. past *bað* and *gat*).

Some common verbs do not adhere to the above patterns.

- Several verbs with 3sg. pres. *-r* show no vowel alternation:
  selja 'deliver' – *sel-**r*** – ***seldi***
  setja 'set' – *set-**r*** – ***setti***
  skilja 'separate' – *skil-**r*** – *sk**i**ldi.*
- The weak verb *segja* 'say' undergoes vowel alternation (3 sing. past ***sagði***) but also inserts *-i-* in the pres. tense (3 sing. pres. *seg-**ir***).
- The weak verb *hafa* 'have' frequently appears in Old Norse texts in two forms. One adds *-r* directly to the stem in the pres. sing. (3 sing. *hef-**r***). The other inserts *-i-* (3 sing. *hef-**ir***) (see 6.5).
- The strong verb *heita* 'be called' also inserts an *-i-* in the pres. sing.: 3 sing. *heit-**ir**.*

7.7. Verbs: Assimilation of the 3rd person singular present-tense ending *-r*.

The ending *-r* of the 3 sing. pres. tense of the verb regularly assimilates to a final *-s* of the verb root: *blæs-**s*** 'blows', *rís-**s*** 'rises'. Assimilation to *-l* or *-n* also sometimes occurs: the example of *þú vil-**l*** was seen in R.S. 4; another common verb is *skín-**n*** 'shines'. Often, however, assimilation does not occur after *-l-* or *-n-*: *myl-**r*** 'crushes', *ven-**r*** 'trains'.

7.8. Verbs: 3rd person plural present-tense endings.

The 3 pl. pres. form of the verb (with the exception of some preterite-present verbs, see 15.1) is identical to the infinitive. Both forms end in *-a*, added to the pres. stem. Examples appear in R.S. 7: *lof**a*** (3 pl. pres.); *mark**a**, segj**a*** (inf.).

7.9. Review paradigms: 3rd person endings (past and pres.) of weak and strong verbs (see 6.3).

	Pres.		**Past**	
	Weak	**Strong**	**Weak**	**Strong**
3sg	(-a/i/–)-r	-r	(-að/ð/d/t)-i	–
3pl	-a	-a	(-að/ð/d/t)-u	-u

Exercises

1. Fill in the appropriate endings.

a. Konung__ var in__ fegrst__ mað__ í England__.

b. Skip____ (def.) var fagr__ ok hvít__. Þat var all__ skip__ bezt.

c. Baldr hét in__ hvít__ ás__. Hann var all__ ás__ bezt__ ok fegrst__.

d. Konung___ gekk til in___ bezt___ skip___. Þat var i___ vænst___ skip.

e. Yngvar___ var vitrast___ konung______ (pl. def.). Hann var son___ Egil___, líknsam___ mann___ ok fagr___.

2. Supply suitable personal names, nouns and adjectives.

a. __________r var __________astr __________anna, __________r ok __________n.

b. Skipit var ______ra skipa __________ast ok __________st.

3. Write the 3 sing. pres. and 3 pl. pres. forms of the following verbs.

a. Weak verbs with vocalic link -*a*-:

Ex.: at kalla (*past* -að-): hann kallar þeir kalla

at elska (*past* -að-): hon __________ þær __________

at lofa (*past* -að-): þat __________ þau __________

at tala (*past* -að-): hann __________ þeir __________

b. Weak verbs without vocalic link:

Ex.: at mæla (*past* -t-): þat mælir þau mæla

at lifa (*past* -ð-): hann __________ þeir __________

at senda (*past* -nd-) hon __________ þær __________

at sýna (*past* -d-): hon __________ þær __________

c. Weak verbs with vowel alternation (5.6):

Ex.: at flytja (*past* flutt-): hann flytr þeir flytja

at berja (*past* barð-): hon __________ þær __________

at kveðja (*past* kvadd-): hon __________ þær __________

at spyrja (*past* spurð-): þat __________ þau __________

d. Strong verbs:

Ex.: at gefa (*past* gaf, gáfu): hann gefr þeir gefa

at bera (*past* bar, báru): þat __________ þau __________

at renna (*past* rann, runnu): hann __________ þeir __________

at rísa (*past* reis, risu): hon __________ þær __________

at skína (*past* skein, skinu): hann __________ þeir __________

VOCABULARY

á *prep* [*w acc*] with respect to
álit *n pl* appearance, countenance
áss *m* god
Baldr *m* Baldr (*mythological name*)
beztr *superl adj* (*see* **góðr**) best
biðja (*pres* biðr, *past sg* bað) *vb* ask
bjartr *adj* bright, radiant
blása (*pres* blæss) *vb* blow
brá (*gen* brár) *f* eyelash
Breiðablik *n* Breidablik ('Broad Gleam') (*mythological place name*)
búa (*pres* býr) *vb* live (in a place), dwell
býr (*inf* **búa**) *vb* dwells

bæði *adv* both
eitt *num* one (*neut*)
eptir *prep* [*w dat*] after, according to
fagr (*superl* fegrstr) *adj* fair, beautiful
fegrð *f* beauty
fegrstr *superl adj* (*see* **fagr**) fairest, most beautiful
frá *prep* [*w dat*] from; about
fyrri *comp adj* former
geta (*pres* getr, *past* gat) *vb* get
gott *nom/acc sg neut of* **góðr**
góðr (*n* gott; *superl* beztr) *adj* good
gras *n* grass, plant, herb
heita (*pres* heitir) *vb* be named, be called
heitir (*inf* **heita**) *vb* is named
himinn (*dat* himni) *m* sky; heaven
hvítastr *superl adj* (*see* **hvítr**) whitest
hvítr (*superl* hvítastr) *adj* white
jafna (*past* -að-) *vb* compare, liken
jafnat (*inf* **jafna**) *ppart* compared, likened
líki *n* body
lofa *vb* praise
lýsa *vb* shine
lýsir (*inf* **lýsa**) *vb* shines
marka *vb* notice; infer
mátt (*inf* **mega**) *vb* (you *sg*) can
mega (*pres* má) *vb* can, may
Óðinn *m* Odin (*mythological name*), the chief god
rísa (*pres* ríss) *vb* rise
sá (*f* sú, *n* þat) *dem pron* that (one)
segja (*past* sagð-) *vb* say, tell
sem *rel pron* who, which, that
skína (*pres* skínn) *vb* shine
svá *adv* so, thus, in this way
tala (*past* -að-) *vb* speak
talaðr (*inf* **tala**) *ppart* spoken
venja (*past* vanð-/vand-) *vb* accustom, train
vera (*ppart* verit) *vb* be
verit (*inf* **vera**) *ppart* been (*nom/acc sg neut*)
vitr (*superl* vitrastr) *adj* wise
vitrastr *superl adj* (*see* **vitr**) wisest
Yngvarr *m* Yngvar (*personal name*)
þar *adv* there
þat *dem pron* that (*nom/acc sg neut of* **sá**)

PHRASES

at segja frá to tell about
á himni in heaven
bæði... ok *conj* both... and
fagr álitum beautiful (in appearance), handsome
fegrð á hár/líki beauty of hair/body
fegrst talaðr most eloquent
hann hafði verit he had been
þar eptir accordingly
þar, sem in the place that

Notes

The North Atlantic World of the Medieval Icelanders.

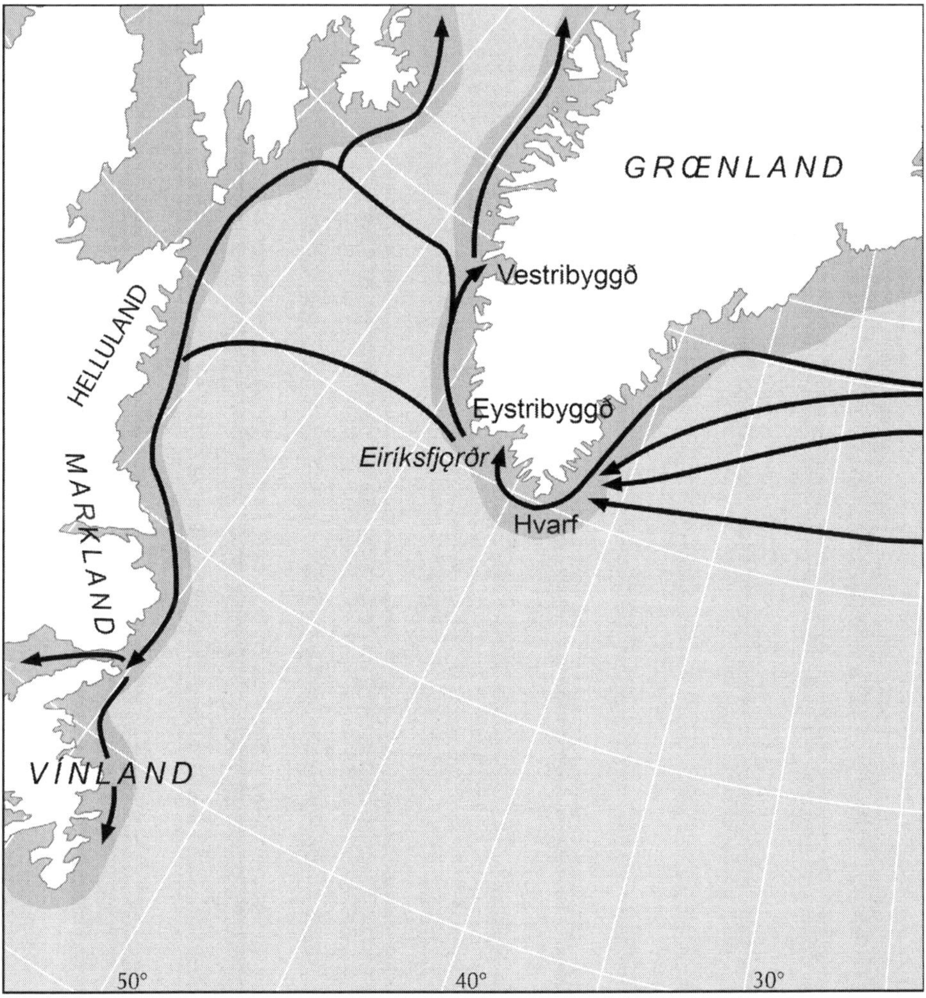

"Wise men report that from Stad in Norway it is a voyage of seven days west to Horn in eastern Iceland, and from Snæfellsnes [in western Iceland] it is four days' sail west to Greenland at the point where the sea is narrowest. It is said that if one sails due west from Bergen to Cape Farewell in Greenland, one passes a half day's sail to the south of Iceland. From Reykjanes in southern Iceland it is five days south to Slyne Head in Ireland, and from Langanes in northern Iceland it is four days northward to Svalbard in the Arctic Sea." (*The Book of Settlements*)

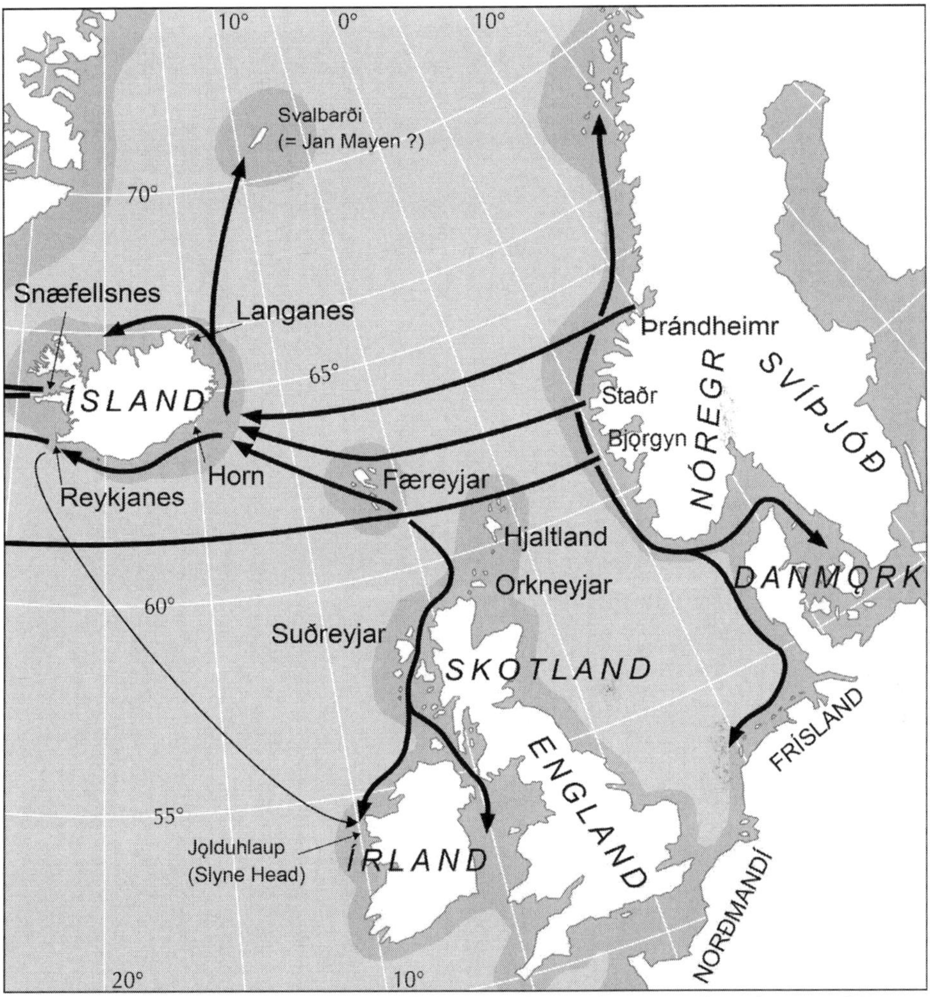

"Svá segja vitrir menn, at ór Nóregi frá Staði sé sjau dœgra sigling í vestr til Horns á Íslandi austanverðu, en frá Snæfellsnesi, þar er skemmst er, er fjǫgurra dœgra haf í vestr til Grœnlands. En svá er sagt, ef siglt er ór Bjǫrgyn rétt í vestr til Hvarfsins á Grœnlandi, at þá mun siglt vera tylft fyrir sunnan Ísland. Frá Reykjanesi á sunnanverðu Íslandi er fimm dœgra haf til Jǫlduhlaups á Írlandi (í suðr; en frá Langanesi á norðanverðu Íslandi er) fjǫgurra dœgra haf norðr til Svalbarða í hafsbotn." (*Landnámabók*)

LESSON 8

Ór *Gunnlaugs sǫgu ormstungu* (9. kap.)

(From the *Saga of Gunnlaug Serpent-Tongue*, Chap. 9)

at this time Sweden [the] Swede
Þenna tíma réð fyrir Svíþjóð Óláfr konungr sœnski, sonr Eiríks

the ambitious
konungs sigrsæla ok Sigríðar innar stórráðu; hann var ríkr konungr

man of ambition near
ok ágætr, metnaðar maðr mikill. Gunnlaugr kom til Uppsala nær

('during')
[the] assembly of (them) [the] Swedes in the spring reached
þingi þeira Svía um várit, ok er hann náði

('meeting')
audience greeted received
konungs fundi, kvaddi hann konunginn. Hann tók honum vel ok

asks who was said he was Icelandic
spyrr, hverr hann væri. Hann kvazk vera íslenzkr maðr. Þar var þá
með Óláfi konungi Hrafn Ǫnundarson.

what of men Iceland
Konungr mælti: "Hrafn," segir hann, "hvat manna er hann á Íslandi?"

the lower bench valiant before
Maðr stóð upp af inum óœðra bekk, mikill ok vaskligr, gekk fyrir

master of the best family
konung ok mælti: "Herra," segir hann, "hann er innar beztu ættar ok

himself bravest
sjálfr inn vaskasti maðr."

let him go sit with
"Fari hann þá ok siti hjá þér," sagði konungr.

8.1. Definite article: Singular feminine.

(1) Ór *Landnámabók* (*Sturlubók*) (112. kap.)

(From the *Book of* Settlements [*Sturla's Book*], Chap. 112)

king of Hordaland Æsa the fair
Hjǫrleifr Hǫrðakonungr átti Æsu **ina** ljósu.

(2) Ór *Egils sǫgu Skalla-Grímssonar* (55. kap.)

(From the *Saga of Egill Skalla-Grimsson*, Chap. 55)

parted with the greatest friendship
Skildusk þeir Aðalsteinn konungr ok Egill með **inni** mestu vináttu.

- The nom. sing. fem. form of the art. is *in*, as in the name of the heroine of *Gunnlaugs saga*: *Helga* ***in*** *fagra*. It appeared suffixed in *kýr-**in*** 'the cow', R.S. 5.
- The acc. sing. fem. is *ina*: *Æsu* ***ina*** *ljósu* 'Æsa the fair'.
- The dat. sing. fem. is *inni*: ***inni*** *mestu vináttu*.
- The gen. sing. fem. is *innar*: *Sigríðar* ***innar*** *stórráðu*, ***innar*** *beztu ættar*.

(For the declension of weak feminine adjectives, f.ex., *fagra*, *ljósu*, etc. in these examples, see 9.1.)

8.2. Definite article: Complete declension (see 4.4, 7.2, 8.1).

At this point we have covered all the forms of the sing. def. art., as well as the gen. pl. Here is the full declension in both singular and plural:

	Masc	**Fem**	**Neut**
Sg *nom*	inn	in	it
acc	inn	ina	it
dat	inum	inni	inu
gen	ins	innar	ins
Pl *nom*	inir	inar	in
acc	ina	inar	in
dat	inum	inum	inum
gen	inna	inna	inna

8.3. Pronouns: Apposition.

In Icelandic a pers. pron. is often placed in apposition to a following noun or nouns. For example, *þeir Þórólfr ok Bjǫrn* (R.S. 4), *þeir Aðalsteinn konungr ok Egill* (R.S. 8.1(2)), *þeira Svía* (R.S. 8). (Note that the gen. form of the pl. pron. *þeir* also ends in *-a*: see 7.1). In these instances, the apposition is complete, i.e., the pron. is in apposition with only the stated nouns that follow.

In other instances, the apposition can be partial. For example, when paired with a single noun: *þeir Þorólfr* would mean 'Thorolf and his companions.' When paired with more than one noun, the apposition may be either complete, as above, or partial; hence *þeir Þórólfr ok Bjǫrn* could also mean 'Thorolf and Bjorn and their companions'. One relies on the context in the sentence to decide which meaning fits best.

8.4. Verbs: 1st and 2nd person past-tense endings.

1. First person singular.

The 1 sing. past ending of weak verbs is *-a*: *ek gerð-**a*** (from *gera* 'make, do'), *ek vild-**a*** (from *vilja* 'want, wish'). Like the 3 sing. ending, it is added after the dental suffix.

The 1 sing. past of strong verbs has no ending; it is identical to the 3 sing. past: *ek var*, *ek bað*, *ek gekk*.

2. Second person singular.

The 2 sing. past ending of weak verbs is *-ir*, added after the dental suffix: *þú gerð-**ir**, þú vild-**ir***.

The 2 sing. past ending of strong verbs is *-t*. The following stem rules apply to this ending.

Special rules affecting the 2 sing. past stem of strong verbs:

- If the 1/3 sing. past form ends in *-t* or *-tt* preceded by a vowel, this changes to *-z* before the addition of the 2 sing. ending *-t*: f.ex., the 1/3 sing. past of *heita* is *hé**t***, so the 2 sing. past is *hét + t* → *hé**z**t*.
- If the 1/3 sing. past form ends in *-ð*, it changes to *-t* before the addition of the 2 sing. ending *-t*: f.ex., the 1/3 sing. past of *ráða* is *ré**ð***, so the 2 sing. past is *réð + t* → *ré**tt***.
- A dental consonant preceded by *-r-*, *-l-*, or *-s-* changes to *-t* and no ending is added: f.ex., the 1/3 sing. past of *verða* is *va**rð***, so the 2 sing. past is *varð + t* → *va**rt***.
- After a long vowel, the ending *-t* doubles: f.ex., the 1/3 sing. past of *sjá* is ***sá***, so the 2 sing. past is *sá**tt***.

3. First person plural.

The 1 pl. past ending of the verb is *-um*. It is added to the past-tense stem: *vér gerð-**um**, vér vár-**um***. When the 1 pl. pron. follows the verb, the *-m* of the ending can be (but is not always) dropped: *gerð**u** vér, vár**u** vér*.

4. Second person plural.

The 2 pl. past verb ending (used with all verbs) is *-uð*: *þér gerð-**uð**, þér vár-**uð***. As with the 1 pl., the final consonant of the ending can be dropped when the pron. follows: *gerð**u** þér, vár**u** þér*. Usage in different Old Icelandic texts varies widely in this respect.

8.5. Verbs: Moods and the subjunctive.

In grammatical terms, the **mood** of a verb indicates the speaker's intention, not his or her emotional state. While "mood" is the accepted grammatical term, "mode" is a more accurate description of the concept.[14] There are three moods (or modes) in Old Norse: indicative, subjunctive, and imperative.

Statements that are presented as being true or factual are in the **indicative mood.** This is by far the most common mood, and most of the verbs in the previous lessons have been in the indicative.

When the verb expresses some degree of uncertainty, potentiality, or wish (something that might be, could be, or would be), it appears in the **subjunctive mood**.

---

[14] The grammatical term "mood" derives from Lat. *modus* meaning 'manner' or 'mode'.

In Old Norse the subjunctive mood is often used in dependent clauses, especially indirect speech. Indirect speech is presented in the subjunct. because it is reported or summarized rather than quoted exactly. Three subjunctives occur in R.S. 8: *hann spyrr, hverr hann **væri*** 'he asks who he **was**' (reporting indirect speech), and ***fari** hann þá ok **siti** hjá þér* '**let him go** then and **let him sit** with you' (both expressing a wish). Certain conjunctions are also regularly followed by the subjunctive, f.ex., *þótt* 'athough': ***þótt** hann **væri** gamall* '**although** he **was** (subjunct.) old' (R.S. 3.9).

Commands are in the **imperative mood** (which will be discussed in 10.1).

8.6. Verbs: 3rd person singular subjunctive endings.

The 3 sing. subjunct. forms, both pres. and past, have the ending *-i* in all verbs: f.ex., 3 sing. pres.: *far**i**, sit**i***, 3 sing. past: *vær**i***.

8.7. Participles: A first look.

A **participle** is a verbal adjective, and all participles are formed from verbs. Old Norse has two types of participles: present and past.

Present participles are easily recognized. They employ the suffix *-and-*, which corresponds to English '-ing': f.ex., ON *verð**and**i* 'becoming', from the verb *verða*. (*Verðandi* [R.S 17] is the name of one of the three Norns, the Norse version of the Fates. See 17.4 for more on pres. participles.)

Past participles are very common and have already appeared in the reading selections: *kallaðr* 'called', *lengt* 'lengthened', *numit* 'taken' (in R.S. 2), *nefndr* 'named' (R.S. 3.9, 5), *verit* 'been' (R.S. 3.9, 7.2), *vígðr* 'ordained' (R.S. 4.5), *orðinn* and *orðit* 'become' (R.S. 6), *jafnat* 'likened', and *talaðr* 'spoken' (R.S. 7).

In addition to being used as adjectives, past participles also have a specialized function in compound tenses. This section looks at the adjectival usage of past participles. The next section considers past participles in compound tenses.

When used as adjectives, past particples take regular adjectival endings, which are added to the ppart. stem. In weak verbs, the ppart. stem is identical to the past-tense stem: *kallað-, nefnd-, talað-, vígð-*. In strong verbs, the ppart. has a special stem (see 10.3.2).

For example, the two past participles that appear in R.S. 7 are *talað**r*** (nom. sing. masc. modifying *hann* 'he') and *jafna**t*** (nom. sing. neut. modifying *gras* 'grass'). Both of these verbs, *tala* 'speak' and *jafna* 'liken', are weak verbs with vocalic link *-a-* (5.3.1), hence the ppart. stem ends in *-að-*: *talað-* and *jafnað-*. As illustrated by *jafnat* and *lengt*, the dental suffix of the stem assimilates to the ending when neut. nom. *-t* is added:

jafnað- + *-t* → *jafna**t***.
lengd- + *-t* → *leng**t***.

8.8. Participles: Past participles in compound tenses.

The nom./acc. neut. ppart. is also used with *hafa* to form compound tenses, similar to English 'have called', 'have taken', etc. These occur frequently. Below are examples of with past participles of weak verbs:

*hann hafði sag**t*** 'he had said' (stem *sagð-* w. dental suffix *-ð-*);
*hann hafði mæl**t*** 'he had spoken' (stem *mælt-* w. dental suffix *-t-*);
*hann hafði dœm**t*** 'he had judged' (stem *dœmd-* w. dental suffix *-d-*);
*hann hafði kasta**t*** 'he had thrown' (stem *kastað-* w. dental suffix *-ð-* preceded by linking vowel *-a-*).

We have seen two examples of such compound tenses in the reading selections, both with the ppart. of strong verbs:

hann hafði numit 'he had taken' (R.S. 2) (inf. *nema*),
hann hafði verit 'he had been' (R.S. 7.2) (inf. *vera*).

Present and Past Perfect

These compound tenses are called **perfect** tenses. The term "perfect" derives from Latin *perfectum* meaning 'completed', because the action is finished with respect to the time of the verb 'have'.

The **present perfect** (***hefir*** *sagt* '**has** said', etc.) employs 'have' in the present tense.

The **past perfect** (***hafði*** *sagt* '**had** said', etc.) employs 'have'in the past tense.

EXERCISES

1. Fill in the appropriate endings.

a. Þeir Egil__ geng__ til Uppsala ok spurð__, hverr in__ sœnsk__ maðr vær__.

b. Gunnlaug__ var kalla___ Ormstunga ('Serpent's Tongue').

c. Skip___ (def.) hafð__ ver___ kalla___ Ormrinn langi ('The Long Serpent').

2. Conjugate the following verbs in the past tense. The 3 sing. and 3 pl. forms are supplied.

a. Weak verbs:

Ex: gera (-ð-):	ek *gerða*,	þú *gerðir*,	hann gerði
	vér *gerðum*,	þér *gerðuð*,	þeir gerðu
lifa (-ð-):	ek ______,	þú ______,	hann lifði
	vér ______,	þér ______,	þeir lifðu
mylja (mulð-):	ek ______,	þú ______,	hann mulði
	vér ______,	þér ______,	þeir mulðu

mæla (-t-): ek ____________, þú ____________, hann mælti
vér ____________, þér ____________, þeir mæltu

senda (-nd-): ek ____________, þú ____________, hann sendi
vér ____________, þér ____________, þeir sendu

b. Strong verbs:

Ex: heita: ek hét, þú hézt, hann hét
vér hétum, þér hétuð, þeir hétu

bera: ek ____________, þú ____________, hann bar
vér ____________, þér ____________, þeir báru

ganga: ek ____________, þú ____________, hann gekk
vér ____________, þér ____________, þeir gengu

skjóta: ek ____________, þú ____________, hann skaut
vér ____________, þér ____________, þeir skutu

standa: ek ____________, þú ____________, hann stóð
vér ____________, þér ____________, þeir stóðu

verða: ek ____________, þú ____________, hann varð
vér ____________, þér ____________, þeir urðu

3. Write the following verbs in the 3 sing. pres. perfect and the 3 sing. past perfect tenses. Each verb is given in the 3 sing. past.

	Pres. perf.	Past perf.
Ex.: hann horfði:	hann hefr horft	hann hafði horft
hon lýsti:	____________	____________
hon svaraði:	____________	____________
hann sagði:	____________	____________
þat nefndi:	____________	____________
hann hafði:	____________	____________
hon mælti:	____________	____________
hon vígði:	____________	____________

4. Write the nom. sing. masc. form of the past participles of the weak verbs in exercise **3**.

____

____

VOCABULARY

bekkr (*dat* bekk) *m* bench
bók *f* book
fara *vb* go, travel
fundr *m* meeting
fyrir *prep* [*w acc*] before, in front of (*motion*)

herra *m* master, sir (NB: *nom ends in* -a)
hjá *prep* [*w dat*] by, beside, with
Hjǫrleifr *m* Hjorleif (*personal name*)
Hrafn *m* Hrafn ('Raven') (*personal name*)
hvat *int pron* what
hverr *int pron* who
Hǫrðakonungr *m* king of Hǫrðaland (in Western Norway)
íslenzkr *adj* Icelandic
kvaddi (*inf* **kveðja**) *vb* greeted (*sg*)
kvazk *refl vb* said of himself (*3sg past of* **kveðask**)
kveða (*past sg* kvað) *vb* say; *refl* **kveðask** (*past sg* kvazk) say of oneself [*w inf*]
kveðja (*past* kvadd-) *vb* greet
landnám *n* 'land-taking', settlement
Landnámabók *f* Book of Settlements
ljóss *adj* light, fair
ljósu *adj* fair (*wk acc sg fem of* **ljóss**)
manna *gen pl* of **maðr**
með *prep* [*w dat*] with (accompanying)
mestr *superl adj* greatest (*see* **mikill**)
mikill (*superl* mestr) *adj* great
ná (*past* -ð-) *vb* [*w dat*] reach
nær *prep* [*w dat*] near (to)
Óláfr *m* Olaf (*personal name*)
óœðri *comp adj* lower
Sigríðr *f* Sigrid (*personal name*)
sitja *vb* sit
sjálfr *adj* self; oneself, himself
skildusk (*inf* **skiljask**, *see* **skilja**) *refl vb* parted from each other
skilja (*past* -d-) *vb* separate, divide; *refl* **skiljask** part from each other
Sturlubók *f* 'Sturla's Book', version of the **Landámabók** made by Sturla Thordarson
Svíar *m pl* the Swedes
Svíþjóð *f* Sweden
sœnskr *adj* Swedish
taka (*past sg* tók) *vb* take, receive
tók (*inf* **taka**) *vb* received ('took') (*sg*)
Uppsalir *m pl* Uppsala ('Upper Halls'), a town in Sweden (*place name*)
vaskastr *superl adj* (*see* **vaskr**) bravest
vaskr *adj* brave, valiant
vár *n* spring (season)
vera *vb* be
væri (*inf* **vera**) *vb* was (*subjunct*)
þeira *pron* of them (*gen of* **þeir**)
þér *pron* you (*pl*)
þing *n* assembly
Æsa *f* Æsa (*personal name*)
ætt *f* family
Ǫnundr *m* Onund (*personal name*)

PHRASES

þenna tíma at this time
hann kvazk vera he said he was
hann tók honum vel he received him well
um várit in the spring

Notes

LESSON 9

Ór *Egils sǫgu Skalla-Grímssonar* (32. kap.)

(From the *Saga of Egil Skalla-Grimsson*, Chap. 32)

Bjǫrn hét hersir ríkr í Sogni, er bjó á Aurlandi; hans son var Brynjólfr,
inheritance father his sons
er arf allan tók eptir fǫður sinn. Synir Brynjólfs váru þeir Bjǫrn
age of news
ok Þórðr; þeir váru menn á ungum aldri, er þetta var tíðenda.
[sea-]farer [engaged] in raiding
Bjǫrn var farmaðr mikill, var stundum í víking, en stundum
trading trips most accomplished
í kaupferðum; Bjǫrn var inn gørviligsti maðr.
it happened one certain summer present [the] Fjords
Þat barsk at á einu hverju sumri, at Bjǫrn var staddr í Fjǫrðum
party certain well-attended girl whom
at veizlu nǫkkurri fjǫlmennri; þar sá hann mey fagra, þá er
he liked very much asked about of what
honum fannsk mikit um. Hann spurði eptir, hverrar ættar hon var;
honum var þat sagt, at hon var systir Þóris hersis Hróaldssonar ok hét
(i.e. proposed)
raised up petition his requested refused
Þóra. Bjǫrn hóf upp bónorð sitt ok bað Þóru, en Þórir synjaði
the match thus autumn
honum ráðsins, ok skildusk þeir at svá gǫrvu. En þat sama haust fekk
himself band of men went boat full-manned north into
Bjǫrn sér liðs ok fór með skútu alskipaða norðr í
[the] Fjords at home took
Fjǫrðu ok kom til Þóris ok svá, at hann var eigi heima. Bjǫrn nam
away brought [her] home him(self) they
Þóru á brott ok hafði heim með sér á Aurland; váru þau þar
('make wedding to')
the winter marry her
um vetrinn, ok vildi Bjǫrn gera brúðlaup til hennar.

9.1. Weak nouns and adjectives: Feminine singular.

Most weak fem. nouns and all weak fem. adjectives end in *-a* in the nom. sing., *-u* in the other cases of the sing. Note that, as in the case of weak masc. and neut. nouns and adjectives, the fem. sing. declensions of weak nouns and adjectives are identical.

nom	-a
acc	-u
dat	-u
gen	-u

Examples of weak nouns from R.S. 9 are nom. *Þór**a***, acc. and gen. *Þór**u*** (NB: the verb *biðja* takes a gen. object); acc. *skút**u*** (nom. *skúta*); and dat.

*veizl**u*** (nom. *veizla*). In addition, nom. *kona* and gen. *kon**u*** appear below in R.S. 9.3.

Examples of adjectives are: nom. *Helga in fagr**a*** 'Helga the fair'; acc. *Æsu ina ljós**u*** 'Æsa the fair' (R.S. 8.1(1)); dat. *inni mest**u** vináttu* 'with the greatest friendship' (R.S. 8.1(2)); gen. *innar bezt**u** ættar* 'of the best family' (R.S. 8).

A small number of weak fem. abstract nouns end in *-i*, f.ex., *ell**i*** 'old age', *æv**i*** 'time, lifetime, age', *grem**i*** 'wrath'. These nouns are indeclinable, having *-i* throughout the singular. For example, acc. *goðagremi* 'wrath of the gods' appears in R.S. 13(3). No weak adjectives end in *-i*.

nom	-i
acc	-i
dat	-i
gen	-i

9.2. Review paradigms: Complete weak noun and adj. endings in the singular (see 4.7, 9.1).

	Masc	Fem	Neut
nom	-i	-a, (-i)	-a
acc	-a	-u, (-i)	-a
dat	-a	-u, (-i)	-a
gen	-a	-u, (-i)	-a

9.3. Strong nouns: Feminine singular.

Ór *Gísla sǫgu Súrssonar* (5. kap.)

(From the *Saga of Gisli Sursson*, Chap. 5)

'Seal-Cliff'
Þórbjǫrn hét maðr ok var kallaðr selagnúpr; hann bjó í Tálknafirði at Kvígandafelli; Þórdís hét kona hans, en Ásgerðr dóttir.

this | woman | Þorkell requests | gets | ('to have') in marriage
Þessarar konu biðr Þorkell Súrsson ok getr hana at eiga, en Gísli

requested | sister | got
Súrsson bað systur Vésteins, Auðar Vésteinsdóttur, ok fekk hana;

dwell | now | both | together
búa nú báðir saman í Haukadal.

- Strong fem. nouns usually have no ending in the nom. sing.: f.ex., *Þórdís*; but the ending *-r* is quite common, especially in personal names: f.ex., *Ásgerð**r**, Auð**r***.

nom	–,	-r
acc	–, (-u),	-i
dat	–, -u,	-i
gen	-ar	

	'beauty'	'earth'	'Ingibjorg'	'Aud'
nom	fegrð	jǫrð	Ingibjǫrg	Auð**r**
acc	fegrð	jǫrð	Ingibjǫrg**u**	Auð**i**
dat	fegrð	jǫrð**u**	Ingibjǫrg**u**	Auð**i**
gen	fegrð**ar**	jarð**ar**	Ingibjarg**ar**	Auð**ar**

- The acc. and dat. sing. forms of most strong fem. nouns have no ending: acc. *fegrð* (R.S. 7), *mey* (R.S. 9; nom. *mær*), dat. *Borg* (R.S. 1), *Svíþjóð* (R.S. 8).
    - A number of strong fem. nouns, however, end in *-u* in the dat. sing.: *jǫrð* 'earth' – acc. *jǫrð* (R.S. 12(2)), dat. *jǫrð**u*** (R.S. 17).
    - Some strong fem. nouns, mostly personal names, have *-u* in both the acc. and dat.: *Ingibjǫrg* – acc./dat. *Ingibjǫrg**u*** (R.S. 6).
    - Strong fem. nouns with nom. sing. *-r* regularly take the ending *-i* in both the acc. and dat. sing.: *Auð**r*** – acc./dat. *Auð**i***.
- The gen. sing. of strong fem. nouns ends in *-ar* in most instances: *Auð**ar***, *Sigríð**ar***.
    - When the root vowel is *-ǫ-* in the nom. sing., the vowel becomes *-a-* in the gen. sing.: *j**a**rðar*, *Ingibj**a**rgar*. (The same alternation occurs in the masc. name *Bjǫrn* – gen. *Bj**a**rnar*, R.S. 1. This vowel change will be explained in Lesson 11.)
    - If the stem of the noun ends in a vowel, the initial *-a-* of the gen. ending is omitted: f.ex., *brár* (R.S. 7) = *brá* + *-ar*.

9.4. Review paradigms: Complete strong noun endings in the singular (see 4.2, 9.3).

	Masc	**Fem**	**Neut**
nom	-r (see 2.1)	–, -r	–
acc	–	–, -i, -u	–
dat	-i	–, -i, -u	-i
gen	-s, -ar	-ar	-s

9.5. Kinship terms in *-ir*: Singular declension.

A very small class of nouns consisting of family members (both masc. and fem.) has the ending *-ir* in the nom. sing. These nouns take *-ur* in the other cases of the singular:

*bróð**ir*** – acc./dat./gen. *bróð**ur***
*dótt**ir*** – acc./dat/gen. *dótt**ur***
*fað**ir*** – acc./dat./gen. *fǫð**ur***[15]
*móð**ir*** – acc./dat./gen. *móð**ur***
*syst**ir*** – acc./dat./gen. *syst**ur***

9.6. Strong adjectives: Singular feminine.

(1) Ór *Hávarðar sǫgu* (1. kap.)

(From the *Saga of Havard*, Chap. 1)

young — of a great family
Hon var **ung** kona ok **stórrar** ættar.

---

[15] The change of root vowel from *faðir* to *fǫður* will be explained in 11.2.2.

(2) Ór *Snorra Eddu* (10. kap.)

(From *Snorri's Edda* [*The Prose Edda*], Chap. 10)

giant / Giant-Land / Night

Nǫrvi hét jǫtunn, er bygði í Jǫtunheimum. Hann átti dóttur, er Nótt

black / dark / was characteristic of her family

hét. Hon var **svǫrt** ok **døkk** sem hon átti ætt til.

nom	–
acc	-a
dat	-ri
gen	-rar

- The nom. sing. fem. form of strong adjectives has no ending: *ung kona, svǫrt, døkk.*
- The acc. sing. fem. ends is *-a*: *mey fagr**a**, skútu alskipað**a**.*
- The dat. sing. fem. ends is *-ri*: *veizlu nǫkkur**ri** fjǫlmenn**ri**.*
- The gen. sing. fem. ends in *-rar*: *stór**rar** ættar.*

The dat. and gen. endings are modified according to the same rules that apply to the nom. sing. masc. ending *-r* (2.1).

9.7. Review paradigms: Complete strong adj. endings in the singular (see 4.6, 9.6).

	Masc	Fem	Neut
nom	-r (see 2.1)	–	-t
acc	-an	-a	-t
dat	-um	-ri (see 2.1)	-u
gen	-s	-rar (see 2.1)	-s

9.8. Verbs: 1st and 2nd person present-tense endings.

1. First person singular.

The 1 sing. pres. of verbs has no ending. It is the same as 3 sing. pres. form (7.6) minus the ending *-r*: *ek kalla* (3 sing. pres. *kalla**r***), *ek segi* (3 sing. pres. *segi**r***, R.S. 4, 5, 8), *ek bið* (3 sing. pres. *bið**r***, R.S. 9.3), *ek spyr* (3 sing. pres. *spyr**r***, R.S. 8).

2. Second person singular.

The 2 sing. pres. of verbs is the same as the 3 sing. pres.: *þú kall**ar**, þú seg**ir**, þú bið**r**, þú spyr**r**.*

3. First person plural.

The 1 pl. pres. verb ending is the same as the past, *-um*: *vér ger**um**, vér bið**um***. It is added to the pres. stem of the verb.

- If the infinitve stem ends in *-j-*, this is retained in the 1 pl.: *vér spyr**jum*** (inf. *spyrja*), *vér seg**jum*** (inf. *segja*), *vér vil**jum*** (inf. *vilja*).
- As with the 1 pl. past (8.4.3), when the pron. follows the verb, the consonant of the ending can be dropped: *vilj**u** vér* for *vilj**um** vér*.

4. Second person plural.

The 2 pl. pres. verb ending is *-ið*: *þér bið**ið**, þér ger**ið**, þér spyr**ið**, þér seg**ið**.*

9.9. Review paradigms: Pres. and past tense endings of verbs (see 7.9, 8.4, 9.8).

	Pres.		Past	
	Weak	Strong	Weak	Strong
1sg	(-a/i/–)-	–	(-að/ð/d/t)-a	–
2sg	(-a/i/–)-r	-r	(-að/ð/d/t)-ir	-t
3sg	(-a/i/–)-r	-r	(-að/ð/d/t)-i	–
1pl	-um	-um	(-að/ð/d/t)-um	-um
2pl	-ið	-ið	(-að/ð/d/t)-uð	-uð
3pl	-a	-a	(-að/ð/d/t)-u	-u

Exercises

1. Fill in the appropriate endings.

a. Þóra in auðg__ hét kon__. Hon var móðir Ásgerð__ in__ væn__ ok Harald__ in__ hárfagr__.

b. Gísl__ bað Helg__ in__ auðg__ ok fekk h____ at eig__.

c. I__ sœnsk__ þing var um vár__ (def.).

d. Fegrð Helg__ in__ auðg__ var mikil. Hon var góð kon__ ok gǫfug__ ætt__.

e. Auð__, kon__ Gísl__ in__ vitr__, var væn kon__ ok stórráð.

f. Þeir Gunnlaugr ok Hrafn stóð__ upp af bekk______ (def.) ok geng__ fyrir konungsson______ (def.).

g. Þeir Eirík__ náð__ fund__ Óláf__ konung__.

h. Konung__ bjó í firð______ (def.).

i. Þorstein__ in__ stór__ stóð á skip______ (def.) ok kvadd__ konung.

2. Fill in the appropriate endings.

a. Maðr hét Gísli. Hann var sonr Ásgerð____, kon__ Þorkel__ in__ mikl__, auðig__ mann__ ok vaen__.

b. Kon__ Gísl__ hét Auð__. Hon var syst___ Véstein__ in__ auðg__, mikil__ mann__ ok vaen__.

c. Véstein__ bað Ásgerð__, dótt___ Gísl__ ok Auð__ ok syst__ Yngvar__.

d. Gísl__ bað Auð__, ágaet__ kon__ ok vitr__.

e. Egil__ var faðir Ásgerð__, væn____ kon__ ok mikil__.

3. Repeat exercise **2**, substituting all names of strong noun form with names of weak noun form. For example, interchange the forms of *Gísli* and *Vesteinn*, or use any other masc. names. For the replacements for the strong fem. names *Auðr* and *Ásgerðr*, use the weak fem. names *Helga* and *Þóra*.

a. ______________________________

____

b. ______________________________

____

c. ______________________________

____

d. ______________________________

e. ______________________________

4. Conjugate the following verbs in the pres. tense. The 3 sing. and 3 pl. forms are supplied.

a. Weak verbs:

Ex: lifa:	ek lifi,	þú lifir,	hann lifir
	vér lifum,	þér lifið,	þeir lifa
elska:	ek ________,	þú ________,	hann elskar
	vér ________,	þér ________,	þeir elska
mæla:	ek ________,	þú ________,	hann mælir
	vér ________,	þér ________,	þeir mæla
spyrja:	ek ________,	þú ________,	hann spyrr
	vér ________,	þér ________,	þeir spyrja

b. Strong verbs:

Ex: biðja:	ek bið,	þú biðr,	hann biðr
	vér biðjum,	þér biðið,	þeir biða
gefa:	ek ________,	þú ________,	hann gefr
	vér ________,	þér ________,	þeir gefa
hefja:	ek ________,	þú ________,	hann hefr
	vér ________,	þér ________,	þeir hefja
rísa:	ek ________,	þú ________,	hann ríss
	vér ________,	þér ________,	þeir rísa

VOCABULARY

aldr *m* age
alskipaðr *adj* fully manned
arfr *m* inheritance
Auðr *f* Aud (*personal name*)
Aurland *n* Aurland (*place name*)
átti (*inf* **eiga**) *vb* had
bað (*inf* **biðja**) *vb* requested (*sg*)
barsk (*inf* **berask**, *see* **bera**) *refl vb* **barsk at** happened
báðir *pron* both (*masc*)
bera (*past sg* bar) *vb* carry, bear; *refl* **berask at** happen
biðja (*pres* biðr, *past sg* bað) *vb* ask; [*w gen*] ask for, request

biðr (*inf* **biðja**) *vb* requests
bónorð *n* request, petition
brott *adv* **á brott** away (*motion*)
brúðlaup *n* wedding
Brynjólfr *m* Brynjolf (*personal name*)
døkkr *adj* dark
eiga (*past* átti) *vb* own, have
elli *f* old age
faðir (*acc/dat/gen* fǫður) *m* father
fannsk (*inf* **finnask**, *see* **finna**) *refl vb* appeared
fara (*past sg* fór) *vb* travel, go
farmaðr *m* traveler, sea-farer
fá (*past sg* fekk) *vb* [*w gen*] get; marry
fekk (*inf* **fá**) *vb* got; married
fell *n* mountain
finna (*past sg* fann) *vb* find; *refl* **finnask** appear
Firðir *m pl* the Fjords (*place name*)
fjǫlmennr *adj* populous, with many people, well attended
fór (*inf* **fara**) *vb* traveled, went
fǫður *m* father (*acc of* **faðir**)
gera (-ð-) *vb* make, do
geta (*pres* getr) *vb* get
getr (*inf* **geta**) *vb* gets
gremi *f* wrath, anger
gǫrr (-v-) *adj* done
gørviligstr *superl adj* (*see* **gørviligr**) most accomplished
gørviligr *adj* accomplished, capable, enterprising
hana *pron* her (*acc of* **hon**)
haust *n* autumn, fall
Hávarðr *m* Havard (*personal name*)
hefja (*past sg* hóf) *vb* raise
heim *adv* (to) home (*motion*)
heima *adv* at home (*location*)
heimr *m* land, region of the world
hennar *pron* (of) her (*gen of* **hon**)
hon (*acc* hana, *gen* hennar) *pron* she
hóf (*inf* **hefja**) *vb* raised (*sg*)
Hróaldr *m* Hroald (*personal name*)
hverr *indef pron* any, anyone
Jǫtunheimar *m pl* Land of Giants
jǫtunn *m* giant
kaupferð *f* trading trip
kona *f* woman, wife
Kvígandafell *n* 'Heifer Mountain' (*place name*)
lið *n* troop, force, band of armed supporters; aid, assistance
mey *f* girl (*acc of* **mær**)
mikit *adv* much (*neut of* **mikill**)
mær (*acc* mey) *f* girl
nam (*inf* **nema**) *vb* took (*sg*)
nema (*past sg* nam) *vb* take
norðr *adv* north
nótt *f* night
nú *adv* now
nǫkkurr *indef pron* one, a certain
Nǫrvi *m* Norvi (*personal name*)
ráð *n* match, marriage
saman *adv* together
selagnúpr *m* 'Seal-Cliff' (*nickname*)
sér *refl pron* to himself (*dat of* **sik**)
sik *refl pron* himself
sinn *refl poss adj* his (own) (refers back to subject)
sitt *refl poss adj* his (own) (*neut of* **sinn**)
skúta *f* small boat, skiff
Sogn *n* Sogn, area in Western Norway (*place name*)
sonr (*gen* -ar; *pl* synir) *m* son
spyrja (spurð-) *vb* ask
staddr *adj* present; located
sumar (*dat* sumri) *n* summer
sú *dem pron* that (one) (*fem of* **sá**)
Súrr *m* Sur (*personal name*)
svartr (*fem* svǫrt) *adj* black
svǫrt *adj* black (*nom sg fem of* **svartr**)
synir *m* sons (*pl of* **sonr**)
synja (*past* -að-) *vb* [*w gen*] refuse, deny
systir (*acc/dat/gen* systur) *f* sister
Tálknafjǫrðr *m* Talknafjord, a fjord in Northwest Iceland
tíðenda *n pl* of news (*gen of* **tíðendi**)
tíðendi *n pl* news, tidings
ungr *adj* young
veizla *f* feast, party
Vésteinn *m* Vestein (*personal name*)
víking *f* sea-raiding
þau *pron* they (*n pl*)
þá *dem pron* that (one) (*acc of* **sú**)
þessarar *dem pron* (of) this (*gen sg fem of* **þessi**)
þessi (*n* þetta) *dem pron* this
þetta *dem pron* this (*neut nom/acc of* **þessi**)
Þorkell *m* Thorkel (*personal name*)
Þóra *f* Thora (*personal name*)
Þórbjǫrn *m* Thorbjorn (*personal

name)
Þórðr *m* Thord (*personal name*)
Þórir *m* Thorir (*personal name*)
ævi *f* time, lifetime, age

PHRASES

at svá gǫrvu thus, this being the case, as things stood
á ungum aldri young, of a young age
biðja konu (*gen*) ask for a woman in marriage
einn hverr one, a certain
er þetta var tíðenda when this happened (lit., 'was of news')
fá sér liðs gather a band of men, get support
gera brúðlaup til marry
geta hana at eiga get her in marriage, marry her
hafa heim með sér bring home with oneself
hefja upp bónorð propose
nema á brott take away, abduct
sem hon átti ætt til which was characteristic for her family
svá at so that
þá er honum fannsk mikit um whom he liked very much

Notes

Suggested Readings: *Viking Language 2*

At this stage, we suggest turning to the longer passages, complete short sagas, and Eddic and Skaldic poetry found in *Viking Language 2: The Old Norse Reader.*

Viking Language 2: The Old Norse Reader (ISBN 978-14-81175265) is a treasure trove of Scandinavian lore with a broad selection of Old Norse sources and runes. The learner chooses from myths, legends, sagas, and runic inscriptions. Several chapters delve deeply into the tales and poems of the Scandinavian gods and heroes. To assist the learner, *The Old Nores Reader* features a large vocabulary and a full reference grammar. Below is the Table of Contents.

www.oldnorse.org
www.juleswilliampress

Viking Language 2: The Old Norse Reader Table of Contents

[16] *Íslendingasögur* (*Sagas of the Icelanders* or *Family Sagas*) is a modern term, hence spelled with modern Icelandic -*ö*- rather than Old Icelandic -*ǫ*-. The same for the modern term *fornaldarsögur* (Legendary Sagas).

Two Runestones from the Parish of Klepp
Runes in the Family Sagas (*Íslendingasögur*)
Runes in *Egils saga Skalla-Grímssonar*
Runes in the Legendary Sagas (*fornaldarsögur*)
Medieval Runes
Medieval Runes from Bergen
Medieval Runes in Commerce
Bryggen Love Runes
Runic Inscriptions in Latin
Key to the Rune Exercises

Chapter 12, Eddic Poetry
Eddic Verse and Its Sources
Eddic Titles
Eddic Tradition - Long Lines and Half Lines

Chapter 13, Eddic Meters
The Four Principal Eddic Meters
Eddic Examples from Mythic Poems

Chapter 14, *The Lay of Thrym* (*Þrymskviða*)
Poetic Devices
Poetic Grammar
Þrymskviða (*The Lay of Thrym*)

Chapter 15, Runes and Eddic Meter from Sweden (*Svíþjóð*)
Two Bällsta Runestones (From Uppland, Sweden)
The Carver and the Carving
A Suggested Translation

Chapter 16, Skaldic Poetry
Skaldic Composition
Heiti and Kennings
Kennings in *Háttatal*: A Series of Examples
Three Skaldic Fragments about Þórr
Classification: The Five Sievers Types
Húsdrápa (*Housepoem*), A Picture Poem of Praise

Chapter 17, The Karlevi Runestone: A Skaldic Poem Carved in Runes on a Baltic Island.
The Karlevi Stone

LESSON 10

Ór *Óláfs sǫgu Tryggvasonar* (108. kap.)

(From the *Saga of Olaf Tryggvason*, Chap. 108)

to some some
Þá mælti Eiríkr jarl við þann mann, er sumir nefna Finn, en sumir

Finnish bowman shoot (you)
segja, at hann væri finnskr – sá var inn mesti bogmaðr: "Skjóttu mann

the bow-room
þann inn mikla í krapparúminu."

shot the arrow struck [the] middle [of] Einar's bow at that moment
Finnr skaut, ok kom ǫrin á boga Einars miðjan í því bili, er

drew [for] the third time the bow broke two pieces
Einarr dró it þriðja sinn bogann. Brast þá boginn í tvá hluti.

broke loudly
Þá mælti Óláfr konungr: "Hvat brast þar svá hátt?"

answers out of your hand
Einarr svarar: "Nóregr ór hendi þér, konungr."

not is likely break happened take my
"Eigi mun svá mikill brestr orðinn," segir konungr, "tak boga minn

shoot with [it] threw the bow
ok skjót af" – ok kastaði boganum til hans.

the bow drew at once beyond [the] point of the arrow
Einarr tók bogann ok dró þegar fyrir odd ǫrvarinnar ok mælti:

too weak sovereign's bow threw back the bow
"Of veikr, of veikr allvalds bogi" – ok kastaði aptr boganum, tók þá

shield his sword
skjǫld sinn ok sverð ok barðisk.

10.1. Verbs: The imperative.

The imperative is the form of the verb used to make commands or requests. The imperative tells someone what to do, f.ex., 'go!'. Expressing one's own intentions (f.ex., 'let's go') is also a type of imperative.

1. Second person singular

The 2 sing. imperative of the verb is the bare pres. stem, which takes one of three forms.

- For weak verbs vocalic link *-a-* (5.3.1), the imperative retains the vocalic link as part of the stem: *kall**a*** 'call!'. In these verbs the imperative looks like the infinitive.

- For most other weak verbs and for strong verbs, the imperative is the same as the bare root: *tak* 'take!' (inf. *taka*), *skjót* 'shoot!' (inf. *skjóta*).
- A few weak verbs have the suffix *-i* in the imperative: *þeg**i*** 'be silent!' (inf. *þegja*).

The pron. *þú* often follows the imperative verb, without changing the meaning: *tak þú* = *tak* ('take!') *skjót þú* = *skjót* ('shoot!'). When the command is empatic (forceful), *þú* is left as a separate word, but in most instances *þú* behaves like a suffix and is joined to the verb in the shortened form *-ðu*: *kalla**ðu*** = *kalla þú* ('call!'), *far**ðu*** = *far þú* ('go!'), *ger**ðu*** = *ger þú* ('do!').

When joined to the verb, the dental consonant of *-ðu* assimilates to the final consonant of the stem according to the same rules (5.4) that determine the form of the dental suffix *-ð-* in the past tense of weak verbs: *skjót**tu***, *tak**tu***.

- When the stem ends in *-nd-*, *-ng-*, and *-ld-*, these consonant clusters sometimes change to *-tt*, *-kk*, and *-lt*. For example, *sta**nd**a*, *ga**ng**a*, and *ha**ld**a* in the imperative become *sta**tt**(u)*, *ga**kk**(tu)*, and *ha**lt**(u)*.

2. Second person plural.

The 2 pl. imperative form is identical to the 2 pl. indic. (see 9.8). For example, *takið* can be either a simple statement 'you (pl.) are taking' or a command 'take!' (adressed to a group). Similarly, *skjótið* can mean either 'you (pl.) are shooting' or 'shoot! (pl.)'.

3. First person plural.

The 1 pl. imperative is the same as the 1 pl. indic.: *gerum* 'we do' or 'let's do', *skjótum* 'we shoot' or 'let's shoot'.

10.2. Stem variation in *-j-* and *-v-*.

The stems of many Icelandic words end in either *-j-* or *-v-*, the presence of which is determined by the ending that follows. Examples are:

Nouns:

masc. *leggr* (*-j-*) 'leg' – gen. sing. *legg**j**ar*, gen. pl. *legg**j**a*
fem. *ey* (*-j-*) 'ísland' – dat. sing. *ey*/*ey**j**u*, gen. sing. *ey**j**ar*, gen. pl. *ey**j**a*
neut. *ríki* (*-j-*) 'power' – gen. pl. *rík**j**a*
fem. *ǫr* (*-v-*) 'arrow' – gen. sing. *ǫr**v**ar*, gen. pl. *ǫr**v**a*

Verbs:

*seg**j**a* 'say' – 3 sing. pres. *segir*
*bið**j**a* 'ask for' – 3 sing. pres. *biðr*
*syng**j**a* (older *syng**v**a*) 'sing' – 3 sing. pres. *syngr*

Adjectives:

miðr (*-j-*) 'middle' – acc. sing. masc. *mið**j**an*, fem. *mið**j**a*, dat. sing. masc. *mið**j**um*, dat. *mið**j**u*, etc.

þriði (-*j*-) 'third' – (always weak) nom. sing. fem. *þrið**ja***, acc./dat./ gen. sing. masc. *þrið**ja***, fem. *þrið**ju***, etc.

døkkr (-*v*-) 'dark' – strong acc. sing. *døkk**van***; weak nom. sing. masc. *døkk**vi***, fem. *døkk**va***, etc.

Pronouns:

hverr (-*j*-) – dat. sing. masc. *hver**jum***, neut. *hver**ju***

The presence of stem-final -*j*- and -*v*- is governed by the following rules:

- Both -*j*- and -*v*-, when present in the stem, appear before the ending -*a*.
- -*j*- does not appear before -*i*.
- -*v*- does not appear before -*u*.
- -*v*- appears before the ending -*i* (f.ex., weak masc. *døk**kvi***) but does not appear before a suffixed article (f.ex., *ǫrin* 'the arrow').
- Neither -*j*- nor -*v*- appears before a consonantal ending.
- Neither -*j*- nor -*v*- appears when there is no ending.

10.3. Verbs: Past participle formation.

Weak verbs and strong verbs form their past participles in manners parallel to the formation of the past tense (5.2).

1. Weak verbs.

The ppart. of weak verbs adds the same dental suffix as the past tense (-*ð*-, -*d*-, or -*t*-, see 5.4). Hence the two stems are the same: *kalla* – past/ppart. stem *kallað*-; *nefna* – past/ppart. stem *nefnd*-; *víga* – past/ppart. stem *vígð*-.

The ppart. adds regular adj. endings to this stem: nom. sing. masc. *kallað-**r*** (R.S. 2), *nefnd-**r*** (R.S. 3.9, 5), *vígð-**r*** (R.S. 4.5), *talað-**r*** (R.S. 7); and nom./acc. sing. neut. *leng**t*** (R.S. 2), *jafna**t*** (R.S. 7).

- A few verbs (f.ex., *lifa* 'live', *vaka* 'awaken', *vilja* 'want') behave differently from the general rule. They attach the dental suffix directly to the stem in the past tense, but insert -*a*- before the ending in the neut. ppart: *vaka* 'awaken': 3 sing. past *vak-ti*; ppart. masc. *vak-tr*, but neut. *vak-**a**-t*.

2. Strong verbs.

Instead of adding a dental suffix, strong verbs form their past participles by changing the stem vowel. The ppart. stem is distinct from the past-tense stem: *t**a**ka* – past *t**ó**k, t**ó**ku* – ppart. *t**e**kinn*. Another example is *syngja* 'sing' – past *s**ǫ**ng, s**u**ngu* – ppart. *s**u**nginn*. English strong verbs show a similar pattern: 't**a**ke' – 't**oo**k' – 't**a**ken'; 's**i**ng' – 's**a**ng' – 's**u**ng'.

The endings of Icelandic strong past participles are identical in form with the article (*tek**inn***, *sung**inn***).[17] Some examples from the reading

---

[17] Technically speaking, the strong ppart. adds the suffix -*in*- (*tek-**in**-*, *sung-**in**-*) followed by adjectival endings. Recall from 2.1 that the -*r*- of these endings

selections are: nom. sing. masc. *bor**inn*** (R.S. 6), from *bera* 'bear'; nom. sing. masc. *orð**inn*** (R.S. 6, 10) and nom. sing. neut. *orð**it*** (R.S. 6), from *verða* 'become'. Other common examples: *ganga* 'go, walk' – ppart. *geng**inn***; *gefa* 'give' – ppart. *gef**inn***; *koma* 'come' – ppart. *kom**inn***.

The ppart. of *taka* shows the full pattern (compare the def. art., 8.2):

	Masc	Fem	Neut
***Sg** nom*	tek-inn	tek-in	tek-it
acc	tek-inn	tek-ina	tek-it
dat	tek-inum	tek-inni	tek-inu
gen	tek-ins	tek-innar	tek-ins
***Pl** nom*	tek-inir	tek-inar	tek-in
acc	tek-ina	tek-inar	tek-in
dat	tek-inum	tek-inum	tek-inum
gen	tek-inna	tek-inna	tek-inna

At this point, you have learned all the principal parts of strong verbs. They are listed in the vocabulary as follows:

fá (fær; fekk, fengu; fengit) *vb* get
liggja (liggr; lá, lágu, legit) *vb* lie
ríða (ríðr; reið, riðu; riðit) *vb* ride
standa (stendr; stóð, stóðu; staðit) *vb* stand

10.4. Verbs: Function of reflexive verbs.

Reflexive verbs have four basic functions: reflexive, reciprocal, passive, and impersonal.

1. Reflexive function.

The reflexive function is used when the action of the verb reflects back onto the subject, that is, when one is doing something to or for oneself. For example, *kýrin fœddisk* 'the cow fed herself' (R.S. 5), from *fœða* 'feed'.

A reflexive verb followed by an infinitive is the regular construction for indirect discourse when the person speaking is reporting something about him- or herself. For example, *hann kvazk vera* (R.S. 8) 'he said he was', lit. 'he said himself to be' (from *kvað*, 3 sing. past of *kveða* 'say'). Note the contrast between this construction and the subjunct. of indirect discourse (8.5), which is used when the person speaking is different from the one being spoken about: *hann spyrr, hverr hann væri* 'he (i.e., the king) asks who he (i.e., Gunnlaug) was' (R.S. 8).

2. Reciprocal function.

The reciprocal function always involves a plural subject. It expresses an action that the verb's subjects perform with regard to each other. For

---

assimilates to stem-final *-n-* according to the Special Stem Rules. The Icelandic suffix *-in-* comes from the same source as English '-en' found on past participles such as 'tak**en**' and 'giv**en**'.

example, *þeir skuldusk* 'they parted', lit. 'they parted from each other' (from *skilja* 'to part, separate'); also *hann barðisk* 'he fought' (R.S. 6, 10), from *berjask* 'to fight', lit. 'strike each other' (from *berja* 'to strike').

3. Passive function.

Reflexive verbs are also used in a passive sense, that is, to indicate that something "is done" or "was done", without necessarily specifying who does or did it. For example: *hjósk skjǫldr Helga* 'Helgi's shield was struck' (*hjósk*, lit. 'struck itself', from *hjó*, 3 sing. past of *hǫggva* 'strike').

4. Use in impersonal constructions.

Reflexive verbs occur frequently in impersonal constructions where the original reflexive function is no longer always clear. These usages are often idiomatic and do not translate literally.

> *honum fannsk mikit um* (R.S. 9) 'he liked very much' (*fannsk* from *finna* 'find')
> *hversu lízk þér á* (R.S. 4) 'how do you like, what do you think of' (*lízk á* from *líta á* 'look at')

Note that in these constructions the logical subject appears in the dative case.

10.5. Reflexive verbs: Formation of the 3rd person.

Reflexive verbs in the 3rd person are formed with the ending *-sk*, a contraction the 3 sing. acc. refl. pron. *sik* (compare the dat. form *sér* in R.S. 9). The infinitive of a refl. verb ends in *-ask*: *berj**ask*** 'fight.' When the verb is conjugated, the ending *-sk* is added to the personal ending of the verb (not to the stem), as the following examples illustrate:

> *barði**sk*** (R.S. 6, 10) = *barði* (3 sing. past of *berja*) + *-sk*
> *bar**sk*** (R.S. 9) = *bar* (3 sing. past of *bera*) + *-sk*
> *fann**sk*** (R.S. 9) = *fann* (3 sing. past of *finna*) + *-sk*
> *skildu**sk*** (R.S. 8.1(2), 9) = *skildu* (3 pl. past of *skilja*) + *-sk*

When *-sk* is added to the verb, the following modifications involving assimilation and loss regularly occur:

- Assimilation after a dental consonant.

  Dental consonant + *-sk* = *-zk*. For example, *kva**zk*** (R.S. 8) = *kvað-* + *-sk*. This is a general type of assimilation and is not limited to this ending; compare the superl. *beztr* 'best' (R.S. 7) = stem *bet-* + *-str*.

- Loss of final *-r* of the personal ending.

  A final *-r* of a personal ending is lost before the ending *-sk*. For example, *lí**zk*** (R.S. 4) = *lítr* + *-sk*. In this case the final *-r* is first lost and the refl. ending is then assimilated to the stem-final *-t*.

Exercises

1. The phrase *kastaði boganum* appeared twice in the R.S.

a. What is the grammatical case of *boganum*? ____________________

b. Why is it in this case? ____

2. Fill in the appropriate endings and missing vowels.

a. Eystein___ stóð á inu stór___ skip___ ok barðisk.

b. Einar___ kast___ð___ in___ sam___ bog___ aptr til Óláf___ konung___.

c. Óláf___ tók in___ veik___ bog___ ok dró h____.

d. In___ stór___ bog___ brast.

3. Fill in the appropriate endings.

a. Kon___ hét Þór___ in ljós___. Hon bjó í stór____ firð___ á Ísland___ hjá Brynjólf___ in____ rík___, góð____ mann___ ok auðg____, ok Helg___ in____ stór___, ágæt____ kon___ ok væn____.

b. Þór___ átti Gísl___ in___ mikl___, gǫfg____ mann ok vitr____. Bjǫrn in___ hvít___ var sonr Gísl___ ok Þór___ ok hann átti Ber___ in___ stórráð___, fagr___ kon___ ok ung___. Bjǫrn var ung___ mað___ ok góð____ ætt____ ok átti stór___ skip. Hann var i víking á ein___ hverj___ haust___ ok fór með it stór___ skip til England___. Þar náði hann fund___ Óláf___ in___ góð___, konung___ England___, ok var með Óláf___ þetta sam___ haust.

4. Commands. Write the 2 sing. imperative of the following verbs. Give both the bare stem and the stem with suffixed *-ðu*.
Ex: flytja (flutt-): flyt / flyttu

a. Weak verbs:

kasta (-að-): ____________ / ____________

kveðja (kvadd-): ____________ / ____________

mæla (-t-): ____________ / ____________

b. Strong verbs:

bera: ____________ / ____________

biðja: ____________ / ____________

þiggja: ____________ / ____________

5. Construct the reflexive form of the following verb forms:

a. at taka ________________, hon tekr ________________,
hon tók ________________, þær tóku ________________.

b. at mæla ______________, hann mælir ______________,
hann mælti ______________, þeir mæltu ______________.

c. at skjóta ______________, þat skýtr ______________,
þat skaut ______________, þau skutu ______________.

6. Translate the following reflexive expressions:

a. Þeir mæltusk við.

____

b. Dagr sezk. (*at setja* 'to set'; 3 sing. pres. *hann setr*)

____

7. Translate the following two sentences and explain the difference:

a. Konungrinn sagðisk vera ríkr maðr.

____

____

b. Konungrinn sagði, at hann væri ríkr maðr.

____

____

VOCABULARY

> Hereafter, verbs in the vocabularies are listed as follows:
> *Weak verbs*: **infinitive** (dental suffix or past-tense stem) *vb* definition
> *Strong verbs*: **infinitive** (3sg. pres.; 3sg. past, 3pl. past; neut. ppart.) *vb* definition

aptr *adv* back
barðisk (*inf* **berjask**, *see* **berja**) *refl vb* fought (*sg*)
berja (barð-) *vb* beat, strike, smite; *refl* **berjask** fight
bil *n* moment
bogi *m* bow
bogmaðr *m* bowman, archer
bresta (brestr; brast, brustu; brostit) *vb* break
brestr *m* break
draga (dregr; dró, drógu; dregit) *vb* pull, draw
døkkr (-v-) *adj* dark
Einarr *m* Einar (*personal name*)
ey (*dat* ey/eyju, *gen* -jar; *pl* -jar) *f* island
fá (fær; fekk, fengu; fengit) *vb* get
finnskr *adj* Finnish
Finnr *m* Finn (*personal name*)
hár *adj* loud
hátt *adv* loudly (*neut of* **hár**)
hendi *dat sg of* **hǫnd**
hǫnd (*dat* hendi) *f* hand
í *prep* [*w acc*] into
kasta (-að-) *vb* [*w dat*] throw
leggr (*gen* -jar; *pl* -ir) *m* leg, limb; hollow bone (of arm and leg)
liggja (liggr; lá, lágu, legit) *vb* lie
miðr (-j-) *adj* middle
minn *poss adj* my, mine
munu (mun, munu; mundi) *vb* will, shall (*futurity*), be likely
oddr *m* point
of *adv* too
orðinn (*inf* verða) *ppart* happened, taken place
ríða (ríðr; reið, riðu; riðit) *vb* ride
ríki (-j-) *n* power
sinn *n* a time, instance
skjóta (skýtr; skaut, skutu; skotit) *vb* shoot

skjǫldr *m* shield
setja (-tt-) *vb* set, put, place
standa (stendr; stóð, stóðu; staðit) *vb* stand
sumir *adj* (*m pl*) some (people)
svara (-að-) *vb* answer
sverð *n* sword
syngja (*older* **syngva**) (syngr; sǫng, sungu; sungit) *vb* sing
Tryggvi *m* Tryggvi (*personal name*)
tvá *num* two (*acc masc of* **tveir**)
tveir (*acc masc* tvá) *num* two
veikr *adj* weak
verða (verðr; varð, urðu; orðit) *vb* become; happen, come to pass (NB: regular loss of initial *v*- before -*o*- and -*u*-)
þegar *adv* at once, immediately
þriði (-j-) *ord num* third
því *dem pron* (to) that (*dat of* **þat**)
ǫr (-v-) *f* arrow

Phrases

eigi mun svá mikill brestr orðinn such a great break is not likely to have occurred
í því bili at that moment
koma á strike
mæla við [*w acc*] speak to
ór hendi þér out of your hand

Notes

LESSON 11

Ór *Fóstbrœðra sǫgu* (23. kap.)

(From the *Saga of the Foster-Brothers*, Chap. 23)

tent
Egill mælti: "Ek var at búð Þorgríms Einarssonar, ok þar er nú mestr
part of the assembly tells story
hluti þingheimsins. Þorgrímr segir þar sǫgu."
about whom story that
Þormóðr mælti: "Frá hverjum er saga sú, er hann segir?"
know fully about whom the story this
Egill svarar: "Eigi veit ek gǫrla frá hverjum sagan er, en hitt veit
entertainingly chair set under out
ek, at hann segir vel frá ok skemmtilega, ok er stóll settr undir hann úti
the tent around listen to the story
hjá búðinni, ok sitja menn umhverfis ok hlýða til sǫgunnar."
you are probably able who
Þormóðr mælti: "Kunna muntu nǫkkurn mann at nefna, þann sem
('in is')
is in the story especially since it is amusing
í er sǫgunni, allra helzt er þú segir svá mikit frá, at gaman sé at."
hero the story
Egill mælti: "Þorgeirr nǫkkur var mikill kappi í sǫgunni, ok svá
[it] seems to me must have been somehow [connected]
virðisk mér sem hann Þorgrímr myndi verit hafa nǫkkut við
('gone very well forward')
the story fought very well likely would like go
sǫguna ok gengit mjǫk vel fram, sem líkligt er. Vilda ek, at þú gengir
to there
þangat."
maybe
"Vera má þat," sagði Þormóðr.

11.1. Strong verbs: Present-stem vowel alternation.

The pres. sing. stem of strong verbs frequently contains a different vowel from that of the pres. pl. stem. For example, *hann gengr – þeir ganga*. Since the 3 pl. pres. is always identical with the inf. (7.8), the vowel of the pres. pl. stem is also the vowel of the inf. stem.

The chart below shows the alternation between the vowels of the pres. sing. and pl. stems of strong verbs. One does not have to memorize every strong verb, only know the pattern of this sound change.

The regular stem vowel alternation in strong verbs

Alternation

Pl		Sing	Examples
a	–	e	at t**a**ka – hann t**e**kr
á	–	æ	at r**á**ða – hann r**æ**ðr
o	–	e	at k**o**ma – hann k**e**mr
ǫ	–	ø	at h**ǫ**ggva – hann h**ø**ggr ('strike')
ú	–	ý	at b**ú**a – hann b**ý**r
jú	–	ý	at dr**jú**pa – hann dr**ý**pr
jó	–	ý	at sk**jó**ta – hann sk**ý**tr
au	–	ey	at hl**au**pa – hann hl**ey**pr ('run')

No alternation

Pl		Sing	Examples
e	–	e	at g**e**fa – hann g**e**fr
ø	–	ø	at s**ø**kkva – hann s**ø**kkr ('sink')
i	–	i	at b**i**ðja – hann b**i**ðr
í	–	í	at r**í**sa – hann r**í**ss
y	–	y	at s**y**ngja – hann s**y**ngr ('sing')
ý	–	ý	at sp**ý**ja – hann sp**ý**r ('spew')
æ	–	æ	at hl**æ**ja – hann hl**æ**r ('laugh')
ei	–	ei	at h**ei**ta – hann h**ei**tir
ey	–	ey	at d**ey**ja – hann d**ey**r ('die')

11.2. Umlaut: An explanation.

The process that changes the vowel of the infinitive and pl. stem into the vowel of the sing. stem in the table above is known as ***i*-umlaut** (also called ***i*-mutation** or **front mutation**). A few basic points of vowel phonetics make umlaut easy to understand.

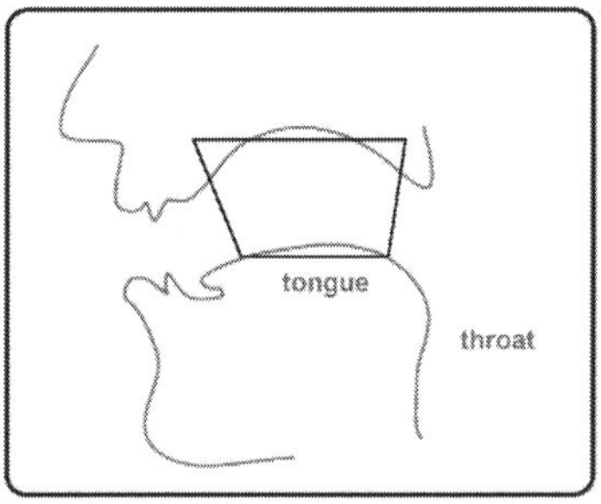

In all languages, two of the factors that differentiate one vowel from another are the position of the tongue in the mouth and the shape of the lips when the vowel is pronounced. Linguists use a space chart to illustrate the position of the vowels in the mouth.

The three cardinal vowels are **i** (as in 'mach**i**ne'), **u** (as in 's**u**e'), and **a** (as in 'f**a**ther'). They are placed in the vowel chart as follows.

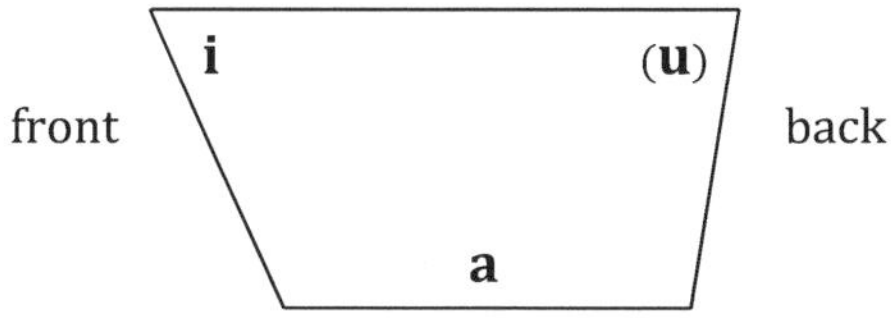

When you say these vowels, notice that the **i** of 'mach**i**ne' is pronounced high in the mouth and toward the front; the **u** of 's**u**e' is pronounced high in the mouth and toward the back; and the **a** of 'f**a**ther' is pronounced low in the mouth and near the center. Note too that the lips are somewhat rounded (indicated by parentheses) when you pronounce **u**, but are not rounded when you pronounce **a** and **i**.

Below are the short and long vowels of Old Icelandic:[18]

Short Vowels

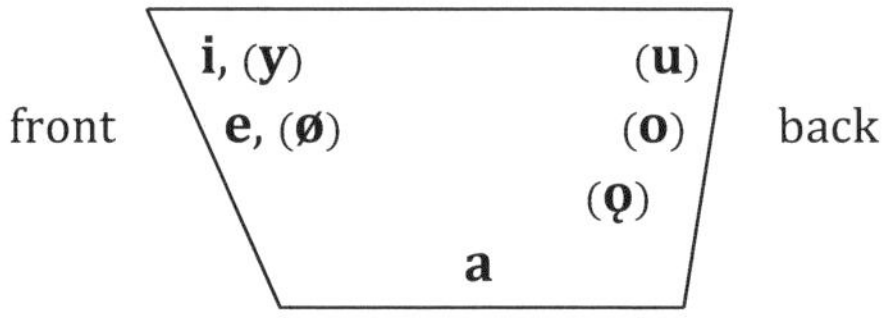

Long Vowels

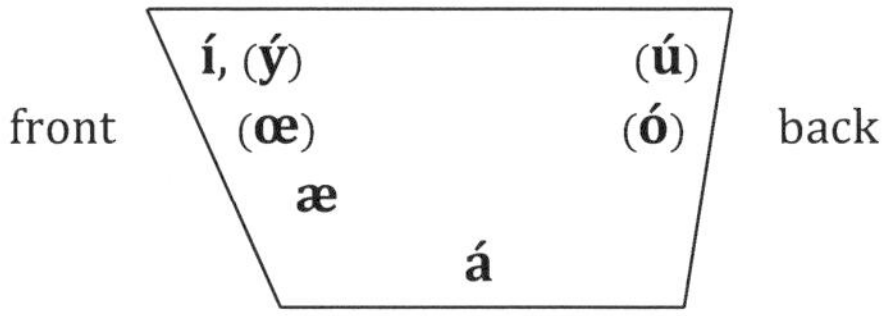

1.* i*-umlaut.

i-umlaut is the result of a historical process in which a vowel was "pulled" forward (and often higher) in the mouth, toward the position of **i**, by an upcoming *-i-* or *-j-* in the next syllable.

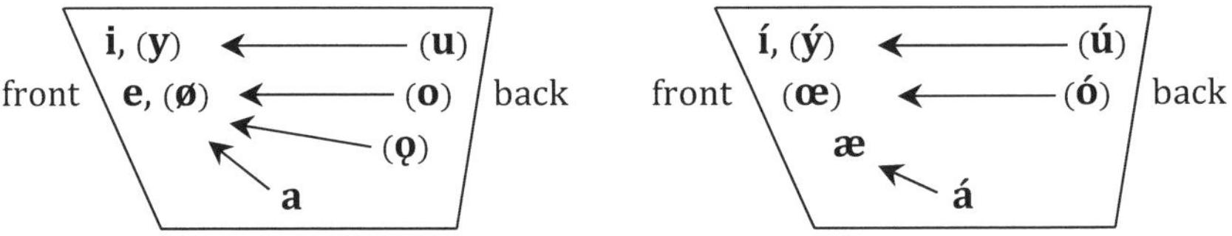

The *-i-* or *-j-* that caused the umlaut has sometimes disappeared by the time of Old Icelandic (although it was present in Proto-Norse, before approximately 700 CE), but its influence survives in the vowel change.

Look again at the above table of sing. and pl. stem vowels. When the vowels alternate, the sing. stem vowel in each instance is the result of moving the pl. stem vowel closer to the position of **i** on the mouth chart.[19] The vowels that do not alternate are **front vowels** to start with, so *i*-umlaut has no effect on them.

2.* u*-umlaut (a~ǫ alternation)

The short vowel *-a-* is regularly replaced by *-ǫ-* when the next syllable contains *-u-* or *-v-*: ***fara*** 'travel' – *vér f**ǫ**rum* 'we travel'; ***hafa*** 'have' – *vér*

[18] The vowels in these charts illustrate the pronunciation of Old Icelandic and not that of Modern Icelandic. For example, in Old Icelandic, *á* was essentially a longer version of *a*; whereas in Modern Icelandic, *á* is pronounced as a diphthong similar to the **ou** in 'h**ou**se'.

[19] Umlaut affects the vowels of dipthongs in the same way it affects individual vowels. For example, *au* → *ey* when affected by *i*-umlaut (*a* → *e* + *u* → *y*).

hǫfum 'we have', *vér hǫfðum* 'we had', *þeir hǫfðu* 'they had'. This process is called ***u*-umlaut** or ***a~ǫ* alternation**.

Frequently, the original *-u-* or *-v-*[20] that triggered this sound change is no longer present in Old Icelandic, but the presence of the vowel *-ǫ-* shows that it existed at an earlier stage of the language. For example, *fǫr* (fem.) 'journey' is from earlier **fǫru*.

As the vowel chart shows, the sound of **ǫ** is the result of raising and backing of an **a** (that is, shifting it toward the position of **u**), and also acquiring lip rounding like **u**.

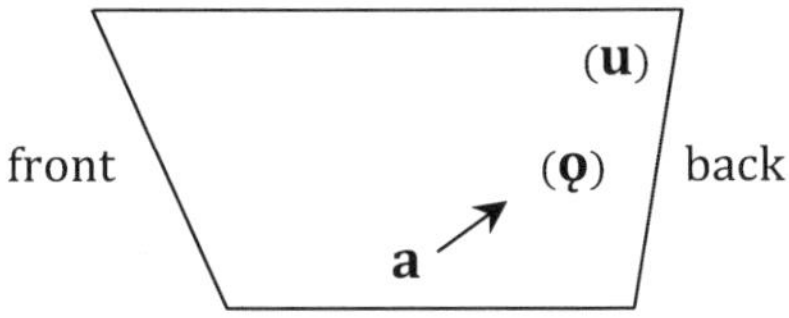

11.3. Weak feminine nouns: *a~ǫ* alternation in the singular.

The declension of the weak fem. noun *saga* illustrates the alternation of *-a-* with *-ǫ-*. In the acc., dat., and gen., the fem. sing. weak ending *-u* regularly triggers *u*-umlaut.

	Indef	Def
Sg *nom*	saga	saga-n
acc	**sǫgu**	**sǫgu**-na
dat	**sǫgu**	**sǫgu**-nni
gen	**sǫgu**	**sǫgu**-nnar

The table at right shows the complete declension of *saga* in all cases of the singular. All of the forms with suffixed article appeared in the R.S. Recall from 4.8 that the article loses its initial *i-* when it is attached to a noun ending in a vowel.

11.4. Strong feminine nouns: *a~ǫ* alternation in the singular.

All strong fem. nouns with root vowel *-a-* also show *a~ǫ* alternation: the nom. and acc. forms, and usually also the dat., contain *-ǫ-*, whereas the gen. retains the original vowel *-a-*: nom./acc./dat. *fǫr* 'journey' – gen. *farar*; nom./acc. *jǫrð* 'earth', dat. *jǫrðu* – gen. *jarðar*. This is due to an ending *-u* that existed at an earlier stage of the language; in some nouns, the ending *-u* remains in the dat. sing. (*jǫrðu*). The complete sing. declension of such fem. nouns is as follows:

	Indef	Def	Indef	Def
Sg *nom*	fǫr	fǫr-in	jǫrð	jǫrð-in
acc	fǫr	fǫr-ina	jǫrð	jǫrð-ina
dat	fǫr	fǫr-inni	jǫrð**u**	jǫrð**u**-nni
gen	farar	farar-innar	jarðar	jarðar-innar

[20] In earlier Icelandic, *v* was pronounced like *w*.

11.5. Strong masculine nouns: *a~ǫ~e* alternation in the singular.

A number of strong masc. nouns show *a~ǫ~e* (or *ja~jǫ~i*) alternation in the singular. Several of these have occurred: nom. *Bjǫrn* (R.S. 4), gen. *Bjarnar* (R.S. 1); dat. *velli* (R.S. 6, 6.6) from *vǫllr* 'field'; *vexti* (R.S. 6) from *vǫxtr* 'growth'; dat. *firði* (R.S. 1, 6.6, 9.3) from *fjǫrðr* 'fjord'; acc. *skjǫld* (R.S. 10) from *skjǫldr* 'shield'.

The complete sing. declension of this type of strong masc. noun can be illustrated by the nouns *vǫllr, ǫrn* 'eagle', *Bjǫrn*, and *skjǫldr*:

	'field'	'eagle'	'Bjorn'	'shield'
***Sg** nom*	v**ǫ**llr	**ǫ**rn	Bj**ǫ**rn	skj**ǫ**ldr
acc	v**ǫ**ll	**ǫ**rn	Bj**ǫ**rn	skj**ǫ**ld
dat	v**e**lli	**e**rni	B**i**rni	sk**i**ldi
gen	v**a**llar	**a**rnar	Bj**a**rnar	skj**a**ldar

Note that the nom. sing. masc. ending *-r* is not added after stem-final *-rn*: *ǫ**rn**, Bjǫ**rn***.

With regard to strong masc. nouns with this three-way alternation *a~ǫ~e* (or *ja~jǫ~i*):

- the gen. retains the original vowel: ***a**rnar, Bj**a**rnar, skj**a**ldar*;
- the nom. and acc. show the influence of *u*-umlaut (***ǫ**rn, Bj**ǫ**rn, skj**ǫ**ldr*), but the original *-u* in the ending that triggered the *a~ǫ* alternation is no longer present;
- in contrast to the nom. and acc. which have lost their ending, the dat. preserves the ending *-i* causing *a~e* alternation (***a**rnar~**e**rni*);
- *Bjǫrn* and *skjǫldr* have *-i-* as the stem vowel in the dat. (*B**i**rni, sk**i**ldi*), the result of *i*-umlaut on the root vowel *-ja-* (shown in the gen. *Bj**a**rnar, skj**a**ldar*).

11.6. Strong feminine noun *hǫnd*: *a~ǫ~e* alternation in the singular.

Only one fem. noun, *hǫnd* 'hand' (9.3), shows *a~ǫ~e* alternation in the singular. The declension is shown at right.

	'hand'
***Sg** nom*	h**ǫ**nd
acc	h**ǫ**nd
dat	h**e**ndi
gen	h**a**ndar

As in the case of the strong masc. nouns with three-way alternation, the original *-u* in the ending that triggered the *a~ǫ* alternation in the nom. and acc. is no longer present, but the dat. ending *-i* that caused the *a~e* alternation is still preserved.

11.7. Strong adjectives: *a~ǫ* alternation in the singular.

Strong adjectives with stem vowel *-a-* (f.ex., *sv**a**rtr* 'black') show *u*-umlaut in three forms of the singular: the dat. masc. (which ends in *-um*, 2.4; f.ex., *sv**ǫ**rtum*), the dat. neut. (which ends in *-u*, 4.5; f.ex., *sv**ǫ**rtu*), and the nom. fem. (which has no ending, 9.6; f.ex., *sv**ǫ**rt*). The following declentions of *svartr* 'black' and *fagr* 'fair' illustrate these *a~ǫ* alternations:

	'black'			'fair'		
	Masc	**Fem**	**Neut**	**Masc**	**Fem**	**Neut**
Sg *nom*	svartr	svǫrt	svart	fagr	fǫgr	fagrt
acc	svartan	svarta	svart	fagran	fagra	fagrt
dat	svǫrtum	svartri	svǫrtu	fǫgrum	fagri	fǫgru
gen	svarts	svartrar	svarts	fagrs	fagrar	fagrs

- Recall (2.1.2) that the final *-r* of *fag**r*** belongs to the stem, and that the initial *-r-* of the ending is dropped: nom. masc. *fag**r***, dat. fem. *fag**ri***, gen. fem. *fag**rar***.

Exercises

1. Fill in the appropriate endings and missing vowels.

a. Þeir Eiríkr kóm___ ok nám___ konu____ á brott, sem sagt er í sǫg______. (all def.)

b. Gísli var faðir Helg___ in_____ f___gr___, þeirar er átti Bjǫrn in___ vitr___.

c. Bjǫrn kom ok nam Helg___ in___ f___gr___ á brott.

d. Jǫrð____ (def.) er stór ok f___gr.

e. Nótt____ (def.) er sv___rt, en dagr_____ (def.) bj___rt___.

f. Brá Baldrs var hvít ok bj___rt.

2. Write the 3 sing. pres. form of the following strong verbs. (See 11.1. Note too that the 3 sing. pres. ending *-r* is added to the stem according to the rules given in 7.7).

Ex: fá 'get'	fær	hefja 'raise'	hefr
aka 'drive'	______________	halda 'hold'	______________
auka 'increase'	______________	liggja 'lie'	______________
bera' carry'	______________	ríða 'ride'	______________
binda 'bind'	______________	sitja 'sit'	______________
blása 'blow'	______________	sjóða 'boil'	______________
draga 'pull'	______________	skína 'shine'	______________
drepa 'kill'	______________	sofa 'sleep'	______________
fljúga 'fly'	______________	standa 'stand'	______________
frjósa 'freeze'	______________	svelgja 'swallow'	______________
geta 'get'	______________	sǫkkva 'sink'	______________
gráta 'cry'	______________	þiggja 'accept'	______________

3. Write the 1 pl. pres. form of the following verbs.

Ex: kalla 'call'	kǫllum	hafa 'have'	hǫfum
banna 'forbid'	______	skapa 'shape'	______
falla 'fall'	______	svara 'answer'	______
halda 'hold'	______	tala 'speak'	______

4. Write the 3 pl. past form of the following verbs.

Ex: leggja (lagð-)	lǫgðu	velja (valð-)	vǫlðu
berja (barð-)	______	segja (sagð-)	______
kveðja (kvadd-)	______	vekja (vakt-)	______

5. Give the title of the following sagas in the dat. (Remember that the preposition *ór* takes the dat.)

Ex.: Gunnlaugs saga ormstungu: ór Gunnlaugs sǫgu ormstungu

Fóstbrœðra saga: ór ______

Hrafnkels saga Freysgoða: ór ______

Magnúss saga Erlingssonar: ór ______

Ragnars saga loðbrókar: ór ______

Vápnfirðinga saga: ór ______

Gísla saga Súrssonar: ór ______

Hávarðar saga: ór ______

VOCABULARY

aka (ekr; ók, óku; ekit) *vb* drive
búð *f* tent, booth
deyja (deyr; dó, dóu; dáit) *vb* die
ekki *indef pron* nothing (*n of* **engi**)
en *conj* than (*w comp*)
engi *indef pron* no one, none (*n* **ekki**)
er *conj* since
fram *adv* forward
frjósa (frýss; fraus, frusu; frosit) *vb* freeze
gaman *n* fun, amusement, pleasure
ganga (gengr; gekk, gengu; gengit) *vb* go, walk
gǫrla *adv* fully, quite
hafa (-ð-) *vb* have
hinn *pron* this (the other)
hitt *dem pron* this (the other) (*n of* **hinn**)
hlaupa (hleypr; hljóp, hljópu; hlaupit) *vb* run
hluti *m* part
hlýða (-dd-) *vb* listen
hlæja (hlær; hló, hlógu; hlegit) *vb* laugh
hǫggva (høggr; hjó, hjoggu; hǫgg(v)it) *vb* strike, hack, hew
jǫrð (*dat* -u) *f* earth
kappi *m* hero, great fighter
koma (kemr; kom, kómu; komit) *vb* come
kunna (kann, kunnu; kunni; kunnat) *vb* be able
líkligr *adj* likely, probable
mega (má, megu; mátti; mátt) *vb* be able
mjǫk *adv* very
munu (mun, munu; mundi) *vb* will, shall (*future*), be likely
myndi (*inf* **munu**) *vb* should, would be likely (*3sg past subjunct*)
nefna (-d-) *vb* name, mention by name
nǫkkut *adv* somewhat, in some degree

sé (*inf* **vera**) *vb* is (*3sg pres subjunct*; *see* 16.2)
sitja (sitr; sat, sátu; setit) *vb* sit
skemmtiliga *adv* entertainingly
spýja (spýr; spjó, spjó; spúit) *vb* spew
stóll *m* chair
svelgja (svelgr; svalg, sulgu; sólgit) *vb* swallow
syngja (syngr; sǫng, sungu; sungit) *vb* sing
sǫkkva (søkkr; sǫkk, sukku; sokkit) *vb* sink
umhverfis *adv* around, round about
undir *prep* [*w acc/dat*] under
úti *adv* outside (*location*)
vilja (vill; vildi; viljat) *vb* want, wish, will
virðask (-rð-) *refl vb* seem, think
vita (veit, vitu; vissi; vitat) *vb* know
þangat *adv* (to) there, thither
þeira *poss pron* their
þingheimr *m* assembly (i.e., those in attendance at a **þing**)
Þorgeirr *m* Thorgeir (*personal name*)
Þorgrímr *m* Thorgrim (*personal name*)
Þormóðr *m* Thormod (*personal name*)

Phrases

allra helzt especially
at gaman sé at that it is amusing
ganga vel fram fight well
kunna muntu at nefna you are probably able to name
myndi verit hafa was likely to have been, must have been
vera má þat maybe, perhaps
vera nǫkkut við be somehow connected with
virðisk mér it seems (seemed) to me
þangat til to there

A Small Icelandic Manuscript. The production of such books made from calfskin began in the century after the Icelandic conversion to Christianity around the year 1000. Christian missionaries and clerics introduced the technique of writing with ink and the use of vellum pages. (Photo Courtesy of Árni Magnússon Manuscript Institute, Reykjavík.)

LESSON 12

(1) Ór *Ragnars sǫgu loðbrókar* (7. kap. 'Frá Ragnarssonum')

(From the *Saga of Ragnar Lodbrok*, Chap. 7 'About the Sons of Ragnar')

the boy with water sprinkled
Var sveinninn vatni ausinn ok nafn gefit ok kallaðr Ívarr. En sá
boy boneless as if cartilage bones should
sveinn var beinlauss ok sem brjósk væri þar, sem bein skyldu vera.
none
Ok þá er hann var ungr, var hann vexti svá mikill, at engir váru hans
equals most handsome in appearance
jafningjar. Hann var allra manna fríðastr sýnum ok svá vitr,
certain greater wise man
at eigi er víst, hverr meiri spekingr hefir verit en hann....
'White-Shirt' fourth
Annarr sonr þeira hét Bjǫrn, inn þriði Hvítserkr, inn fjórði Rǫgnvaldr.
most valiant as soon as
Þeir váru miklir menn allir ok inir frœknustu, ok þegar þeir máttu
something undertake of every kind skills wherever
nǫkkut at hafask, námu þeir alls konar íþróttir. Ok hvert sem þeir
poles because walk
fóru, lét Ívarr bera sik á stǫngum, því at hann mátti eigi ganga, ok
should plans whatever did
skyldi hann hafa ráð fyrir þeim, hvat sem þeir hǫfðusk at.

(2) Ór *Heimskringlu* (1. kap.)

(From *Heimskringla* or the *History of the Kings of Norway*, Chap. 1)[21]

orb mankind inhabit bay-cut
Kringla heimsins, sú er mannfólkit byggvir er mjǫk vágskorin;
seas large the oceans into the earth sea
ganga hǫf stór ór útsjánum inn í jǫrðina. Er þat kunnigt, at haf
the Straits of Gibraltar Jerusalem's Land (i.e., Israel)
gengr frá Nǫrvasundum ok alt út til Jórsalalands.

12.1. Demonstrative pronouns: *sá* 'that, that one' and *þessi* (*sjá*) 'this, this one'.

Sá. Individual forms of the dem. pron. *sá* 'that (one)' have appeared in the reading selections: *sá* (R.S. 5, 6.6, 10, 12(1)), *sú* (R.S. 5, 11, 12(2)), *þat* (R.S. 3, 7, 9), *þann* (R.S. 6, 10, 11), *þá* (R.S. 9), *þeiri* (R.S. 6), *því*

[21] *Heimskringla* means 'Orb of the World' but is usually referred to as the *History of the Kings of Norway*.

(R.S. 10, 12(1)). The neut. sing. forms (*þat*, etc.) are also employed as the neut. pron. 'it' (R.S. 4, 5, 9, 11, 12(2)).

Þessi. In addition to *sá*, 'that (one)', Old Norse has the dem. pron. *þessi* 'this (one)'. *Þessi* refers to an object that is close, while *sá* refers to an object that is further away. The acc. sing. masc. *þenna* appeared in R.S. 6.6 and R.S. 8, and neut. sing. *þetta* appeared in R.S. 2 and R.S. 9. Here are *sá* and *þessi* side by side.

	sá 'that'			**þessi (sjá) 'this'**		
	Masc	**Fem**	**Neut**	**Masc**	**Fem**	**Neut**
Sg *nom*	sá	sú	þat	þessi/sjá	þessi/sjá	þetta
acc	þann	þá	þat	þenna	þessa	þetta
dat	þeim	þeiri	því	þessum	þessari	þessu
gen	þess	þeirar	þess	þessa	þessarar	þessa
Pl *nom*	þeir	þær	þau	þessir	þessar	þessi
acc	þá	þær	þau	þessa	þessar	þessi
dat	þeim	þeim	þeim	þessum	þessum	þessum
gen	þeir(r)a	þeir(r)a	þeir(r)a	þessara	þessara	þessara

- The pl. forms of *sá* are identical in all genders with the pl. pers. pronouns (5.1).
- The dem. pronouns *sá* and *þessi* agree in gender and number with noun they modify: nom. *sá maðr* 'that man', *þessi maðr* 'this man'; acc. *þann mann* 'that man', *þessa mann*, etc.
- When *sá* and *þessi* are followed by an adj., the adj. is weak (3.2): nom. *sá/þessi góð**i** maðr* 'that/this good man'; acc. *þann/þessa góð**a** mann* 'that/this good man', etc.

12.2. Relative particles *er* and *sem*.

A rel. clause is introduced by a rel. particle, which can be either *sem* or *er*. Often the rel. particle is preceded by a form of the dem. pron. *sá* in agreement with the noun to which it refers in the preceding clause. The rel. particles and the dem. pronouns are bolded in the following examples. Note that when the dem. pron. appears in these examples, it appears together with the rel. particle.

> Bjǫrn hét hersir ríkr í Sogni, **er** bjó á Aurlandi; hans son var Brynjólfr, **er** arf allan tók eptir fǫður sinn. (R.S. 9)
>
> Þar sá hann mey fagra, **þá er** honum fannsk mikit um. (R.S. 9)
>
> Kringla heimsins, **sú er** mannfólkit byggvir (R.S. 12(2))
>
> Kunna muntu nǫkkurn mann at nefna, **þann sem** í er sǫgunni. (R.S. 11)

In the following examples, the dem. pron. is part of the preceding clause:

> Frá hverjum er saga **sú**, **er** hann segir? (R.S. 11)

Þá mælti Eiríkr jarl við **þann** mann, **er** sumir nefna Finn. (R.S. 10)
Kom ǫrin á boga Einars miðjan í **því** bili, **er** Einarr dró it þriðja sinn bogann. (R.S. 10)

***Er* and *sem* as conjunctions.**
Er can also be used as a conjunction of time, meaning 'when':

Þeir váru menn á ungum aldri, **er** þetta var tíðenda. (R.S. 9)
Ok **er** hann náði konungs fundi, kvaddi hann konunginn. (R.S. 8)
Þat var einn dag, **er** þeir Þórólfr ok Bjǫrn gengu ofan til skipsins. (R.S. 4)

Both *er* and *sem* can also be used as other types of conjunctions (all examples are from R.S. 11):

allra helzt ***er*** 'especially **since**'
svá virðisk mér ***sem*** 'so it seems to me **as if**'
sem *líkligt er* '**as** is likely, **as** might be expected'

Sem also occurs with the adv. *þar* as a conjunction of place, meaning 'in the place that'.

Hann býr **þar, sem** heitir Breiðablik. (R.S. 7)

12.3. Strong nouns: Plural of all genders.

1. Masc. nom. and acc. pl.
The nom. pl. of masc. strong nouns ends in *-ar* or *-ir*: *hest**ar*** ('horses'), *vin**ir*** ('friends').

- In most instances, masc. nouns with gen. sing. *-s* take the nom. pl. ending *-ar* (gen. sing. *hest**s***, nom. pl. *hest**ar***), whereas masc. nouns with gen. sing. *-ar* take the nom. pl. ending *-ir* (gen. sing. *vin**ar***, nom. pl. *vin**ir***).

Strong Noun Endings

	Masc	Fem	Neut
Pl *nom*	-ar, -ir	-ar, -ir, -(i)r	(ǫ)–
acc	-a, -i	-ar, -ir, -(i)r	(ǫ)–
dat	-um	-um	-um
gen	-a	-a	-a

Superscript (i) or (ǫ) indicates that the ending triggers *i*-umlaut or *u*-umlaut (11.2).

The acc. pl. has the same form as the nom. minus the final *-r*: acc. pl. *hest**a*** and *vin**i***.

- Three masc. nouns (in addition to the kinship nouns in 14.8 below) end in *-r* in both the nom. and acc. pl. These nouns are: *fótr* 'foot', nom./acc. pl. ***fætr*** (the ending triggers *i*-umlaut; see 11.2.1); *fingr* 'finger', nom./acc. pl. *fingr*; *vetr* 'winter', nom./acc. pl. *vetr*.

2. Fem. nom. and acc. pl.
The nom. and acc. pl. of the fem. declension are in all ways identical, including those of the article, strong adjectives, weak adjectives, nouns, and pronouns. In the strong noun declension, they end in *-ar*, *-ir*, or *-r*: *far**ar***, *ætt**ir***, *bæk**r*** ('books').

- The nom./acc. pl. ending *-r* triggers *i*-umlaut (11.2.1): ***bók***, pl. *b**œ**kr*; *hǫnd* (stem *h**a**nd-*), pl. *h**e**nd**r***.

3. Neut. nom. and acc. pl.

The nom. and acc. pl. of strong neut. nouns are identical. They have no ending, and in most instances are the same as the nom. and acc. neut. sing.: *blót* 'a sacrifice' or 'sacrifices', *sverð* 'a sword' or 'swords'.[22] If the root vowel is *-a-*, it changes to *-ǫ-* in the nom./acc. pl. due to *u*-umlaut: *l**a**nd*, pl. *l**ǫ**nd* ('lands'). Like strong fem. nouns (f.ex., *f**ǫ**r* 'journey', 11.2.2; 11.4), the *u*-ending that originally triggered the umlaut is no longer present.

4. Dat. and gen. pl. (all genders).

The dat. pl. ending is *-um* for nouns of all genders: *hest**um***, *meyj**um***, *hǫnd**um***, *sverð**um***. The gen. pl. ending of all strong nouns is *-a* (see 7.1): *hest**a***, *mey**a***, *hand**a***, *sverð**a***.

- Plural forms of monosyllabic nouns ending in *-á* show contraction in all forms: nom./acc. pl. *brá**r*** (= *brá-ar*), dat. pl. *brá**m*** (= *brá-um*), gen. pl. *brá* (= *brá-a*); so also nom./acc. pl. *ár*, dat. pl. *ám*, gen. pl. *á*.

12.4. Weak nouns: Plural of all genders.

The nom. pl. ending of weak masc. nouns is *-ar*. Like strong masc. nouns, the acc. pl. of weak masc. nouns is the same as the nom. without *-r*: nom. *goð**ar***, acc. *goð**a***.

The nom. and acc. pl. of weak fem. nouns both have the ending *-ur* (which triggers *u*-umlaut): *kon**ur*** (R.S. 13(2)), *s**ǫ**g**ur*** (R.S. 16).

The nom. and acc. pl. of weak neut. nouns end in *-u* (which triggers *u*-umlaut): *hj**ǫ**rt**u***.

Weak Noun Endings

	Masc	Fem	Neut
***Pl** nom*	-ar	-ur	-u
acc	-a	-ur	-u
dat	-um	-um	-um
gen	-a	-na	-na

The dat. pl. of weak nouns of all genders ends in *-um*: *goð**um***, *s**ǫ**g**um***, *hj**ǫ**rt**um***.

The gen. pl. ending of weak masc. nouns is *-a*, but fem. and neut. weak nouns have a stem-final *-n-* before the gen. pl. *-a*: f.ex., *sag**na*** from fem. *saga*; *hjart**na*** from neut. *hjarta*.

- The gen. pl. of *kona* 'woman' is *kv**e**n**na***, with an irregular change in the root vowel; *hún var allra* **kvenna** *fríðust* 'she was of all women most beautiful'.

---

[22] Compare English words such as 'deer' and 'sheep', which are the same in the singular and plural. These were neut. nouns in Old English.

12.5. Review paradigms: Noun endings, sing. and pl.

	Strong			Weak		
	Masc	**Fem**	**Neut**	**Masc**	**Fem**	**Neut**
Sg *nom*	-r (see 2.1)	(ǫ)–, -r	–	-i	-a	-a
acc	–	(ǫ)–, -i, -u	–	-a	-u	-a
dat	-i	(ǫ)–, -i, -u	-i	-a	-u	-a
gen	-s, -ar	-ar	-s	-a	-u	-a
Pl *nom*	-ar, -ir	-ar, -ir, -(i)r	(ǫ)–	-ar	-ur	-u
acc	-a, -i	-ar, -ir, -(i)r	(ǫ)–	-a	-ur	-u
dat	-um	-um	-um	-um	-um	-um
gen	-a	-a	-a	-a	-na	-na

Exercises

1. Fill in the appropriate endings and missing vowels.

a. Þeir tók__ skip___ (def.) sem váru þar ok fór__ á brott.

b. Fǫr___ (def.) frá Nóreg__ til Ísland__ er l__ng ok h__rð. (*harðr* 'hard')

2. Fill in the missing forms of the dem. pron. *sá*.

	Masc	**Fem**	**Neut**
Sg *nom*	sá	________	þat
acc	________	þá	________
dat	________	________	________
gen	________	________	þess
Pl *nom*	________	________	________
acc	________	þær	þau
dat	________	________	þeim
gen	þeira	________	________

3. Fill in the missing forms of the dem. pron. *þessi*.

	Masc	**Fem**	**Neut**
Sg *nom*	þessi	________	________
acc	________	________	þetta
dat	þessum	________	________
gen	________	________	________
Pl *nom*	________	þessar	þessi
acc	þessa	________	________
dat	________	________	________
gen	________	þessara	________

4. Strong nouns. Decline the following nouns in the singular and plural.

	Masc	Fem	Neut
Sg *nom*	hestr	fǫr	land
acc	___	___	___
dat	___	___	___
gen	___	___	___
Pl *nom*	___	___	___
acc	___	___	___
dat	___	___	___
gen	___	___	___

5. Weak nouns. Decline the following nouns in the singular and plural.

	Masc	Fem	Neut
Sg *nom*	goði	saga	hjarta
acc	___	___	___
dat	___	___	___
gen	___	___	___
Pl *nom*	___	___	___
acc	___	___	___
dat	___	___	___
gen	___	___	___

Vocabulary

alt *adv* all the way
ausa (eyss; jós, jósu/jusu; ausit) *vb* sprinkle, pour
bein *n* bone
beinlauss *adj* boneless
brjósk *n* cartilage
byggva = **byggja** (bygð-) *vb* inhabit
engi *indef pron* no one; (*pl*) none
fjórði *adj* fourth
fríðastr *superl of* **fríðr**
fríðr *adj* beautiful, handsome, fine
frœkn *adj* bold, daring, valiant
frœknustu *wk m pl of* frœknastr, *superl of* **frœkn**
fǫr *f* journey
haf *n* sea
harðr *adj* hard
hvert *adv* to where
Hvítserkr *m* Hvitserk ('White-Shirt') (*personal name*)
hǫf *pl of* **haf**
inn *adv* in, into
Ívarr *m* Ivar (*personal name*)
íþrótt (*pl* -ir) *f* skill, feat, accomplishment
jafningi (*pl* -jar) *m* equal, match
Jórsalaland *n* 'Jerusalem's Land', Israel (*place name*)
konar *gen sg of obs* ***konr** *m* kind, sort
kringla *f* disc, circle
langr *adj* long
mannfólk *n* mankind
mikill (*comp* meiri) *adj* big, large, great
meiri *comp adj* greater (*see* **mikill**)
Njáll *m* Njal (*personal name*)

nǫkkurr (*n* nǫkkut) *indef pron* some, somebody; (*n*) something
Nǫrvasund *n pl* Straits of Gibraltar (*place name*)
ráð *n* plan
Rǫgnvaldr *m* Rognvald (*personal name*)
sem *conj* [*w subjunct*] as if
serkr *m* shirt
skarpr *adj* sharp
skulu (skal, skulu; skyldi) *vb* shall (necessity)
skyldi, **skyldu** (*inf* **skulu**) *vb* should
spekingr *m* wise man, sage
sveinn *m* boy, lad
sýn *f* sight, appearance
útsjár *m* ocean
vatn *n* water
vágskorinn *adj* indented (cut) with bays
víss *adj* certain, sure
þegar *conj* as soon as

Phrases

alls konar of every kind, of all kinds
fríðastr sýnum most handsome, finest in appearane
nǫkkut hafask at undertake ('have at') something
hvat sem whatever
hvert sem (to) wherever
inn í into
því at because

Notes

LESSON 13

(1) Ór *Egils sǫgu Skalla-Grímssonar* (25. kap.)

(From the *Saga of Egil Skalla-Grimsson*, Chap. 25)

prepared for trip before chose
Skalla-Grímr bjósk til ferðar þeirar, er fyrr var frá sagt; hann valði

servants his (own) neighbors strongest
sér menn af heimamǫnnum **sínum** ok nábúum þá er váru **sterkastir**

in strength boldest of them were at hand twelve for
at afli ok **hraustastir**, þeira er til váru.... Tólf váru þeir til

strongest many shapeshifters
fararinnar,[23] ok **allir** inir sterkustu menn ok **margir** hamrammir.

(2) Ór *Egils sǫgu Skalla-Grímssonar* (25. kap.)

(From the *Saga of Egil Skalla-Grimsson*, Chap. 25)

early prepared their (own)
Snemma um várit bjuggu þeir Kveld-Úlfr skip sín; þeir hǫfðu[24]

great naval force prepared ships
mikinn skipakost ok góðan, bjuggu tvá knǫrru **mikla** ok hǫfðu á

each thirty able-bodied in addition
hvárum þrjá tigu manna, þeira er **liðfœrir** váru ok um fram konur

young people ready sailed away sailed
ok ungmenni.... En er þeir váru **búnir**, þá sigldu þeir í brott; þeir sigldu

islands many islands
í eyjar þær, er Sólundir heita; þat eru **margar** eyjar ok **stórar** ok svá

are likely few
mjǫk **vágskornar**, at þat er mælt, at þar munu **fáir** menn vita **allar**

harbors
hafnir.

(3) Ór *Egils sǫgu Skalla-Grímssonar* (57. kap.)

(From the *Saga of Egil Skalla-Grimsson*, Chap. 57)

turned back I call to witness
Þá snerisk Egill aptr ok mælti hátt: "Þat skírskota ek undir þik,

hear case
Arinbjǫrn, ok þik, Þórðr, ok þá menn **alla** er nú heyra mál mitt, **lenda**

lawmen common people forbid lands
menn ok lǫgmenn ok alla alþýðu, at ek banna jarðir þær **allar** er

has owned rent work profits from [them]
átt hefr Bjǫrn Brynjólfsson, at byggja ok vinna ok **allra** gagna af

---

[23] Hint: *farar-innar* is the gen. sing. of fem. *fǫr* with the suffixed def. art. (11.4).

[24] Hint: see 6.5 for the conjugation of *hafa*.

make use forbid all other
at neyta. Banna ek þér, Berg-Ǫnundr, ok **ǫllum ǫðrum** mǫnnum,

foreign native noble common
útlenzkum ok **innlenzkum**, **tignum** ok **ótignum**, en hverjum er þat

does I charge with breaking the law of the land wrath of the gods trucebreaking
gjǫrir legg ek við lagabrot landsréttar, goðagremi ok griðarof."

(4) Ór *Egils sǫgu Skalla-Grímssonar* (66. kap.)

(From the *Saga of Egil Skalla-Grimsson*, Chap. 66)

all children promising oldest
Ǫll váru bǫrn Egils **mannvæn** ok vel viti **borin**; Þorgerðr var ellzt barna Egils.

13.1. Strong adjectives: Plural.

Strong pl. adj. endings correspond to those of the article (8.2):

	Strong Adj Endings			Article		
	Masc	Fem	Neut	Masc	Fem	Neut
Pl nom	-ir	-ar	–(ǫ)	in**ir**	in**ar**	in
acc	-a	-ar	–(ǫ)	in**a**	in**ar**	in
dat	-um	-um	-um	in**um**	in**um**	in**um**
gen	-ra (2.1)	-ra (2.1)	-ra (2.1)	in**na**	in**na**	in**na**

- The nom. pl. masc. of strong adjectives ends in *-ir*: *all**ir***, *marg**ir***, *sterkast**ir***, *hraustast**ir*** (R.S. 13(1) above).
- The acc. pl. masc. ending is *-a*: *all**a***, *lend**a*** (R.S. 13(3) above).
- The nom. and acc. pl. fem. ending of strong adjectives is *-ar*: *all**ar***, *marg**ar***, *stór**ar*** (R.S. 13(2) and (3) above).
- Like the nom. and acc. pl. of strong neut. nouns (12.3.3), the neut. nom./acc. pl. of strong adjectives has no ending (*mannvæn*, *borin*), and adjectives with the stem vowel *-a-* (f.ex., ***a**llr*) show *a~ǫ* alternation: ***ǫ**ll* (R.S. 13(4) above).
- The dat. pl. ending of all strong adjectives is *-um*: *innlenzk**um***, *útlenzk**um*** (R.S. 13(3) above), *sín**um*** (R.S. 13(1) above), *góð**um***. As expected, adjectives with the stem vowel *-a-* show *a~ǫ* alternation: ***ǫ**ll**um***, ***ǫ**ð**rum*** (R.S. 13(3) above).
- Disyllabic adjectives (3.5) lose the vowel of the second syllable when the ending is added: *tign**um***, *ótign**um*** (= (*ó-*)*tigin-* + *-um*) (R.S. 13(3) above). Note, however, that *mannvænn* in R.S. 13(4) is not a disyllabic adj. but a compound of *mann-* plus the monosyllabic adj. *vænn* 'promising', so the vowel *-æ-* in this word is not lost when the ending *-um* is added: *mannvæn**um***.
- Recall (7.1) that the gen. pl. ending of all strong adjectives is *-ra* (with regular assimilation after *-l*, *-n*, *-s* according to the Special Stem Rules of 2.1): *all**ra***, *góð**ra***, *mikil**la***, *væn**na***, *fag**ra***.

13.2. Review paradigms: Complete endings of strong adjectives (see 9.7, 13.1).

	Masc	Fem	Neut
Sg *nom*	-r (see 2.1)	–(ǫ)	-t
acc	-an	-a	-t
dat	-um	-ri (see 2.1)	-u
gen	-s	-rar (see 2.1)	-s
Pl *nom*	-ir	-ar	–(ǫ)
acc	-a	-ar	–(ǫ)
dat	-um	-um	-um
gen	-ra (see 2.1)	-ra (see 2.1)	-ra (see 2.1)

The similarities of case forms noted in the list below can be seen in the chart above:

(a) nom. sing. fem. = nom. pl. neut. = acc. pl. neut.
(b) nom. sing. neut = acc. sing. neut.
(c) acc. sing. fem. = acc. pl. masc.
(d) dat. sing. masc. = dat. pl. (all)
(e) gen. sing. masc. = gen. sing. neut.
(f) nom. pl. fem. = acc. pl. fem.

The same identities are present in the declension of the art. (8.2) and for the most part also in the declension of the dem. pronouns (12.1, with the exception of identity (a), where the nom. sing. fem. *sú* is different).

13.3. The adjective *annarr* '(an)other, second'.

The adj. *annarr* means 'other, another, one of two'. It is also an ordinal number meaning 'second'. We have encountered several forms already: *annat* (R.S. 2), *annan* (R.S. 5), *annarr* (R.S. 7, 12(1)), and *ǫðrum* (R.S. 13(3)). The full declension is as follows:

	Masc	Fem	Neut
Sg *nom*	annarr	ǫnnur	annat
acc	annan	aðra	annat
dat	ǫðrum	annarri	ǫðru
gen	annars	annarrar	annars
Pl *nom*	aðrir	aðrar	ǫnnur
acc	aðra	aðrar	ǫnnur
dat	ǫðrum	ǫðrum	ǫðrum
gen	annarra	annarra	annarra

Annarr is always declined strong. The declension looks complicated, but most of the differences in the paradigm are the result of three regular sound changes:

- *u*-umlaut (11.2.2): ***ǫ**nn**ur**, **ǫ**ð**rum**, **ǫ**ð**ru***;
- loss of the vowel of the second syllable upon addition of an ending that begins with a vowel (3.5): *aðra, aðrir, ǫðrum*, etc.;

- the change of *-nn-* to *-ð-* when followed directly by *-r*: *a**ðr**a*, *a**ðr**ir*, *ǫ**ðr**um*, etc. This change also takes place in the nom. sing. of the noun *maðr* (stem *mann-*; see 2.6).

In the nom./acc. sing. neut., **ann**art*** was simplified to *ann**at***. In the acc. sing. masc., **ann**aran*** became *ann**an***.

13.4. Weak adjectives: Plural.

The following passages contain examples of weak adjectives.

(1) Ór *Egils sǫgu Skalla-Grímssonar* (25. kap.)

(From the *Saga of Egil Skalla-Grimsson*, Chap. 25)

twelve for strongest many
Tólf váru þeir til fararinnar, ok allir inir **sterkustu** menn ok margir
shapeshifters
hamrammir.

(2) Ór *Ynglinga sǫgu* (29. kap.)

(From the *Saga of the Ynglings*, Chap. 29)

fond of saddle horses horses
Aðils konungr var mjǫk kærr at góðhestum; hann átti ina **beztu** hesta í þann tima.

(3) Ór *Egils sǫgu Skalla-Grímssonar* (36. Kap.)

(From the *Saga of Egil Skalla-Grimsson*, Chap. 36)

friendly terms
Þórir var þá í inum **mestum** kærleikum við konung.

(4) Ór *Egils sǫgu Skalla-Grímssonar* (77. kap.)

(From the *Saga of Egil Skalla-Grimsson*, Chap. 77)

west the wood
Er þeir koma vestr af skóginum ok segja þessi tíðendi Nóregskonungi,
expectation harsh treatment
þá eigu vér[25] af honum ván inna **mestu** afarkosta.

The accompanying chart gives the pl. endings of weak adjectives. They are the same for all genders (masc., fem., and neut.).

Sg *nom*	-u
acc	-u
dat	-um
gen	-u

- Nom. and acc. pl. end in *-u*: *inir sterkust**u** menn*, *ina bezt**u** hesta*.
- Dat. pl. ends in *-um*: *inum meist**um** kærleik**um***.
- Gen. pl. ends in *-u*: *inna mest**u** afarkosta*.

All the examples from the above readings are superlatives. Superlative adjectives are frequently preceded by the article and are declined weak

[25] Recall from 8.4.3 that the *-m* of the 1 pl. ending may be dropped when the pron. follows; *eigu vér* (= *eigu**m** vér*) is an example.

in such instances. In the pl., they are far more frequent than other weak adjectives.

13.5. *u*-umlaut: *a~u* alternation.

Section 11.2.2 explained that *u*-umlaut changes the vowel *-a-* to *-ǫ-* in stressed syllables (the first syllable). This is called *a~ǫ* alternation. In unstressed syllables, the regular alternation is *a~u*. For example, *sterk**a**str* becomes *sterk**u**stu* in the weak plural (*inir sterk**u**stu menn*).

Both alternations (*a~ǫ* and *a~u*) can occur in the same word: f.ex., *v**a**sk**a**str* bravest' becomes *v**ǫ**sk**u**stu* in the weak pl.: *allir inir v**ǫ**sk**u**stu menn*.

These two alternations are characteristic of weak verbs with vocalic link *-a-* when a personal ending in *-u-* is added. For example:

*k**a**lla* (*-að-*) – pres. *vér k**ǫ**llum*, past *vér k**ǫ**ll**u**ðum*, *þér k**ǫ**ll**u**ðuð*, *þeir k**ǫ**ll**u**ðu*.

elska (*-að-*) – past *vér elsk**u**ðum*, *þér elsk**u**ðuð*, *þeir elsk**u**ðu*.

13.6. Review paradigms: Complete endings of weak adjectives and nouns (see 9.2, 12.4, 13.4).

Weak nouns and adjectives have the same endings in the singular. There are differences between the weak and strong endings in the plural.

	Weak Adjectives			Weak Nouns		
	Masc	Fem	Neut	Masc	Fem	Neut
Sg *nom*	-i	-a	-a	-i	-a	-a
acc	-a	-u	-a	-a	-u	-a
dat	-a	-u	-a	-a	-u	-a
gen	-a	-u	-a	-a	-u	-a
Pl *nom*	-u	-u	-u	-ar	-ur	-u
acc	-u	-u	-u	-a	-ur	-u
dat	-um	-um	-um	-um	-um	-um
gen	-u	-u	-u	-a	-na	-na

13.7. Adjectives: Examples of complete declensions.

Section 6.7 introduced a list of common adjectives found in the sagas and gave the declensions in the singular. Here are full declensions in the singular and plural.

Using *stórr* 'big' as the model:

	Strong			Weak		
	Masc	Fem	Neut	Masc	Fem	Neut
Sg *nom*	stór-r	stór	stór-t	stór-i	stór-a	stór-a
acc	stór-an	stór-a	stór-t	stór-a	stór-u	stór-a
dat	stór-um	stór-ri	stór-u	stór-a	stór-u	stór-a
gen	stór-s	stór-rar	stór-s	stór-a	stór-u	stór-a

Pl *nom*	stór-ir	stór-ar	stór	stór-u	stór-u	stór-u
acc	stór-a	stór-ar	stór	stór-u	stór-u	stór-u
dat	stór-um	stór-um	stór-um	stór-um	stór-um	stór-um
gen	stór-ra	stór-ra	stór-ra	stór-u	stór-u	stór-u

Using *heill* 'healthy' as the model:

	Strong			**Weak**		
	Masc	**Fem**	**Neut**	**Masc**	**Fem**	**Neut**
Sg *nom*	heil-**l**	heil	heil-t	heil-i	heil-a	heil-a
acc	heil-an	heil-a	heil-t	heil-a	heil-u	heil-a
dat	heil-um	heil-**l**i	heil-u	heil-a	heil-u	heil-a
gen	heil-s	heil-**l**ar	heil-s	heil-a	heil-u	heil-a
Pl *nom*	heil-ir	heil-ar	heil	heil-u	heil-u	heil-u
acc	heil-a	heil-ar	heil	heil-u	heil-u	heil-u
dat	heil-um	heil-um	heil-um	heil-um	heil-um	heil-um
gen	heil-**l**a	heil-**l**a	heil-**l**a	heil-u	heil-u	heil-u

Using *lítill* as the model:

	Strong			**Weak**		
	Masc	**Fem**	**Neut**	**Masc**	**Fem**	**Neut**
Sg *nom*	lítil-**l**	lítil	líti-**t**	li**tl**-i	li**tl**-a	li**tl**-a
acc	li**tl**-an	li**tl**-a	líti-**t**	li**tl**-a	li**tl**-u	li**tl**-a
dat	li**tl**-um	lítil-**l**i	li**tl**-u	li**tl**-a	li**tl**-u	li**tl**-a
gen	lítil-s	lítil-**l**ar	lítil-s	li**tl**-a	li**tl**-u	li**tl**-a
Pl *nom*	li**tl**-ir	li**tl**-ar	lítil	li**tl**-u	li**tl**-u	li**tl**-u
acc	li**tl**-a	li**tl**-ar	lítil	li**tl**-u	li**tl**-u	li**tl**-u
dat	li**tl**-um	li**tl**-um	li**tl**-um	li**tl**-um	li**tl**-um	li**tl**-um
gen	lítil-**l**a	lítil-**l**a	lítil-**l**a	li**tl**-u	li**tl**-u	li**tl**-u

Exercises

1. Fill in the appropriate endings and missing vowels.

a. __ll b__rn Egils váru f__gr ok v__sk.

b. Spjót___ (def.) váru sk__rp ok l__ng. (*spjót* neut. 'spear')

c. Hross___ (def.) váru sv__rt ok f__gr. (*hross* neut. 'horse')

d. Rewrite the previous sentence in the singular.

---

2. Fill in the appropriate endings and missing vowels.

Skalla-Grím__ valð__ sér marg__ vask__ menn til ferð_______ (def.). Þeir tók__ með sér m__rg__ góð__ hesta ok m__rg góð skip. All___ vár__ þeir sterk___ ok stór___ ok __ll váru skip___ (def.) in bezt___. Á ___ll skip_____ (def.) váru m___rg spjót ok sverð. Síðan fór___ þeir til m___rg___ land___.

3. Change from singular to plural or vice versa.

inn stóri maðr ______________________

ins vaska manns ______________________

inum góða manni ______________________

inir beztu menn ______________________

inum vǫskustum mǫnnum ______________________

ina sterku menn ______________________

it bezta spjót ______________________

inu góða hrossi ______________________

in fǫgru skip ______________________

inum góðum hestum ______________________

stórum hrossum ______________________

góðan mann ______________________

vǫskum manni ______________________

stórum hestum ______________________

fǫgr skip ______________________

langt sverð ______________________

góðs hests ______________________

4. Write the strong forms of the adjectives *stórr* and *langr* in the following cases:

	stórr	**langr**
a. nom. sing. fem. = nom./acc. pl. neut.:	__________	__________
b. nom./acc. sing. neut.:	__________	__________
c. acc. sing. fem. = acc. pl. masc.:	__________	__________
d. dat. sing. masc. = dat. pl. (all):	__________	__________
e. gen. sing. masc./neut.:	__________	__________
f. nom./acc. pl. fem.:	__________	__________

5. Write the adj. *annarr* in the following case forms:

a. nom. sing. fem. = nom./acc. pl. neut.: __________

b. nom./acc. sing. neut.: __________

c. acc. sing. fem. = acc. pl. masc.: __________

d. dat. sing. masc. = dat. pl. (all): __________

e. gen. sing. masc./neut.: __________

f. nom./acc. pl. fem.: __________

6. Conjugate the following weak verbs with vocalic link *-a-*.

	kalla	**svara**	**tala**
Pres *1sg*	ek ______	ek ______	ek ______
2sg	þú ______	þú ______	þú ______
3sg	hon ______	þat ______	hann ______
1pl	vér ______	vér ______	vér ______
2pl	þér ______	þér ______	þér ______
3pl	þær ______	þau ______	þeir ______
Past *1sg*	ek ______	ek ______	ek ______
2sg	þú ______	þú ______	þú ______
3sg	hon ______	þat ______	hann ______
1pl	vér ______	vér ______	vér ______
2pl	þér ______	þér ______	þér ______
3pl	þær ______	þau ______	þeir ______

Vocabulary

af *adv* from; off
afarkostir *m pl* harsh terms or treatment
afl *n* strength
allr (*pl n* ǫll, *dat* ǫllum) *adj* all
alþýða *f* the common people, the public
annarr (*pl dat* ǫðrum) *adj* other
aptr *adv* back
Arinbjǫrn *m* Arinbjorn (*personal name*)
átt (*inf* **eiga**) *ppart* owned (*sg*)
banna (-að-) *vb* forbid, prohibit
barn *n* child
bera (berr; bar, báru; borit) *vb* carry, bear
berg *n* rock, boulder
brott *adv* **í brott** away (*motion*)
búa (býr; bjó, bjuggu; búit) *vb* dwell, prepare; *refl* **búask** prepare (oneself)
búnir (*inf* **búa**) *ppart* prepared (*nom pl masc*)
byggja (bygð-) *vb* inhabit, dwell; rent, let out
eiga (á, eigu; átti; átt) *vb* own
ellztr *superl adj* oldest
ey (*pl* -jar) *f* island
fár *adj* few
ferð *f* trip, journey
fram *adv* forward
fyrr *adv* before
gagn *n* advantage, benefit, produce, revenue
gjǫrir *var of* **gerir** (*inf* **gera**) *vb* does
goðagremi *f* wrath of the gods
griðarof *n pl* breach of the peace, trucebreaking
hamrammr *adj* fierce, furious in battle (*lit.* 'shape-mighty'; used of warriors who 'changed shape', i.e., went berserk)
heimamaðr *m* servant
hestr *m* horse
heyra (-ð-) *vb* hear
hraustr *adj* bold
hvárr *indef pron* each (of two)
hǫfn (*pl* hafnir) *f* harbor
innlenzkr *adj* native
knǫrr (*pl acc* knǫrru) *m* ship; merchant vessel
kærr *adj* dear
lagabrot *n* lawbreaking
landsréttr *m* law of the land

leggja (lagði, lagt/lagit) *vb* lay, place; set, fix, arrange
liðfœrr *adj* able-bodied
lǫgmaðr *m* lawman, lawyer
mannvænn *adj* promising
margr *adj* many
mál *n* case, affair
mikinn *acc sg masc of* **mikill**
munu (mun, munu; mundi) *vb* will, be likely
nábúi *m* neighbor
neyta (-tt-) *vb* [*w gen*] make use of
ótiginn *adj* not noble (of family), of common descent
sigla (-d-) *vb* sail
skipakostr *m* naval force
skírskota (-að-) *vb* refer to, appeal to
skógr *m* forest, woods
snemma *adv* early, soon
snerisk (*inf* **snúask**) *refl vb* turned (himself) (*sg*)
snúa (snýr; snøri/sneri; snúit) *vb* turn; *refl* **snúask** turn oneself
Sólundir *pl* Solundir, islands off the west coast of Norway (*place name*)
stórskip *n* large ship
tiginn *adj* noble (of family)
tólf *num* twelve
ungmenni *n* young people, children
útlenzkr *adj* foreign
ván *f* expectation, prospect
velja (valð-) *vb* choose, select
vestr *adv* west, westwards
vinna (vinnr; vann, unnu; unnit) *vb* work; till, cultivate (land)
Ynglingar *m pl* line of early Swedish kings
þrír *num* three; **þrír tigir** *num* [*w gen*] thirty
þrjá *num* three (*masc acc of* **þrír**)
ǫðrum *dat pl of* **annarr**
ǫll *nom/acc pl neut of* **allr**
ǫllum *dat pl of* **allr**
Ǫnundr *m* Onund (*personal name*)

PHRASES

átt hefr = **hefr átt** has owned
banna jarðir at byggja ok vinna forbid lands to be rented and worked
búask til prepare (oneself) for
kærr at fond of
lagabrot landsréttar breaking the law of the land
leggja við accuse of, charge with, declare guilty of or subject to
sterkr at afli strong
um fram in addition
vera til exist, be at hand
þat skírskota ek undir þik I call you to witness

Notes

LESSON 14

Ór *Ynglinga sǫgu* (3. Kap. 'Frá brœðrum Óðins')

(From the *Saga of the Ynglings*, Chap. 3 'About Odin's Brothers')

had brothers the one the other
Óðinn átti tvá brœðr. Hét annarr Vé, en annarr Vílir. Þeir brœðr hans
ruled the realm away
stýrðu ríkinu, þá er hann var í brottu. Þat var eitt sinn, þá er Óðinn
had traveled far long stayed to [the] gods [it] seemed
var farinn langt í brot ok hafði lengi dvalzk, at Ásum þótti
improbable his [returning] home divide
ørvænt hans heim. Þa tóku brœðr hans at skipta arfi hans, en
a little later
konu hans, Frigg, gengu þeir báðir at eiga. En litlu síðar kom Óðinn
heim. Tók hann þá við konu sinni.

14.1. Numerals.

The first four numerals are declined in Icelandic. Several examples of *einn* 'one', *tvá* 'two', and *þrír* 'three' have already occurred: acc. sing. masc. *einn* (R.S. 3.9, 4), nom. sing. neut. *eitt* (R.S. 7), acc. sing. neut. *eitt* (R.S. 14), dat. sing. neut. *einu* (R.S. 9); acc. pl. masc. *tvá* (R.S. 10, 13(2), 14); acc. pl. masc. *þrjá* (R.S. 13(2)).

Numerals decline similarly to strong adjectives:

	einn 'one'			**tveir 'two'**		
	Masc	**Fem**	**Neut**	**Masc**	**Fem**	**Neut**
nom	einn	ein	eitt	tveir	tvær	tvau
acc	einn	eina	eitt	tvá	tvær	tvau
dat	einum	einni	einu	tveim(r)	tveim(r)	tveim(r)
gen	eins	einnar	eins	tveggja	tveggja	tveggja

	þrír 'three'			**fjórir 'four'**		
	Masc	**Fem**	**Neut**	**Masc**	**Fem**	**Neut**
nom	þrír	þrjár	þrjú	fjórir	fjórar	fjǫgur
acc	þrjá	þrjár	þrjú	fjóra	fjórar	fjǫgur
dat	þrim(r)	þrim(r)	þrim(r)	fjórum	fjórum	fjórum
gen	þriggja	þriggja	þriggja	fjǫgurra	fjǫgurra	fjǫgurra

Einn is also used as an indef. pron. It means 'a, an, a certain one' in the singular and 'some' in the plural. The endings follow Special Stem Rule 2.1.1 (nom. sing. masc. *ein**n***, dat. sing. fem. *ein**n**i*, gen. sing. fem. *ein**n**ar*, gen. pl. *ein**n**a*).

	Masc	Fem	Neut
***Pl** nom*	einir	einar	ein
acc	eina	einar	ein
dat	einum	einum	einum
gen	einna	einna	einna

The numerals above four are indeclinable. The numbers five through twenty are as follows.

5	fimm	9	níu	13	þrettán	17	sjautján
6	sex	10	tíu	14	fjórtán	18	átján
7	sjau	11	ellifu	15	fimmtán	19	nítján
8	átta	12	tólf	16	sextán	20	tuttugu

14.2. Verbs: Weak verbs with vowel alternation.

It was noted in 5.6 that certain weak verbs have different vowels in the pres. and past stems. These verbs have a root consisting of a short vowel followed by a single consonant, and their infinitve has stem-final *-j-*: *kveð**j**a, seg**j**a, vel**j**a, hygg**j**a,*[26] *spyr**j**a.*

The past stem of these verbs preserves the basic vowel, whereas the pres. stem and inf. show the effect of *i*-umlaut caused by the stem-final *-j-*.[27] This *-j-* no longer appears in the singular forms, but its effect continues in the umlauted stem vowel: *hann kv**e**ðr, hann v**e**lr; hann h**y**ggr, hann sp**y**rr.* The verb *segja* is exceptional in that *-i-* (from the original *-j-*) remains in the pres. forms (*ek seg**i**, þú/hann seg**ir***).

As explained (5.6), the most common vowel alternations between pres. and past are *-e-* ~ *-a-* and *-y-* ~ *-u-*:

Examples of *-e-* ~ *-a-* and *-y-* ~ *-u-*vowel alternations:

Pres Past	Inf	3sg Pres	3sg Past
e – a	at kv**e**ðja	hann kv**e**ðr	hann kv**a**ddi
	at s**e**gja	hann s**e**gir	hann s**a**gði
	at v**e**lja	hann v**e**lr	hann v**a**lði
y – u	at h**y**ggja	hann h**y**ggr	hann h**u**gði
	at sp**y**rja	hann sp**y**rr	hann sp**u**rði

14.3. Reflexive possessive adjective.

The poss. Pronouns 'his', 'her(s)', 'its', and 'their(s)' can be ambiguous in English, because these pronouns do not clarify whether the possessor is the same person as the subject of the sentence or is someone else. For

---

[26] The double *-gg-* of *hy**gg**ja* is a later development. The past tense *hugði* shows the basic stem *hu**g**-* with a single *-g-*.

[27] This process is *j*-umlaut, which is parallel to *i*-umlaut (11.2.1). The sound **j** (like the **y** in the English words '**y**es' and '**y**ou') is similar to the sound **i**, but is pronounced more rapidly and functions as a consonant. It involves the same tongue position in the mouth as **i** (high and front), exerting the same umlauting influence on the stem vowel in the preceding syllable. It is common to consider *i*-umlaut and *j*-umlaut as the same process, "*i*/*j*-umlaut" or "front mutation".

example, in 'Thorolf greeted Eirik beside **his ship**', it is not possible to determine who owns the ship. Is it Thorolf's ship or is it Eirik's (or someone else's) ship?

Old Norse avoids this confusion by employing two ways to express possession in the 3rd person. On the one hand, if the possessive 'his', 'her', 'its', or 'their' refers back to the subject of the sentence or clause, then *sinn*, a special refl. poss. adj.[28] is used. One often translates *sinn* as 'his own', 'her own', 'its own', or 'their own'. On the other hand, when the possessive refers to persons or things other than the subject of the sentence, then the gen. pron. *hans, hennar, þess*, or *þeira* is used.

In the example of Thorolf greeting Eirik 'beside **his** ship', it would be *hjá skipi* ***sínu*** if it were Thorolf's own ship, but *hjá skipi* ***hans*** if it were someone else's (f.ex., Eirik's) ship.

This difference is also illustrated in this lesson's R.S. When Odin's brothers took his (Odin's) wife:

þeir gengu báðir at eiga konu ***hans***.

But when Odin took back his own wife:

Tók hann þá við konu ***sinni***.

The refl. poss. adj. *sinn* declines like the numeral *einn* (14.1):

	Masc	**Fem**	**Neut**
Sg *nom*	sinn	sín	sitt
acc	sinn	sína	sitt
dat	sínum	sinni	sínu
gen	síns	sinnar	síns
Pl *nom*	sínir	sínar	sín
acc	sína	sínar	sín
dat	sínum	sínum	sínum
gen	sinna	sinna	sinna

- Note that all vowels followed by only one *n* are long (accented).
- Several of these forms have been encountered in earlier reading selections: acc. sing. masc. *tók þá skjǫld* ***sinn*** (R.S. 10; NB: do not confuse this form with the neut. noun *sinn* 'time' which also appears in R.S. 10 and in R.S. 14); acc. sing. neut. *Bjǫrn hóf upp bónorð* ***sitt*** (R.S. 9); acc. pl. masc. *stórlyndr við* ***sína*** *menn* (R.S. 6), acc. pl. neut. *bjuggu þeir Kveld-Úlfr skip* ***sín*** (R.S. 13(2)); and dat. pl. masc. *grimmr* ***sínum*** *óvinum* (R.S. 6); *hann valði sér menn af heimamǫnnum* ***sínum*** (R.S. 13(1)).

[28] English has poss. pronouns, while Old Norse distinguishes the declinable poss. adj. *sinn* from the indeclinable gen. pronouns *hans, hennar*, etc.

The following passage has additional examples of the refl. poss. adj.

Ór *Egils sǫgu Skalla-Grímssonar* (59. Kap.)
(From the *Saga of Egil Skalla-Grimsson*, Chap. 59)

sons his power
Haraldr inn hárfagri setti sonu **sína** til ríkis í Nóregi, þá er hann tók at
grow old made of sons his
eldask, gerði Eirík konung yfirkonung sona **sinna** allra, ok er Haraldr
seventy (of) winters delivered hands
hafði verit sjau tigu vetra konungr, þá seldi hann í hendr Eiríki
son his kingdom
syni **sínum** ríki.

14.4. Declension of *sonr* in the singular and plural.

The declension of the masc. noun *sonr* is somewhat irregular (see R.S. 3, 6.6, 9, 14.3, 15). The chart below gives the singular and plural of *sonr*.

	Sing	**Pl**
nom	sonr	synir
acc	son	sonu (syni)
dat	syni	sonum
gen	sonar	sona

14.5. Suffixed article: Plural.

When suffixed to pl. forms in *-ar*, *-ir*, and *-r* (masc. and fem., nom. and acc.), the article loses its initial *i-*, in the same way that it does after forms ending in a vowel: *hestar* + *inir* = *hestar**nir***, likewise *hlutir**nir***, *hendr**nir***.

When the dat. pl. art. *inum* is attached to a noun (ending in *-um*), the resultant ending *-uminum* is contracted to *-unum*: *skip**unum***.

Since the detached article in the masc. dat. sing. is also *inum*, the sing. and pl. forms of masc. dat. nouns can be confused unless attention is paid to two points:

- the weak adj. forms and the isolated noun forms are different:
  sing.: af inum sterk**a** hest**i**
  pl.: af inum sterk**um** hest**um**
- the forms of the suffixed art. are different:
  sing.: af hest**i**num
  pl: af hest**u**num

14.6. Review paradigms: Suffixed art. in the sing. and pl.

The tables below summarize the suffixed article in all cases of the singular and plural. The strong nouns *hestr, staðr, fǫr, jǫrð, á*, and *skip*, and the weak nouns *goði, saga*, and *hjarta* have been used examples.

Strong nouns:

	Masc		Fem			Neut
	'horse'	**'place'**	**'journey'**	**'earth'**	**'river'**	**'ship'**
Sg *nom*	hestr-inn	staðr-inn	fǫr-in	jǫrð-in	á-in	skip-it
acc	hest-inn	stað-inn	fǫr-ina	jǫrð-ina	á-na	skip-it
dat	hesti-num	stað-inum	fǫr-inni	jǫrðu-nni	á-nni	skipi-nu
gen	hests-ins	staðar-ins	farar-innar	jarðar-innar	ár-innar	skips-ins
Pl *nom*	hestar-nir	staðir-nir	farar-nar	jarðir-nar	ár-nar	skip-in
acc	hesta-na	staði-na	farar-nar	jarðir-nar	ár-nar	skip-in
dat	hestu-num	stǫðu-num	fǫru-num	jǫrðu-num	á-num	skipu-num
gen	hesta-nna	staða-nna	fara-nna	jarða-nna	á-nna	skipa-nna

Weak nouns:

	Masc	Fem	Neut
	'chieftain'	**'story'**	**'heart'**
Sg *nom*	goði-nn	saga-n	hjarta-t
acc	goða-nn	sǫgu-na	hjarta-t
dat	goða-num	sǫgu-nni	hjarta-nu
gen	goða-ns	sǫgu-nnar	hjarta-ns
Pl *nom*	goðar-nir	sǫgur-nar	hjǫrtu-n
acc	goða-na	sǫgur-nar	hjǫrtu-n
dat	goðu-num	sǫgu-num	hjǫrtu-num
gen	goða-nna	sagna-nna	hjartna-nna

14.7. Suffixed article: Contraction with monosyllabic strong nouns ending in a vowel.

As mentioned earlier (4.8, 14.5), the article regularly contracts when suffixed to a noun ending in a vowel. The following reading selection contains an exception to that rule. The exception occurs when both the art. and the noun are monosyllabic, that is, both have just one syllable: f.ex., *á* + *-in* = *áin* ('the river'). When either the noun or the art. has more than one syllable (is polysyllabic), the normal rule comes into play and the art. loses its initial *i-*: acc. *á* + *ina* = ***ána***; dat. *á* + *inni* = ***ánni***; gen. *á* + *innar* = ***ánnar***.

Ór *Njáls sǫgu* (146. Kap.)

(From *Njal's Saga*, Chap. 146)

rode east Arnarstakk's Heath
Riðu þeir Þorgeirr austr á Arnarstakksheiði.[29] Er nú ekki at segja frá

---

[29] *Arnarstakksheiðr* is the heath beside a mountain in the south of Iceland. The mountain is named *Arnarstakkr* ('Eagle's Haystack') because it is shaped like a haystack. *Arnarstakkr* is a compound of *ǫrn* (masc.) 'eagle', gen. *arnar* + *stakkr* (masc.) 'haystack'.

before came Old Woman's Valley River
ferð þeira, fyrr en þeir kómu til Kerlingardalsár;[30] **áin** var mikil.
rode along horses saddles rode
Riðu þeir upp með **ánni**, því at þeir sá þar hross með sǫðlum. Riðu þeir
were sleeping dale stood spears
þangat til ok sá, at menn sváfu í dœl nǫkkurri, ok stóðu spjót
below took the spears carried [them]
þeira ofan frá þeim; þeir tóku spjótin ok báru út á **ána**.

14.8. Kinship terms in the plural.

The small class of nouns consisting of family members (9.5) follows a distinct pattern in the pl. These nouns end in *-r* in the nom. and acc. pl. and have a stem-final *-r-* before the dat. pl. ending *-um* and the gen. pl. ending *-a*. The stem vowel shows *i*-umlaut throughout the pl.

The chart below gives both the singular and the plural.

	Masc		**Fem**		
	faðir	**bróðir**	**móðir**	**systir**	**dóttir**
Sg *nom*	faðir	bróðir	móðir	systir	dóttir
acc	fǫður	bróður	móður	systur	dóttur
dat	fǫður	bróður	móður	systur	dóttur
gen	fǫður	bróður	móður	systur	dóttur
Pl *nom*	f**e**ð**r**	br**œ**ð**r**	m**œ**ð**r**	s**y**st**r**	d**œ**t**r**
acc	f**e**ð**r**	br**œ**ð**r**	m**œ**ð**r**	s**y**st**r**	d**œ**t**r**
dat	f**e**ð**rum**	br**œ**ð**rum**	m**œ**ð**rum**	s**y**st**rum**	d**œ**t**rum**
gen	f**e**ð**ra**	br**œ**ð**ra**	m**œ**ð**ra**	s**y**st**ra**	d**œ**t**ra**

Exercises

1. Fill in the appropriate endings.

a. Hross___ gengu upp með á____ ok kona__ gekk hjá þeim. (all def.)

b. Hross___ horfði á á___ ok gekk síðan til á_______. (all def.)

c. Á___ (def.) var fegrst um vár___.

d. Spjót___ stóðu hjá búð_____ (sg.) ok skip____ var í á____. (all def.)

e. Repeat sentence **d**, making the subject of the first clause singular and the subject of the second clause plural.

---

[30] *Kerlingardalsár* (*Kerling-ar* + *dal-s* + *ár*) literally means 'Old woman's valley's river' (that is, 'River of the Old Woman's Valley'). It is in the gen. case because it follows the prep. *til*. The last element of this compound is *ár* (= *á* + *-ar*) 'of a river', showing the contraction (loss of *-a-*) in the gen. sing. fem. ending *-ar* (see the last bullet point under 9.3).

2. Supply a poss. pron. (*hans*) or refl. poss. adj. (*sinn*) in the appropriate case.

a. Egill fór til Englands með mǫnnum ________. Hann fór aptr til Nóregs með fǫður ________.

b. Bjǫrn náði fundi Þóris. Hann hóf upp bónorð ________ ok bað systur ________.

c. Þórir vildi ekki gefa honum systur ________.

d. Óðinn stýrði ríki ________, þá er hann var heima, en brœðr ________ stýrðu ríki ________, þá er hann var i brottu.

3. Write the infinitive of the weak verbs with vowel shift of which the 3 sing. past forms are:

Ex: barði 'struck'	berja	muldi 'crushed'	mylja
dvalði 'delayed'	________	smurði 'anointed'	________
flutti 'conveyed'	________	tamdi 'tamed'	________
hulði 'hid'	________	vakti 'wakened'	________
hvatti 'whetted'	________	valði 'chose'	________
lamdi 'beat'	________	þusti 'rushed'	________

4. Change the nouns in **bold type** from singular to plural, and make any other necessary changes.

a. **Sonr** konungs stýrði ríkinu eptir hann.

____

b. Hann heyrði tíðendi um dauða **bróður** síns. (*dauði* masc. 'death')

____

c. Nǫrvi átti **dóttur**, svǫrt ok døkk.

____

d. Þá var Bjarni heima með **systur** sinni.

____

Vocabulary

Arnarstakkr *m* 'Eagle's Haystack', a mountain in the south of Iceland (*place name*)
Arnarstakksheiðr *f* Heath of Arnarstakkr (*place name*)
austr *adv* east
átján *num* eighteen
átta *num* eight
brottu *adv* **í brottu** away (*location*)
dvelja (dvalð-) *vb* delay, defer; *refl* **dveljask** stay
dœl *f* dale, hollow
ellifu *num* eleven
fimm *num* five
fimmtán *num* fifteen
fjórtán *num* fourteen
Frigg *f* Frigg, wife of Odin (*mythological name*)
heiðr *f* heath
hross *n* horse
hvetja (hvatt-) *vb* whet, sharpen
hylja (hulð-) *vb* hide, cover
Kerlingardalsá *f* 'River of the Old Woman's Valley' (*place name*)

langt *adv* far
lemja (lamd-) *vb* beat, thrash
lengi *adv* long, a long time
litlu *adv* a little
nítján *num* nineteen
níu *num* nine
ríða (ríðr; reið, riðu; riðit) *vb* ride
ríki (-j-) *n* realm, kingdom; power
selja (-d-) *vb* deliver, hand over
sex *num* six
sextán *num* sixteen
síð *adv* late
síðar *comp adv* (*see* **síð**) later
sjau *num* seven; **sjau tigir** *num* [*w gen*] seventy
sjautján *num* seventeen
smyrja (smurð-) *vb* anoint, 'smear'
sofa (sefr; svaf, sváfu; sofit) *vb* sleep
spjót *n* spear
stakkr *m* haystack
stýra (-ð-) *vb* [*w dat*] rule, govern
sváfu (*inf* **sofa**) *vb* were sleeping
sǫðull *m* saddle
temja (tamd-) *vb* tame
tíu *num* ten
tuttugu *num* twenty
Vé *m* Ve, brother of Odin (*mythological name*)
Vílir *m* Vili, brother of Odin (*mythological name*)
þrettán *num* thirteen
þykkja (þótt-) *vb* seem
þysja (þust-) *vb* rush
ǫrn (*gen* arnar) *m* eagle

Phrases

annarr ... annarr ... the one ... the other ...
fyrr en before
litlu síðar a little later
ofan frá below
setja til ríkis put in power
selja i hendr turn over (to)
sjau tigu for seventy years (lit. winters)
upp með up along

Notes

LESSON 15

Ór *Egils sǫgu Skalla-Grímssonar* (81. kap.)

(From the *Saga of Egil Skalla-Grimsson*, Chap. 81)

then (whether) 'Seer' here
Síðan stóð Egill upp ok mælti hátt: "Hvárt er Ǫnundr sjóni hér í
the assembly slope
þingbrekkunni?"

am happy
Ǫnundr kvazk þar vera, – "ek em feginn orðinn, Egill, er þú ert
('stands between')
improve here impedes
kominn; mun þat allt bœta til um þat, er hér stendr milli máls manna."

('seeks with suits')
(whether) are you responsible for this that your prosecutes
"Hvárt ræðr þú því, er Steinarr, sonr þinn, sœkir sǫkum
drawn crowd
Þorstein, son minn, ok hefir dregit saman fjǫlmenni, til þess at gera at
outlaw
Þorstein urðarmanni?"

('unreconciled')
cause that at odds have
"Því veld ek eigi," segir Ǫnundr, "er þeir eru ósáttir, hefi ek þar
('laid to')
said words asked be reconciled
lagt til mǫrg orð ok beðit Steinar sættask við Þorstein...."

quickly clear whether
"Brátt mun þat," segir Egill, "ljóst verða, hvárt þú mælir þetta af
('that')
earnestness or insincerity think the latter less remember
alvǫru eða hégóma, þótt ek ætla þat síðr vera munu. Man ek
('would seem')
those to each (of the two) of us would have seemed unlikely we (two)
þá daga, at hvárumtveggja okkrum mundi þykkja ólíkligt, at vit
would prosecute each other or restrain our
myndim sǫkum sœkjask eða stilla eigi sonu okkra, at þeir
('travel not with')
not commit folly such hear here is in prospect seems to me
fari eigi með fíflsku slikri, sem ek heyri, at hér horfisk til. Sýnisk mér
counsel while we (two) are alive near located dispute
þat ráð, meðan vit erum á lífi ok svá nær staddir deilu þeira, at
('under us') ('set down')
we (two) take in our hands settle [it] let [them]
vit takim mál þetta undir okkr ok setim niðr, en látim eigi þá

	('incite') drive		sons	our		pack-horses
Tungu-Odd ok Einar	etja	saman	sonum	okkrum	sem	kapalhestum."

15.1. Preterite-present verbs: Present tense.

As mentioned earlier (3.7), modial auxiliary verbs are helping verbs ('can', 'may', 'shall', 'will', etc.) that are used with an infinitive to express characteristics such as ability, possibility, necessity, intention, etc. Most modal auxiliaries (with the major exceptions of *hafa*, *vera*, and *vilja*) belong to a small but important class of verbs known as **preterite presents**.

Preterite presents are so called because their present tense is formed like the preterite (past tense)[31] of strong verbs. Pret.-pres. endings are identical to the past-tense endings of strong verbs (shown at right; see also 6.2, 8.4, 9.9). Also like strong verbs, pret.-pres. verbs often have different stem vowels in sing. and pl. pres. (6.4): *þat má, þeir megu; þat skal, þeir skulu*, etc.

1sg	–
2sg	-t
3sg	–
1pl	-um
2pl	-uð
3pl	-u

Below are the three most common pret.-pres. auxiliaries, declined in the pres. tense: *mega* ('be able to, may'), *munu* ('will, shall [*futurity*]; be likely'), and *skulu* ('shall [*necessity*], must'):

Pres. tense of pret.-pres. verbs (modal auxiliaries)

	mega	**munu**	**skulu**
1sg	má	mun	skal
2sg	mátt	munt	skalt
3sg	má	mun	skal
1pl	megum	munum	skulum
2pl	meguð	munuð	skuluð
3pl	megu	munu	skulu

- Several examples have appeared in the readings:
  - *þú mátt* (R.S. 7), *þat má* (R.S. 11), both from *mega*;
  - *muntu* (R.S. 11) (= *munt þú*, 10.1.1), *þat mun* (R.S. 10, 15), *fáir menn munu* (R.S. 13(2)), all from *munu*.
- ***Munu*** and ***skulu*** are unique in that their infinitives end in *-u* instead of *-a*. In these pret.-pres. verbs, the 3 pl. pres. is the same as the inf.: *at mun**u*** (R.S. 15) – *þeir mun**u*** (R.S. 13(2)); *at skul**u*** – *þeir skul**u***.
- In most other pret.-pres. verbs (with the exception of *muna*, see 15.3), the 3 pl. pres. is different from the inf.: *at kunn**a*** (R.S. 11) – *þeir kunn**u***; *at meg**a*** – *þeir meg**u*** (R.S. 16 below).

---

[31] Preterite is from the Latin word *præteritum* meaning 'past'. It is used grammatically to decribe a simple past tense such as *tók* ('took') as distinct from a perf. tense such as *hefir tekit* ('has taken') and *hafði tekit* ('had taken').

- When the 2 sing. ending *-t* is added to a stem ending in a vowel, it is doubled: *má**tt***.

In addition to the modal auxiliaries, there are a few other pret.-pres. verbs. We have already seen *muna* 'remember': *ek man* (R.S. 15); and *vita* 'know': *ek veit* (R.S. 11). Other common examples are *eiga* 'own, be married to', *kunna* 'know; be able', and *þurfa* 'need'. These verbs are conjugated as follows:

Pres. tense of pret.-pres. verbs

	eiga	**kunna**	**muna**	**vita**	**þurfa**
1sg	á	kann	man	veit	þarf
2sg	átt	kannt	mant	veizt	þarft
3sg	á	kann	man	veit	þarf
1pl	eigum	kunnum	munum	vitum	þurfum
2pl	eiguð	kunnuð	munið	vituð	þurfuð
3pl	eigu	kunnu	muna	vitu	þurfu

15.2. *Munu* 'will, shall, be likely' vs. *muna* 'remember'.

The modal auxiliary verb *munu* 'will, shall, be likely (expressing futurity or probability)' can be confused with the verb *muna* 'to remember' (f.ex., *ek man* R.S. 15). In addition to having different infinitives, these two verbs are distinguishable in several other ways:

- *Munu* has the root vowel *-u-* in the pres. sing. (*ek m**u**n* 'I will'), while *muna* has the vowel *-a-* (*ek m**a**n* 'I remember').
- *Munu* has past endings in the pres. pl. (*mun**um***, *mun**uð***, *mun**u***), whereas *muna* has normal pres. endings (*mun**um***, *mun**ið***, *mun**a***). Only the 1 pl. *munum* is the same in both verbs.
- Because *munu* is a modal auxiliary, it is regularly accompanied by an infinitive: *fáir menn munu **vita*** 'few men are likely **to know**' (R.S. 13(2)), *brátt mun þat ljóst **verða*** 'that will quickly **become** clear' (R.S. 15).

15.3. Preterite-present verbs: Past tense.

Preterite-present verbs in the past tense have the same endings as weak verbs in the past tense (shown at right; see also 5.5, 9.9): 3 sing. *át**ti*** (R.S. 3.9, 6, 6.6, 8.1(1), 9.6(2), 13.4(2), 14), *mát**ti*** (R.S 12(1)) *mun**di*** (R.S. 15); 3 pl. *mát**tu*** (R.S 12(1)). In addition, the past stem usually has a dental suffix like weak verbs (see 5.3.2): *á**tt**-*, *má**tt**-*, *mun**d**-*.

1sg	-a
2sg	-ir
3sg	-i
1pl	-um
2pl	-uð
3pl	-u

Here is the past tense of the seven most common pret.-pres. verbs (see 15.1 for the pres.):

Past tense of pret.-pres. verbs

	mega	**munu**	**skulu**
1sg	mátta	munda	skylda
2sg	máttir	mundir	skyldir
3sg	mátti	mundi	skyldi
1pl	máttum	mundum	skyldum
2pl	máttuð	munduð	skylduð
3pl	máttu	mundu	skyldu

	eiga	**kunna**	**muna**	**vita**	**þurfa**
1sg	átta	kunna	munda	vissa	þurfta
2sg	áttir	kunnir	mundir	vissir	þurftir
3sg	átti	kunni	mundi	vissi	þurfti
1pl	áttum	kunnum	mundum	vissum	þurftum
2pl	áttuð	kunnuð	mundið	vissuð	þurftuð
3pl	áttu	kunnu	munda	vissu	þurftu

- *Kunna* 'know; be able' and *vita* 'know' have distinctive past-tense stems: *kunn-* and *viss-*. The expected dental suffix has assimilated to the final consonant of the stem.
- *Kunna* has the same forms in the pres. pl. and past pl.
- *Munu* and *muna* are identical in the past sing. and 1 pl., but differ in the 2 pl. and 3 pl. forms.
- Two other pret.-pres. verbs are *kná* 'know how, be able', which follows the conjugation of *mega*, and *unna* 'love', which follows the congjuagtion of *kunna*.

15.4. Verbs: More on *vera*.

	Pres	**Past**
1sg	em	var
2sg	er-**t**	var-**t**
3sg	er	var
1pl	er-**um**	vár-**um**
2pl	er-**uð**	vár-**uð**
3pl	er-**u**	vár-**u**

In the pres. tense, *vera* conjugates as a pret.-pres. verb. The strong past endings are added to the stem *er-*, except in the 1st person where *em* is used.

In the past tense, *vera* conjugates as a strong verb, with regular strong past endings added to the stems *var-* (sing.) and *vár-* (pl.). Because of this, the sing. and pl. of *vera* employ the same endings but the stems are different.

15.5. Verbs: Present subjunctive (see also 8.5, 8.6).

The pres. subjunct. is characterized by the presence of -*i*- in all endings except the 1 sing. (which ends in -*a*). This -*i*- in the ending does not cause *i*-umlaut (11.2.1).

1sg	-a
2sg	-ir
3sg	-i
1pl	-im
2pl	-ið
3pl	-i

With *fara* and *taka* as examples, we have seen: *hann far**i*** (R.S. 8), *þeir far**i**, vit tak**im*** (both in R.S. 15). Note that the 3 sing. and 3 pl. forms are identical (*hann fari, þeir fari*).

Pres. subjunct. of *fara* and *taka*

	fara	taka
1sg	fara	taka
2sg	farir	takir
3sg	fari	taki
1pl	farim	takim
2pl	farið	takið
3pl	fari	taki

Other examples are: *hann sit**i*** (R.S. 8), *vit lát**im*** (R.S. 15), *þú eig**ir**, vér et**im**, vér ger**im**, þér ráð**ið**, þér ger**ið*** (all in R.S. 16 below).

15.6. Verbs: Impersonal constructions expressing opinion or belief.

Icelandic employs several impersonal constructions to express opinion or belief. These constructions consist of a verb in the 3 sing. plus a dat. pron., and are equivalent to the English expressions 'it appears to me' and 'it seems to me'.

Often the verb is reflexive: *virðisk mér* 'it seems to me' (R.S. 11), from *virðask*; *sýnisk mér* 'it appears to me' (R.S. 15), from *sýnask*. The non-refl. verb *þykkja* is also common: *Ásum þótti* 'it seemed to the Æsir' (R.S. 14), *hvárumtveggja okkrum mundi þykkja* 'it would have seemed to each of us' (R.S. 15). Old English possessed a parallel construction which survived into Shakespearean times as 'methinks, methought'. These expressions do not mean 'I think, I thought', but 'to me it seems, to me it seemed' (pres. and past). Because they are impersonal expressions ('[it] seems', '[it] appears'), the verb is in the 3 sing. and the pronoun is usually omitted; f.ex.:

> *Ásum þótti* '[it] seemed to the Æsir' (R.S. 14).

Sometimes the neut. pron. *þat* 'it' accompanies the verb; f.ex.:

> *óráðligt sýnisk mér **þat*** '**it** seems inadvisable to me' (from *Fóstbrœðra saga*, ch. 1).

In this example, the presence of *þat* implies a certain sense of emphasis, and one could also translate using 'that'.

In Old Icelandic, verbs in dependent clauses that follow these impersonal constructions are in the subjunctive; f.ex.:

***Sýnisk mér** þat ráð ... at vit **takim** mál þetta undir okkr ok **setim** niðr, en **látim** eigi þá Tungu-Odd ok Einar etja saman sonum okkrum sem kapalhestum* (R.S. 15).

EXERCISES

1. Conjugate the following pret.-pres. verbs in the pres. and past tenses.

	eiga	**mega**	**skulu**	**vita**
Pres *1sg*	________	________	________	________
2sg	________	________	________	________
3sg	________	________	________	________
1pl	________	________	________	________
2pl	________	________	________	________
3pl	________	________	________	________
Past *1sg*	________	________	________	________
2sg	________	________	________	________
3sg	________	________	________	________
1pl	________	________	________	________
2pl	________	________	________	________
3pl	________	________	________	________

2. Identify whether the following phrases contain the verb *munu* 'will, shall, be likely' or *muna* 'remember'.

Ex.: þér munið _muna_

a. ek mun ________

b. þú mant ________

c. þeir muna ________

d. þér munduð ________

e. þau mundu ________

f. þær munda ________

g. Engi maðr mundi þá fyrri daga. ________

h. Engi maðr mundi þurfa at berjask. ________

i. Translate sentences **g** and **h**.

g. ________________________________

h. ________________________________

3. Supply the correct form of the pronoun, noun, or name in parentheses.

a. (þú) ________ sýnisk

b. (konungr) ________ þótti

c. sýndisk (Bjǫrn) ________

d. (Gísli) ________ virðisk

e. (hann) ________ þótti

f. (vér) ________ mundi þykkja

g. (menn) ________ þykkir

h. virðisk (þeir) ________

4. Give the pres. subjunct. form of the verb in parentheses.

Ex.: Sýnisk Þórólfi at Eiríkr (hyggja) <u>hyggi</u> vandliga at skipinu.

a. Mér sýnisk, konungsson, at þú (hyggja) ________ vandliga at skipinu.

b. Svá virðisk yðr sem ek (vilja) ________ vera yfirmaðr yðarr?

c. Ásum þykkir ørvænt at Óðinn ________ heim koma.

d. Agli þykkir at Steinarr (fara) ________ með fíflsku. (NB: *Agli*, dat. of *Egill*)

e. Agli þykkir at Steinarr ok Þorsteinn (fara) ________ með fíflsku.

VOCABULARY

alvara *f* earnestness
brátt *adv* quickly
bœta (-tt-) *vb* to better, improve
draga (dregr; dró, drógu; dregit) *vb* pull, draw
etja (att-) *vb* [*w dat*] incite, egg on
feginn *adj* happy, glad, pleased
fíflska *f* folly, foolishness
fjǫlmenni *n* crowd
hégómi *m* insincerity
hér *adv* here
horfa (-ð-) *vb* look
hvárrtveggja *indef pron* each (of two)
hvárt *conj* whether (often used to introduce a yes/no question)
leggja (lagð-) *vb* lay
láta (lætr; lét, létu; látit) *vb* let, allow
líf *n* life
ljóss *adj* clear
meðan *conj* while
milli *prep* [*w gen*] between
muna (man, muna; mundi; munat) *vb* remember
munu (mun, munu; mundi) *vb* will, shall (*futurity*), be likely
myndim (*inf* **munu**) *vb* (we) would, should (*1pl past subjunct*)
nær *adv* near, nearly
okkarr *poss adj* our (two)
okkr *pron* us (two) (*acc of* vit)
orð *n* word
ósáttr *adj* unreconciled, at odds
ráð *n* counsel, advice
ráða (ræðr; réð, réðu; ráðit) *vb* [*w dat*] counsel, advise; plan, arrange
síðan *adv* then, afterwards
síðr *comp adv* less
skulu (skal, skulu; skyldi) *vb* shall (necessity)
slíkr *adj* such
staddr *adj* located
Steinarr *m* Steinar (*personal name*)
sýnask (-d-) *refl vb* seem
sœkja (sótt-) *vb* seek
sǫk *f* lawsuit
Tungu-Oddr *m* Tungu-Odd (*personal name*)
valda (veldr; olli, ollu; valdit) *vb* [*w dat*] cause
vit *pron* we (two)
ætla (-að-) *vb* think

PHRASES

á lifi alive
bœta til um improve
etja hestum incite horses (to fight)
fara með fíflsku commit folly
horfask til be in prospect
hvárt ræðr þú því are you responsible for this
leggja til orð say
setja niðr settle (a dispute)
standa milli impede
sýnisk mér it seems to me
sættask við be reconciled with
sœkja sǫkum prosecute
taka undir sik take charge of
þótt ek ætla þat síðr mun vera although I think that is less likely

LESSON 16

Ór *Njáls sǫgu* (58. kap.)

(From *Njal's Saga*, Chap. 58)

Ríða þeir brœðr nú til Hlíðarenda. Gunnarr var heima ok gekk út;

welcome
Kolskeggr gekk út með honum ok Hjǫrtr, bróðir þeira, ok fagna þeim

intended
vel ok spurðu, hvert þeir ætlaði at fara.

farther (to) us own
"Eigi lengra," segja þeir; "oss er sagt, at þú eigir hest góðan, ok vilju

we offer horse-fight
vér bjóða þér hestaat."

small can
Gunnarr svarar: "Litlar sǫgur megu ganga frá hesti mínum; hann er

unproved in all respects
ungr ok óreyndr at ǫllu."

surmised this would [be] proud of
"Hildigunnr gat þess til," segja þeir, "at þú myndir góðr af hestinum."

why spoke you
"Hví tǫluðuð þér um þat?" segir Gunnarr.

no one would dare
"Þeir menn váru," segja þeir, "er mæltu, at engi myndi þora at etja

our
við várn hest."

dare maliciously
"Þora mun ek at etja," segir Gunnarr, "en gráliga þykki mér þetta

mælt."

('intend')
we agree
"Skulu vér til þess ætla þá?" segja þeir.

('prevail in')
(to) you your attain
"Þá mun yðr fǫr yðvar þykkja bezt," segir Gunnarr, "ef þér ráðið

this ask (of) you we
þessu, en þó vil ek þess biðja yðr, at vér etim svá hestunum, at vér

('make to others pleasure')
entertain others no trouble you no
gerim ǫðrum gaman, en oss engi vandræði ok þér gerið mér enga

('[it] is not to be helped but I')
shame you me I will be forced to
skǫmm. En ef þér gerið til mín sem til annarra, þá er eigi ráðit, nema ek

('bend it to you')
deal with you you difficult bear up
sveigja þat at yðr, at yðr mun þykkja hart undir at búa. Mun ek þar
('before')
first
eptir gera, sem þér gerið fyrir."

('how to them [it] had gone')
how they had made out
Ríða þeir þá heim. Spurði Starkaðr at, hversu þeim hefði farizk.
said promised
Þeir sǫgðu, at Gunnarr gerði góða ferð þeira; – "hann hét at etja
we determined when horse-fight should it appeared
hesti sínum, ok kváðu vér á, nær þat hestavíg skyldi vera. Fannsk þat á
in all to be inferior to us he was evasive
í ǫllu, at honum þótti sik skorta við oss, ok bazk hann undan."

often appear slow to stir up
"Þat mun opt á finnask," segir Hildigunnr, "at Gunnarr er seinþreyttr
trouble hard to handle can not escape
til vandræða, en harðdrægr, ef hann má eigi undan komask."

16.1. Verbs: Past subjunctive.

The past subjunct. endings are identical to the pres. subjunct. endings (15.5), but the stems are different. For example, earlier reading selections have shown the following past subjunctives:

*hann væ**ri*** (R.S. 3.9, 8, 10, 12(1))
*þeir ætlaði**i**, þat hefð**i*** (R.S. 16)
*hann mynd**i*** (R.S. 11, 16), *þú mynd**ir*** (R.S. 16), *vit mynd**im*** (R.S. 15)

1sg	-a
2sg	-ir
3sg	-i
1pl	-im
2pl	-ið
3pl	-i

Formation of the past subjunctive stem.

Inf		Past indic		Past subjunct
kalla	–	kallað-	–	hann/þeir kallaði
hafa	–	h**a**fð-	–	hann/þeir h**e**fði
vera	–	þeir v**á**ru	–	hann/þeir v**æ**ri

The past subjunct. is characterized by *i*-umlaut of the stem vowel in all verbs except weak verbs with vocalic link *-a-* (5.3.1).

- In these weak verbs with vocalic link *-a-*, the past subjunct. stem is the same as the past indic.: f.ex., *kallað-*.
- In the remaining weak verbs, the past subjunct. employs the stem of the past indicative with *i*-umlaut where applicable (11.2.1): f.ex., past indic. ***h**a**fð-*** → past subjunct. ***hefð-***.
- In strong verbs, the past subjunct. stem is based on the 3 pl. past indic. stem with *i*-umlaut where applicable: f.ex., 3 pl. past ***vár**-u* → past subjunct. ***vær-***.

The same stem vowel occurs throughout the entire past subjunct.: *hann væri, þeir væri* (vs. *hann v**a**r, þeir v**á**ru*). In addition to the vowels listed in the table in 11.1, the stem vowels *-ó-* and *-u-* also undergo alternations in the past subjunctive.

Past indic		Past subjunct	Examples
ó	–	œ	koma – þeir k**ó**mu – hann/þeir k**œ**mi
u	–	y	munu – þeir m**u**ndu – hann/þeir m**y**ndi

16.2. The verb *vera*: Present and past subjunctive.

The pres. subjunct. of *vera* is irregular. The special stem *sé-* is employed, and the vowels of the regular subjunct. endings are dropped.

	Sing	Pl
1	ek sé	vér sé**m**
2	þú sé**r**	þú sé**ð**
3	hann / hon / þat sé	þeir / þær / þau sé

The past subjunct. of *vera* is regular, based on the stem *vær-*:

	Sing	Pl
1	ek væra	vér værim
2	þú værir	þú værið
3	hann / hon / þat væri	þeir / þær / þau væri

16.3. Personal pronouns: 1st and 2nd person dual.

In addition to sing. *ek* 'I', *þú* 'you' and pl. *vér* 'we', *þér* 'you' (3.6), Old Norse also employs **dual** pronouns, *vit* 'we two' and *þit* 'you two'. *Vit* and *þit* refer to only two people, while *vér* and *þér* refer to three or more people.

Dual pronouns

	1st		2nd	
***Dual** nom*	vit	'we'	þit/it	'you'
acc	okkr	'us'	ykkr	'you'
dat	okkr	'(to) us'	ykkr	'(to) you'
gen	okkar	'of us'	ykkar	'of you'

Dual pronouns use the regular plural form of the verb. For example:

Vit erum 'we [the two of us] are' (R.S. 15)
Vér erum 'we [more than two] are'
Vit sǫgðum 'we [the two of us] said'
Vér sǫgðum 'we [more than two] said'

Þit eruð 'you [the two of you] are'
Þér eruð 'you [more than two] are'
Þit sǫgðuð 'you [the two of you] said'
Þér sǫgðuð 'you [more than two] said'

The presence of the -*u*- in the ending causes *a*~*ǫ* alternation (11.2.2) in the verb stem: *vit tǫ**ku**m*, *þit tǫ**kuð*** (from *taka*), *vit sǫgð**u**m*, *þit sǫgð**uð*** (from *segja*), etc.

16.4. Adjectives: Possessive adjectives.

Declinable poss. adjectives exist in the 1st and 2nd persons. These poss. adjectives are all based on the gen. form of the corresponding pers. pron. (see 3.6).

Pers. pron.	**Gen.**	**Poss. adj.**
ek 'I'	*mín* 'of me'	*minn* 'my'
þú 'you (sing.)'	*þín* 'of you (sing.)'	*þinn* 'your (sing.)'
—	*sín* 'of oneself'	*sinn* 'one's own'
vit 'we two'	*okkar* 'of us two'	*okkarr* 'our (dual)'
þit 'you two'	*ykkar* 'of you two'	*ykkarr* 'your (dual)'
vér 'we'	*vár* 'of us'	*várr* 'our (pl.)'
þér 'you (pl.)'	*yðar* 'of you (pl.)'	*yðarr* 'your (pl.)'

The poss. adjectives *minn* 'my' and *þinn* 'your (sing.)' are declined like *sinn* (14.3).

Poss. adjectives *minn* and *þinn*

	minn 'my'			**þinn 'your (sing.)'**		
	Masc	**Fem**	**Neut**	**Masc**	**Fem**	**Neut**
Sg *nom*	minn	mín	mitt	þinn	þín	þitt
acc	minn	mína	mitt	þinn	þína	þitt
dat	mínum	minni	mínu	þínum	þinni	þínu
gen	míns	minnar	míns	þíns	þinnar	þíns
Pl *nom*	mínir	mínar	mín	þínir	þínar	þín
acc	mína	mínar	mín	þína	þínar	þín
dat	mínum	mínum	mínum	þínum	þínum	þínum
gen	minna	minna	minna	þinna	þinna	þinna

Dual and pl. poss. adjectives *okkarr*, *ykkarr*, *várr*, and *yðarr*

The other poss. adjectives, *okkarr* 'our (dual)', *ykkarr* 'your (dual)', *várr* 'our (pl.)', *yð(v)arr* 'your (pl.)' are declined like regular strong adjectives: f.ex., acc. pl. masc. *sonu okkra*, dat. *sonum okkrum*, *hvárumtveggja okkrum* (all in R.S. 15).

	okkarr 'our (dual)'			**ykkarr 'your (dual)'**		
	Masc	**Fem**	**Neut**	**Masc**	**Fem**	**Neut**
Sg *nom*	okkarr	okkur	okkart	ykkarr	ykkur	ykkart
acc	okkarn	okkra	okkart	ykkarn	ykkra	ykkart
dat	okkrum	okkarri	okkru	ykkrum	ykkarri	ykkru
gen	okkars	okkarrar	okkars	ykkars	ykkarrar	ykkars
Pl *nom*	okkrir	okkrar	okkur	ykkrir	ykkrar	ykkur
acc	okkra	okkrar	okkur	ykkra	ykkrar	ykkur
dat	okkrum	okkrum	okkrum	ykkrum	ykkrum	ykkrum
gen	okkarra	okkarra	okkarra	ykkarra	ykkarra	ykkarra

	várr 'our (pl.)'			**yð(v)arr 'your (pl.)'**		
	Masc	**Fem**	**Neut**	**Masc**	**Fem**	**Neut**
Sg *nom*	várr	vár	várt	yð(v)arr	yður	yð(v)art
acc	várn	vára	várt	yð(v)arn	yðra	yð(v)art
dat	várum	várri	váru	yðrum	yð(v)arri	yðru
gen	várs	várrar	várs	yð(v)ars	yð(v)arrar	yð(v)ars
Pl *nom*	várir	várar	vár	yðrir	yðrar	yður
acc	vára	várar	vár	yðra	yðrar	yður
dat	várum	várum	várum	yðrum	yðrum	yðrum
gen	várra	várra	várra	yð(v)arra	yð(v)arra	yð(v)arra

There are no poss. adjectives in the 3rd person. Instead, the gen. pronouns *hans, hennar, þess,* and *þeira* are used as indeclinable poss. pronouns: *sonr* ***hans*** (R.S. 3), *spenum* ***hennar*** (R.S. 5), *yfirmaðr* ***þeira*** (R.S. 2), etc.

16.5. The indefinite pronoun *hvárrtveggja.*

The indef. pron. *hvárrtveggja* 'each of two, both' is composed of *hvárr* 'each' + *tveggja*, gen. pl. of the numeral *tveir* 'two' (14.1). Only *hvárr-* is declined in this compound pronoun: *til hvár**s**tveggja* 'to each of two' (gen. sing. masc.), *í hvár**u**tveggja liði* 'in each army' (dat. sing. neut.), *hvár**ir**tveggja* 'both (men)' (nom. pl. masc.), etc. In the 1st and 2nd persons, this pronoun is regularly followed by a poss. adj. instead of a gen. pron.: *hvárumtveggja* ***okkrum*** 'each of the two of us' (R.S. 15). In the 3rd person it is a regular gen. pronoun: *hvárrtveggja þeira*, 'each of the two of them.'

Exercises

1. Indicative to Subjunctive, Present and Past. Write the 3 sing. and 3 pl. pres. and past subjunct. forms of the following verbs.

a. Weak Verbs	**Pres**	**Past**
Ex: hafa (*past stem* hafð-):	hann _hafi_	hann _hefði_
	þeir _hafi_	þeir _hefði_
dvelja (*past stem* dvalð-):	hon ______	hon ______
	þær ______	þær ______
fagna (*past stem* fagnað-):	hann ______	hann ______
	þeir ______	þeir ______
gera (*past stem* gerð-):	þat ______	þat ______
	þau ______	þau ______
spyrja (*past stem* spurð-):	hon ______	hon ______
	þær ______	þær ______

b. Strong Verbs	**Pres**	**Past**
Ex: halda (*3 pl. past* heldu):	hon haldi	hon heldi
	þær haldi	þær heldi
bjóða (*3 pl. past* buðu):	hann ____	hann ____
	þeir ____	þeir ____
bera (*3 pl. past* báru):	þat ____	þat ____
	þau ____	þau ____
hlaupa (*3 pl. past* hljópu):	hann ____	hann ____
	þeir ____	þeir ____
taka (*3 pl. past* tóku):	hon ____	hon ____
	þær ____	þær ____

2. Past Subjunctive to Indicative. Provide the requested forms of the following verbs on the basis of the 3 sing. past subjunct.

a. Weak Verbs. The 3 sing. past subjunct. of each verb is given. Supply the (1) past-tense indic. stem, (2) 3 sing. past indic., and (3) inf. forms of the verb.

Ex: þat berði:	(1) past indic. stem: barð-	
	(2) þat barði	(3) at berja
hon legði:	(1) past indic. stem: ____	
	(2) hon ____	(3) at ____
hon skipti:	(1) past indic. stem: ____	
	(2) hon ____	(3) at ____
hann velði:	(1) past indic. stem: ____	
	(2) hann ____	(3) at ____
þat ætlaði:	(1) past indic. stem: ____	
	(2) þat ____	(3) at ____

b. Strong Verbs. The 3 sing. past subjunct. of each verb is given. Supply the (1) 3 pl. past indic., (2) 3 sing. past indic., and (3) inf. forms of the verb.

Ex: hann bæri:	(1) þeir báru	
	(2) hann bar	(3) at bera
hon gengi:	(1) þær ____	
	(2) hon ____	(3) at ____
hon gæti:	(1) þær ____	
	(2) hon ____	(3) at ____
þat kœmi:	(1) þau ____	
	(2) þat ____	(3) at ____

hann stœði: (1) þeir ______________

(2) hann ____________ (3) at ____________

3. Complete the paradigm of *vera* in the indicative and subjunctive.

		Indicative	Subjunctive
Pres.:	ek	em	___________
	þú	___________	sér
	hann	___________	___________
	vér	___________	sém
	þér	eruð	___________
	þeir	___________	___________

		Indicative	Subjunctive
Past:	ek	___________	væra
	þú	vart	___________
	hann	___________	___________
	vér	várum	___________
	þér	___________	værið
	þeir	___________	___________

4. Supply a gen. pron. (*mín, þín, vár, yðar*) or a poss. adj. (*minn, þinn, várr, yðarr*) in the appropriate case.

a. Farðu leið þ____ og kom þá aptr til m____. (*leið* fem. 'way, road')

b. Þórólfr gekk ofan til skips m_____.

c. Steinarr, sonr þ_____, sœkir sǫkum Þorstein, son m_____.

d. Góð þykki mér fǫr m____.

e. Litlar sǫgur megu ganga frá hesti þ______.

f. Þér skuluð ekki láta vánda menn komask í milli yð____ og v____.

g. Þat skaltu segja konungi yð_____, at Haraldr Svíakonungr fór þessa leið. (*Svíakonungr* 'king of the Swedes')

h. Engi mun þora at etja við yð____ hesta.

i. Bróðir þ________ bað systur m________, en faðir m________ vildi ekki gefa honum dóttur sína.

Vocabulary

af *prep* [*w dat*] of

bjóða (býðr; bauð, buðu; boðit) *vb* offer

eiga (á, eigu; átti; átt) *vb* own

fagna (-að-) *vb* [*w dat*] welcome

geta (getr; gat, gátu; getit) *vb* [*w gen*] guess

Gunnarr *m* Gunnar (*personal name*)

harðr *adj* hard

heita (heitir; hét, hétu; heitit) *vb* promise

Hildigunnr *f* Hildigunn (*personal

name)
Hjǫrtr *m* Hjort ('Deer') (*personal name*)
Hlíðarendi *m* Hlidarendi, a farm in southern Iceland (*place name*)
hví *adv* why
Kolskeggr *m* Kolskegg (*personal name*)
leið *f* way, road
lengra *adv* farther
mega (má, megu; mátti; mátt) *vb* be able
nema *conj* but (that), except
nær *conj* when
opt *adv* often
oss *pron* us (*pl*) (*acc/dat of* **vér**)
óreyndr *adj* unproved
seinþreyttr *adj* slow to stir up; **seinþreyttr til vandræða** slow to be drawn into a quarrel
skǫmm *f* shame, disgrace
Starkaðr *m* Starkad (*personal name*)
undan *adv* away
Svíakonungr *m* king of the Swedes
vandræði *n pl* trouble
várr *poss adj* our (*pl*)
vér *pron* we (*pl*)
yðarr *poss adj* your (*pl*)
yðr *pron* you (*acc/dat of* **þér**)
þér *pron* you (*pl*)
þora (-ð-) *vb* dare
þó *adv* yet, nevertheless
ætla (-að-) *vb* think, intend; agree

Phrases

at ǫllu in all respects
biðjask undan be evasive
finnask á appear
gera gaman entertain
geta til suppose, surmise
hversu þeim hefði farizk how they had made out
komask undan escape
kveða á fix, determine

Notes

LESSON 17

Ór *Snorra Eddu* (15., 17. kap.)

(From *Snorri's Edda*, Chaps. 15, 17)

the ash Urd's Well Norns chief places of the gods
Frá askinum, Urðarbrunni, nǫrnum ok hǫfuðstǫðum goðanna.

the chief place the holy place
Þá mælti Gangleri: "Hvar er hǫfuðstaðrinn eða helgistaðrinn
goðanna?"

hall
Hárr svarar: "Þat er at aski Yggdrasils. Þar stendr salr einn fagr undir
askinum við brunninn, ok ór þeim sal koma
three maidens they 'Fate' 'Becoming' 'Debt' these
þrjár meyjar, þær er svá heita: Urðr, Verðandi, Skuld. Þessar meyjar
shape life them Norns yet more
skapa mǫnnum aldr. Þær kǫllum vér nornir. Enn eru fleiri nornir,
each shape life
þær er koma til hvers barns, er borit er, at skapa aldr, ok eru þessar
god-kinned others of elves the third of dwarves
goðkunnigar, en aðrar álfa ættar, en inar þriðju dverga ættar."

can (the) heaven
Þá mælti Gangleri: "Mikil tíðendi kannt þú at segja af himninum?
more of chief places Urd's Well
Hvat er þar fleiri hǫfuðstaða en at Urðarbrunni?"

places magnificent place
Hárr segir: "Margir staðir eru þar gǫfugligir. Sá er einn staðr þar, er
Elf-Land people Light-Elves
kallaðr er Álfheimr. Þar byggvir fólk þat, er Ljósálfar heita, en
Dark-Elves down unlike much more unlike
Døkkálfar búa niðri í jǫrðu, ok eru þeir ólíkir sýnum ok miklu ólíkari
('fairer')
in reality Light-Elves more beautiful sun
reyndum. Ljósálfar eru fegri en sol sýnum, en døkkalfar eru
blacker pitch yet place none
svartari en bik. Þar er enn sá staðr, er Breiðablik er kallaðr, ok engi er
more beautiful walls
þar fegri staðr. Þar er ok sá, er Glitnir heitir, ok eru veggir hans
pillars posts red gold roof silver yet
ok steðr allar ok stólpar af rauðu gulli, en þak hans af silfri. Þar er enn
end at bridgehead
sá staðr, er Himinbjǫrg heita. Sá stendr á himins enda við brúarsporð,

heaven
þar er Bifrǫst kemr til himins. Þar er enn mikill staðr, er Valaskjálf
owns the gods thatched with pure silver
heitir. Þann stað á Óðinn. Þann gerðú goðin ok þǫkðu skíru silfri,
('high-seat')
hall throne
ok þar er Hliðskjálfin í þessum sal, þat hásæti, er svá heitir, ok þá
('all regions')
sees over the whole world southern
er Alfǫðr sitr í því sæti, þá sér hann of alla heima. Á sunnanverðum
heaven's end hall most beautiful brighter the sun
himins enda er sá salr, er allra er fegrstr ok bjartari en sólin, er
has perished
Gimlé heitir. Hann skal standa, þá er bæði himinn ok jǫrð hefir farizk,
inhabit place just for all ages
ok byggja þann stað góðir menn ok réttlátir of allar aldir."

17.1. Adjectives: Declension of comparative adjectives.

Reading Selection 16 has several comp. adjectives:

fleiri – referring to *nornir* (nom. pl. fem.)
fegri – referring to *staðr* (nom. sing. masc.) and *Ljósálfar* (nom. pl. masc.)
svartari – referring to *Døkkálfar* (nom. pl. masc.)
bjartari – referring to *salr* (nom. sing. masc.)

Comparative adjectives have a special declension:

	Masc	Fem	Neut
Sg *nom*	-i	-i	-a
acc	-a	-i	-a
dat	-a	-i	-a
gen	-a	-i	-a
Pl *nom*	-i	-i	-i
acc	-i	-i	-i
dat	-um	-um	-um
gen	-i	-i	-i

Compare this with the weak adj. declension (13.6). Even when used in weak adj. position, comp. adjectives take comp. adj. endings: *inna fyrr**i** konunga* (R.S. 7.2).

17.2. Adjectives: Formation of comparatives.

The comp., like the superl. (7.4), is formed with either of two suffixes. The comp. suffixws are *-ar-* and *-r-*.

Comparative adverbs add no further endings: *meir* (R.S. 2), *fyrr* (R.S. 13(1), 14.7), *síðar* (R.S. 14).

Comparative adjectives add the appropriate comp. ending (17.1) after *-ar-* or *-r-*: *svart**ar-i*** and *feg**r-i*** in the R.S. above.

When the comp. suffix is *-r-*, the stem vowel often undergoes *i*-umlaut (11.2.1): *fagr – fegri, smár* 'small' – *smæri*. The relationship of the stem vowel in the positive and comp. forms is:

Positive form	Comp with *-r*	Examples
a	e	f**a**gr – f**e**gri
á	æ	sm**á**r – sm**æ**ri
ǫ	ø	þr**ǫ**ngr 'narrow' – þr**ø**ngri
ó	œ	st**ó**rr – st**œ**rri
u	y	**u**ngr – **y**ngri
(j)ú	ý	dj**ú**pr 'deep' – d**ý**pri

See 7.4 for a similar change in the formation of the superl. with *-st-, fagr – fegri – fegrstr*; so also *smár – smæri – smæstr, stórr – stœrri – stœrstr, ungr – yngri – yngstr*, etc. When the adj. stem has a front vowel to begin with, *i*-umlaut has no effect and the vowel remains unchanged in the comp. and superl.: *vænn – vænni – vænstr.*

Using *stœrri* 'bigger' as an example, comp. adjectives decline as follows.

	Masc	Fem	Neut
Sg *nom*	stœrr**i**	stœrr**i**	stœrr**a**
acc	stœrr**a**	stœrr**i**	stœrr**a**
dat	stœrr**a**	stœrr**i**	stœrr**a**
gen	stœrr**a**	stœrr**i**	stœrr**a**
Pl *nom*	stœrr**i**	stœrr**i**	stœrr**i**
acc	stœrr**i**	stœrr**i**	stœrr**i**
dat	stœrr**um**	stœrr**um**	stœrr**um**
gen	stœrr**i**	stœrr**i**	stœrr**i**

17.3. Adjectives and adverbs: Irregular comparatives and superlatives.

A few Icelandic comparatives and superlatives are formed from stems that are different from the simple (positive) adjective. These irregular forms are sometimes called **suppletive** paradigms, because parts of the paradigm were "supplied" from different words. Several of these irregular forms correspond to English, where for example 'good' employs 'better' and 'best' for the comp. and superl., while 'bad' employs 'worse' and 'worst'. Below are the most common of these adjectives.

adj.: *góðr – betri – beztr* (be) 'good' – 'better' – 'best'
adv.: *vel – betr – bezt* (do) 'well' – 'better' – 'best'

adj.: *illr – verri – verstr* (be) 'bad' – 'worse' – 'worst'
adv.: *illa – verr – verst* (do) 'badly' – 'worse' – 'worst'

adj.: *lítill – minni – minnstr* (be) 'little' – 'littler' – 'littlest'
adv.: *lítt – minnr – minnst* (do) 'little' – 'less' – 'least'

adj.: *mikill – meiri – mestr* 'big' – 'bigger' – 'biggest'
adv.: *mjǫk – meir(r) – mest* 'much, very' – 'more' – 'most'

adj.: *margr – fleiri – flestr* 'many' – 'more' – 'most'
(no corresponding adv.)

adj.: *gamall – ellri – ellstr* 'old' – 'older' – 'oldest'
(no corresponding adv.)]

adj. *fyrri – fyrstr* 'former' – 'first, foremost'
adv. *fyrr – fyrst* 'before, earlier' – 'first, earliest'
(no corresponding positive forms)

17.4. Verbs: Present participles.

As mentioned earlier (8.7), participles are verbal adjectives, and Old Norse has two types of participles: pres. and past. Pres. participles employ the suffix *-and-* (corresponding to English '-ing') and are easily recognized. For example, the pres. part. *Verð**and**i* 'Becoming', from the verb *verða* 'become', appears in the R.S. as the name of one of the Norns.

Pres. participles have the same special declension as comp. adjectives (17.1). Using *verðandi* as an example:

	Masc	Fem	Neut
Sg *nom*	verðand**i**	verðand**i**	verðand**a**
acc	verðand**a**	verðand**i**	verðand**a**
dat	verðand**a**	verðand**i**	verðand**a**
gen	verðand**a**	verðand**i**	verðand**a**
Pl *nom*	verðand**i**	verðand**i**	verðand**i**
acc	verðand**i**	verðand**i**	verðand**i**
dat	verðǫnd**um**	verðǫnd**um**	verðǫnd**um**
gen	verðand**i**	verðand**i**	verðand**i**

- Note that the fem. sing. ends in *-i*. This explains the ending *-i* of the name of the Norn *Verðandi*.

17.5. Verbs: Preterite infinitive.

The preterite infinitive is a special form of the infinitive that appears chiefly in three verbs: *munu*; *skulu*; and *vilja*. The pret. inf. is formed by adding the ending *-u* to the weak past-tense stem of the verb.

munu 'will, shall' (futurity) – pret. inf. *mundu*
skulu 'shall, must' (necessity) – pret. inf. *skyldu*
vilja 'want, wish' – pret inf. *vildu*

- The pret. inf. is identical in form with the 3 pl. past.

The pret. inf. only occurs in one type of construction, called the **accusative with infinitive**, because the main verb is followed by an object in the acc. case followed by an infinitive. When the main verb is in the pres. tense, a normal inf. (f.ex., *munu*) follows; but when the main verb is in the past, a pret. inf. (f.ex., *mundu*) follows. Note that in both examples below, the object *hana* is in the acc.

Pres. tense: *Ek* ***hygg*** *hana* ***munu*** *heim koma* 'I **think** she (lit. 'her') **will** come home'.

Past tense: *Ek* ***hugða*** *hana* ***mundu*** *heim koma* 'I **thought** she (lit. 'her') **would** come home'.

This type of construction is frequent with reflexive verbs (10.5.1):

Pres.: *Hann* ***kvezk munu*** *fara* 'he **says** he (lit. 'says himself') **will** go'.

Past: *Hann* ***kvazk mundu*** *fara* 'he **said** he (lit. 'said himself') **would** go'.

Ór *Þorsteins þætti stangarhǫggs* (3. Kap.)

(From the *Tale of Thorstein Staff-Struck*, Chap. 3)

Ok er þeir kómu þar, þá spurði hann, hvert þeir ætluðu, en þeir

search for should/must
sǫgðusk hrossa leita **skyldu.**"

17.6. Nouns: Plural of strong nouns with *a~ǫ~e* alternation.

Nouns showing *a~ǫ~e* (or *ja~jǫ~i*) alternation in the sing. (see 11.5 and 11.6) also show this alternation in the plural. Masculine *vǫllr, ǫrn, skjǫldr*, and fem. *hǫnd* illustrate the patterns:

	Masc 'field'	'eagle'	'shield'	**Fem** 'hand'
Sg *nom*	v**ǫ**llr	**ǫ**rn	skj**ǫ**ldr	h**ǫ**nd
acc	v**ǫ**ll	**ǫ**rn	skj**ǫ**ld	h**ǫ**nd
dat	v**e**lli	**e**rni	sk**i**ldi	h**e**ndi
gen	v**a**llar	**a**rnar	skj**a**ldar	h**a**ndar
Pl *nom*	v**e**llir	**e**rnir	sk**i**ldir	h**e**ndr
acc	v**ǫ**llu	**ǫ**rnu	skj**ǫ**ldu	h**e**ndr
dat	v**ǫ**llum	**ǫ**rnum	skj**ǫ**ldum	h**ǫ**ndum
gen	v**a**lla	**a**rna	skj**a**lda	h**a**nda

Exercises

1. Fill in the appropriate endings and missing vowels.

a. Marg____ hǫfuðstað___ eru á himn___ ok all___ eru þeir fegr__ ok bjartar__ en hǫfuðstað_____ (def.) á jǫrð_____ (def.). Óðin__ átt__ hǫfuðstað sem Valaskjálf hét__, en in__ vitr___ nornir átt__ fagr__ hǫfuðstað undir ask_____ (def.).

b. Egil__ valð__ sér góð__ menn ok sterk__ ok fór með þeim til Himinbj__rg__ (pl.).

c. Supply exercise **b** with a plural subject and make other necessary changes.

____

____

d. Ljósálfar er__ ljós___ álf___ sem bú__ í þeim stað, er Álfheim__ heit___.

e. Urðr ok Skuld er__ vitr___ norn___, er skap__ m__rg___ mǫnn___ aldr.

2. Supply the missing comparatives and superlatives (see 17.3.). The forms listed have appeared in the Reading Selections.

Positive form	Comparative	Superlative
Ex.: góðr 'good'	betri	beztr (R.S. 7)
bjartr 'bright'	bjartari (R.S. 17)	___________
gamall 'old'	___________	ellztr (R.S. 13)
gørviligr 'accomplished'	___________	gørviligstr (R.S. 9)
hraustr 'bold'	___________	hraustastr (R.S. 13)
hvítr 'white'	___________	hvítastr (R.S. 7)
margr 'many'	fleiri (R.S. 17)	___________
mikill 'big'	___________	mestr (R.S. 8(2))
mjǫk 'much' (adv.)	meir (R.S. 2)	___________
sið 'late' (adv.)	síðar (R.S. 14)	___________
sterkr 'strong'	___________	sterkastr (R.S. 13)
vaskr 'brave'	___________	vaskastr (R.S. 8)
vitr 'wise'	___________	vitrastr (R.S. 7)

3. Change the adjectives in the following phrases to their corresponding comparatives.

a. vitr hǫfðingi: ________________

b. inn gamli bróðir: ________________

c. góðan hest: ________________

d. inn unga svein: ________________

e. ina góðu hesta: ________________

f. inum vaska bogmanni: ________________

g. inum sterkum nábúum: ________________

h. stórt haf: ________________

i. stór hǫf: ________________

j. inu smá skipi: ________________

k. ins hvíta grass: ________________

l. djúp á: ________________

m. in djúpa á: ________________

n. fagra mey: ________________

o. með mikilli vináttu: ________________________

p. svartrar nætr: __________________ (NB: nætr, gen. of nótt)

q. margar eyjar ok stórar: ________________________

r. inna bjartra sala: _______________________

VOCABULARY

Alfǫðr *m* 'All-Father,' a name of Odin
askr *m* ash tree
Álfheimr *m* 'Land of the Elves' (*place name*)
álfr *m* elf
Bifrǫst *f* the rainbow bridge to heaven
bik *n* pitch
bjartr *adj* bright, radiant
brunnr *m* well
djúpr *adj* deep
dvergr *m* dwarf
endi *m* end
engi *indef pron* none, no one
enn *adv* yet
farask (fersk; fórsk, fórusk; farizk) *refl vb* perish
fleiri *adj* more
fólk *n* people
Gimlé *n* Gimle (*place name*)
Glitnir *m* Glitnir (*place name*)
goð *n* god
gull *n* gold
gǫfugligr *adj* magnificent
hásæti *n* throne
Himinbjǫrg *n pl* 'Heaven Mountains' (*place name*)
Hliðskjálf *f* name of Odin's throne
hverr *indef pron* each
hǫfuðstaðr *m* capital, chief place
meyjar *pl of* **mær**
miklu *adv* [*w comp*] much
mær *f* girl, maiden
niðri *adv* down (in)
norn *f* Norn
of *prep* [*w acc/dat*] over (*distance*); for, during (*time*)
ólíkr *adj* unlike, different
réttlátr *adj* just
réttr *adj* straight; right, just
salr *m* hall
silfr *n* silver
sjá (sér; sá, sá(u); séð) *vb* see
skapa (-að-) *vb* shape, form
skírr *adj* pure
Skuld *f* Skuld ('Debt'), one of the Norns
smár *adj* small
staðr *m* place
stoð (*pl* steðr) *f* pillar
stólpi *m* post
sunnanverðr *adj* southern
svartr *adj* black
Urðarbrunnr *m* 'Urd's Well' (*place name*)
Urðr *f* Urd ('Fate'), one of the Norns
Valaskjálf *f* 'Vali's Seat' (*place name*)
veggr *m* wall
Verðandi *f* Verdandi ('Becoming', *pres part of* **verða**), one of the Norns
við *prep* [*w acc*] at
Yggdrasill *m* the tree of life
þekja (þakð-) *vb* thatch
þessar *dem pron* these (*fem pl nom/acc*)
þrǫngr *adj* narrow
þær *pron* they (*fem pl nom/acc*)

PHRASES

fegri sýnum more beautiful (in appearance)
of alla heima over all regions, over the whole world
ólíkr sýnum different in appearance

Appendix 1
Pronunciation Guide to Old Icelandic
(With a Discussion of Modern Icelandic Pronunciation)

Reconstruction of Old Icelandic sounds is by nature approximate. In most instances we infer the pronunciation from spellings in manuscripts and rhymes in poetry. There was no standard spelling. Writers and poets often employed their personal or regional pronunciation, and sounds sometimes changed over decades and centuries.

Stress in Old Norse and Old and Modern Icelandic typically falls on the first syllable of the word. For example, *kona*, *gerði*, and *konungr* are pronounced ***ko**-na*, ***ger**-ði*, and ***kon**-ungr*. Compounds have secondary stress on the first syllable of the second element. For example, the syllable *-móð-* in ***kon**unga**móð**ir* ('mother of kings') has secondary stress.

Old Icelandic Vowels

Vowels are sounds made by the unobstructed passage of air through the mouth. Old Norse vowels are classified as long or short. For most vowels, length is indicated by an acute accent, *á*, *é*, *í*, *ó*, *ú*, *ý*. The vowels *æ* and *œ* (sometimes spelled *ǿ*) are always long.

Long vowels in Old Icelandic were longer versions of the corresponding short vowels. For example, *a* and *á* were articulated alike, but *á* was originally longer in duration. Below is a chart showing the pronunciation of Old Icelandic vowels around the beginning of the 13th century. By this time, *á* had acquired rounding and merged into a long, low, round back vowel like the **au** in c**au**ght.

The vowels *au*, *ei*, and *ey* are diphthongs, with the tongue gliding from the first vowel to the position of the second. For example, *ei* begins with *e* and glides towards *i*.

Vowel	Old Icelandic Pronunciation	Examples
a	as **a** in f**a**ther, but shorter	*f**a**ðir*
á	as **au** in c**au**ght, with rounded lips and longer than *ǫ*	*l**á**ta*
e	as **e** in b**e**t	*b**e**kkr*
é	as **e** in b**e**t, but longer	*þ**é**r*
i	**i** in s**i**n	*s**i**nn*
í	as **ee** in s**ee**n	*l**í**ta*
o	as **o** in s**o**le, but shorter	*k**o**na*
ó	as **o** in b**o**at	*bj**ó**ða*
u	as **oo** in t**oo**k	*s**u**mar*
ú	as **oo** in m**oo**n	*b**ú**a*

y	as **ee** in s**ee**n, but pronounced with rounded lips; as in German *für*	*systir*
ý	as **ee** in s**ee**n, but pronounced with rounded lips; as in German *für*, but longer	*býðr*
æ	as **a** in n**a**p, but longer	*lætr*
œ	as **e** in b**e**t, but longer and pronounced with rounded lips; as in German *können*	*dœl*
ø	as **e** in b**e**t, but pronounced with rounded lips; as in German *können*. By early thirteenth century *ø* merged with *ǫ*.	*søkkva*
ǫ	as **au** in c**au**ght, pronounced with rounded lips and shorter than ***á***	*kǫttr*
au	as **ou** in h**ou**se	*n**au**ð*
ei	as **ei** in v**ei**n	*h**ei**ta*
ey	Old Icelandic *e* + *y*	*h**ey**ra*

Old Icelandic Consonants

Consonants are sounds made by a narrowing or closure of the vocal tract, which results in obstruction of the free flow of air. The Old Icelandic consonants *b, d, h, k, l, m, n, s,* and *t* were probably similar to the corresponding sounds in modern English.

Old Icelandic distinguished the pronunciation of single and double consonants. Double letters form long consonants; for instance, the *-mm-* in *ste**mm**a* is pronounced twice as long as the *-m-* in *hei**m**a*. In words that employ stop consonants (*p, t, k, b, d, g*) like *sta**dd**r* and *li**gg**ja*, the lengthening results in a pause before the release of air forming the consonant. We can hear a similar distinction in English between the single **k** in 'bee keeper' vs. the double **kk** in 'boo**kk**eeper', or the single **d** in 're**d** eye' vs. the double **dd** in 're**d d**ye'.

In Old Icelandic *f* and *v* were likely pronounced using both the lower and upper lips.

Below is a pronunciation chart for the Old Icelandic consonants that differ from English.

Consonant	Old Icelandic Pronunciation	Examples
f	1) at the beginning of a word: as ***f*** in **f**ather	***f**aðir*
	2) in the middle or at the end of a word: as **v** in ha**v**e	*ha**f**a*
g	1) at the beginning of word or after *n*: as **g** in **g**ood	***g**óðr, lan**g**r*
	2) preceding *s* or *t*: as **ch** in Scots English lo**ch**	*la**g**t*
j	as **y** in **y**es	***j**arl*
p	as **p** in **p**in	***p**enningr*
	preceding *s* or *t*: as ***f*** in a**f**ter	*e**p**tir*
r	trilled as Scots English **r**	***r**auðr*

s	as **s** in **s**it, not as English **z**	***s**itja*
v	as **w** in **w**est or **v** in **v**est	***v**estr*
þ	as **th** in **th**ing	***þ**ing*
ð	as **th** in **th**is, bro**th**er	*bró**ð**ir*
x	as **chs** in Scots English lo**chs**	*ø**x***
z	as **ts** in prin**ts**	*brau**z**k*

Modern Icelandic Pronunciation

A trend in teaching Old Norse-Icelandic is to read the texts with Modern Icelandic pronunciation. For those interested in reading the texts with the modern pronunciation, the following two charts provide guidance. Much of the grammar and basic vocabulary of Old Icelandic come into Modern Icelandic with few changes, and employing modern pronunciation is a good start to learning Modern Icelandic.

Modern Icelandic Vowels

In the 14th century, Icelandic long vowels began to mutate into diphthongs (a sequence of two vowel sounds pronounced together). As a result, many of the long vowels in Modern Icelandic differ from the corresponding short vowels in quality as well as length. In Modern Icelandic, the short vowels *a*, *e*, and *o* are still pronounced much as they were in Old Icelandic. However, the long vowels have changed. In most instances, Modern Icelandic long *á* resembles the diphthong **ou** in English 'h**ou**se'. Long *é* is pronounce like **ye** in English '**ye**s', and long *ó* is like the long **o** in English 'g**o**' or the **ow** of 'sn**ow**', with a glide toward **w** at the end.

Modern *y* and *ý* have lost their lip rounding and merged with *i* and *í*. The diphthong *ey* has also merged with *ei*. On the other hand, modern *au* has acquired lip rounding.

Soon after the beginning of the 13th century, *ø* merged with *ǫ*, represented by *ö*. The merged vowel is pronounced as a mid (i.e., half-low) front rounded vowel, like *ö* in German *sch**ö**n*. In addition, *œ* merged with *æ*, both now represented by *æ*, and this merged vowel is pronounced like Modern English long **i** as in mile.

Vowel	Modern Icelandic Pronunciation	Examples
a	as **a** in f**a**ther	*f**a**ðir*
	before *ng* and *nk*: as **ou** in h**ou**se	*l**a**ngr*
á	as **ou** in h**ou**se	*l**á**ta*
e	as **e** in b**e**t	*b**e**kkr*
é	as **ye** in **ye**s	*þ**é**r*
i	**i** in s**i**n	*s**i**nn*
í	as **ee** in s**ee**n	*l**í**ta*
o	as **o** in s**o**le	*k**o**na*
ó	as **o** in g**o**	*bj**ó**ða*
ö	as **u** in c**u**t, but with rounded lips	*k**ö**ttr*

u	as **u** in p**u**t	*s**u**mar*
ú	as **oo** in m**oo**n	*b**ú**a*
y	as **i** in s**i**n	*s**y**stir*
ý	as **ee** in s**ee**n	*b**ý**ðr*
æ	as **i** in m**i**le	*l**æ**tr, d**æ**l*
au	as **ay** in h**ay**, but with rounded lips	*n**au**ð*
ei, ey	as **ei** in v**ei**n	*h**ei**ta, h**ey**ra*

Modern Icelandic Consonants

The consonants *h, k, l, m, n* are pronounced much as in Modern English.

As in English, the consonants *p, t, k* are pronounced voiceless (with no vibration of the vocal cords). Unlike English, the consonants *b, d, g* are also pronounced voiceless.

The two consonant series *p, t, k* and *b, d, g* are distinguished from each other by the presence of aspiration (a puff of air) following *p, t, k*, while *b, d* and *g* are not aspirated.

In Modern Icelandic (and English), the letters *f* and *v* are pronounced with the lower lip in contact with the upper teeth.

Consonant	Modern Icelandic Pronunciation	Examples
f	1) at the beginning of a word: as ***f*** in **f**ather	***f**aðir*
	2) before *n* or *l*: as Modern Icelandic **p**	*na**f**n, ka**f**li*
	3) elsewhere: as **v** in ha**v**e	*ha**f**a*
g	1) at the beginning of word or after *n*: as **g** in **g**ood, but voiceless	***g**óðr, lan**g**r*
	2) preceding *s* or *t*: as **ch** in Scots English lo**ch**	*la**g**t*
	3) after vowels and before *a, u, ð, r*: as **ch** in Scots English lo**ch**, but voiced	*flu**g**a*
	4) between a vowel and a following *i* or *j*: as **y** in **y**es	*ei**g**i, se**g**ja*
	5) between *ó, á, ú*, and a following *a, u*: silent	*fljú**g**a*
	6) in sequences *-angt* and *-angs*: silent	*lan**g**t, lan**g**s*
j	as **y** in **y**es	***j**arl*
p	as **p** in **p**in	***p**enningr*
	preceding *s* or *t*: as ***f*** in a**f**ter	*e**p**tir*
r	trilled as Scots English **r**	***r**auðr*
s	as **s** in **s**it, not as English **z**	***s**itja*
v	as **v** in **v**est	***v**estr*
þ	as **th** in **th**ing	***þ**ing*
ð	as **th** in bro**th**er	*bró**ð**ir*
x	as **chs** in Scots English lo**chs**	*ø**x***
z	as **ts** in prin**ts**	*brau**z**k*
hv	most commonly pronounced as **kv**	***hv**ítr*

A few double consonants in Modern Icelandic have special pronunciations.

- *pp*, *tt*, and *kk* are pronounced with a preceding pause resembling a weakly pronounced *h*. For example, *upp*, *dóttir*, and *ekki* are pronounced [u^{h}pp], [dó^{h}ttir], and [e^{h}kki]. This is called **pre-aspiration**.
  pp is pronounced as *f* in *father* when it precedes *t*: *keppti* [kefti].
- *nn* sounds like [tn] when it follows a vowel with an accent mark or diphthong at the end of a word: *einn* [eitn].
- *ll* sounds like [tl] when preceding a vowel, *r*, or *n*: *kalla* [katla], *allr* [atlr]. It also has this pronunciation at the end of words: *mikill* [mikitl]. Before *t*, *d*, and *s*, double *ll* is pronounced like a single *l*: *alls* [als], *allt* [alt]. In loan words and nicknames *ll* is pronounced as long *l*: *mylla* 'mill' [milla] and *Kalli* [kalli].
- The sequences *rn* and *rl* usually are pronounced [rtn] and [rtl]: *Bjarni* [bjartni], or *karlar* [kartlar].

Sequences of three consonants are often simplified at the end of a syllable. For example, the *b* in *ku**mbl*** is silent and the word is pronounced [kuml], similar to the English pronunciation of 'twelfth' as [twelth] in quick speech. When the sequence occurs over a syllable break, all three consonants are pronounced, f.ex., *la**ndn**ám* (the syllable breaks between *land-* and *-nám*).

Appendix 2
Reference Grammar
of Old Norse – Old Icelandic

ARTICLE

	Masc	Fem	Neut
Sg *nom*	inn	in	it
acc	inn	ina	it
dat	inum	inni	inu
gen	ins	innar	ins
Pl *nom*	inir	inar	in
acc	ina	inar	in
dat	→	inum	←
gen	→	inna	←

NOUNS: Strong

	Masc			Endings
Sg *nom*	hest-**r**	stað-**r**	bekk-**r**	-r*
acc	hest	stað	bekk	–
dat	hest-**i**	stað-**i**	bekk	-i, –
gen	hest-**s**	stað-**ar**	bekk**j**-**ar**	-s, -ar
Pl *nom*	hest-**ar**	stað-**ir**	bekk-**ir**	-ar, -ir
acc	hest-**a**	stað-**i**	bekk-**i**	-a, -i
dat	hest-**um**	st**ǫ**ð-**um**	bekk**j**-**um**	-um
gen	hest-**a**	stað-**a**	bekk**j**-**a**	-a

	Fem						Endings
Sg *nom*	fǫr	jǫrð	Bjǫrg	á	heið-**r**	bók	(ǫ)–, -r
acc	fǫr	jǫrð	Bjǫrg-**u**	á	heið-**i**	bók	(ǫ)–, (-u), -i
dat	fǫr	jǫrð-**u**	Bjǫrg-**u**	á	heið-**i**	bók	(ǫ)–, -u, -i
gen	far-**ar**	jarð-**ar**	Bjarg-**ar**	á-**r**	heið-**ar**	bók-**ar**	-ar
Pl *nom*	far-**ar**	jarð-**ir**		á-**r**	heið-**ar**	bœk-**r**	-ar, -ir, -(i)r
acc	far-**ar**	jarð-**ir**		á-**r**	heið-**ar**	bœk-**r**	-ar, -ir, -(i)r
dat	fǫr-**um**	jǫrð-**um**		á-**m**	heið-**um**	bók-**um**	-um
gen	far-**a**	jarð-**a**		á	heið-**a**	bók-**a**	-a

	Neut			Endings
Sg *nom*	skip	barn	líki	–
acc	skip	barn	líki	–
dat	skip-**i**	barn-**i**	lík-**i**	-i
gen	skip-**s**	barn-**s**	líki-**s**	-s
Pl *nom*	skip	bǫrn	líki	(ǫ)–
acc	skip	bǫrn	líki	(ǫ)–
dat	skip-**um**	bǫrn-**um**	lík-**um**	-um
gen	skip-**a**	barn-**a**	lík-**a**	-a

Kinship Terms

			Endings
fað-**ir**	móð-**ir**	syst-**ir**	-ir
fǫð-**ur**	móð-**ur**	syst-**ur**	-ur
fǫð-**ur**	móð-**ur**	syst-**ur**	-ur
fǫð-**ur**	móð-**ur**	syst-**ur**	-ur
feð-**r**	mœð-**r**	syst-**r**	-(i)r
feð-**r**	mœð-**r**	syst-**r**	-(i)r
feð-**rum**	mœð-**rum**	syst-**rum**	-(i)rum
feð-**ra**	mœð-**ra**	syst-**ra**	-(i)ra

a~ǫ~e Alternation

	Masc			Fem
Sg *nom*	vǫll-**r**	ǫrn	skjǫld-**r**	hǫnd
acc	vǫll	ǫrn	skjǫld	hǫnd
dat	vell-**i**	ern-**i**	skild-**i**	hend-**i**
gen	vall-**ar**	arn-**ar**	skjald-**ar**	hand-**ar**
Pl *nom*	vell-**ir**	ern-**ir**	skild-**ir**	hend-**r**
acc	vǫll-**u**	ǫrn-**u**	skjǫld-**u**	hend-**r**
dat	vǫll-**um**	ǫrn-**um**	skjǫld-**um**	hǫnd-**um**
gen	vall-**a**	arn-**a**	skjald-**a**	hand-**a**

---

* With modifications, see Section 2.1.

Strong Nouns with Suffixed Article

	Masc		Fem			Neut
Sg *nom*	hestr-**inn**	staðr-**inn**	fǫr-**in**	jǫrð-**in**	á-**in**	skip-**it**
acc	hest-**inn**	stað-**inn**	fǫr-**ina**	jǫrð-**ina**	á-**na**	skip-**it**
dat	hesti-**num**	stað-**inum**	fǫr-**inni**	jǫrðu-**nni**	á-**nni**	skipi-**nu**
gen	hests-**ins**	staðar-**ins**	farar-**innar**	jarðar-**innar**	ár-**innar**	skips-**ins**
Pl *nom*	hestar-**nir**	staðir-**nir**	farar-**nar**	jarðir-**nar**	ár-**nar**	skip-**in**
acc	hesta-**na**	staði-**na**	farar-**nar**	jarðir-**nar**	ár-**nar**	skip-**in**
dat	hestu-**num**	stǫðu-**num**	fǫru-**num**	jǫrðu-**num**	á-**num**	skipu-**num**
gen	hesta-**nna**	staða-**nna**	fara-**nna**	jarða-**nna**	á-**nna**	skipa-**nna**

NOUNS: Weak

	Masc	Fem			Neut		Endings		
Sg *nom*	bog-**i**	tung-**a**	sag-**a**	ell-**i**	aug-**a**	hjart-**a**	-i	-a, -i	-a
acc	bog-**a**	tung-**u**	sǫg-**u**	ell-**i**	aug-**a**	hjart-**a**	-a	-u, -i	-a
dat	bog-**a**	tung-**u**	sǫg-**u**	ell-**i**	aug-**a**	hjart-**a**	-a	-u, -i	-a
gen	bog-**a**	tung-**u**	sǫg-**u**	ell-**i**	aug-**a**	hjart-**a**	-a	-u, -i	-a
Pl *nom*	bog-**ar**	tung-**ur**	sǫg-**ur**		aug-**u**	hjǫrt-**u**	-ar	-ur	-u
acc	bog-**a**	tung-**ur**	sǫg-**ur**		aug-**u**	hjǫrt-**u**	-a	-ur	-u
dat	bog-**um**	tung-**um**	sǫg-**um**		aug-**um**	hjǫrt-**um**	→	-um	←
gen	bog-**a**	tung-**na**	sag-**na**		aug-**na**	hjart-**na**	-a	-na	←

Weak Nouns with Suffixed Article

	Masc	Fem			Neut	
Sg *nom*	bogi-**nn**	tunga-**n**	saga-**n**	elli-**n**	auga-**t**	hjarta-**t**
acc	boga-**nn**	tungu-**na**	sǫgu-**na**	elli-**na**	auga-**t**	hjarta-**t**
dat	boga-**num**	tungu-**nni**	sǫgu-**nni**	elli-**nni**	auga-**nu**	hjarta-**nu**
gen	boga-**ns**	tungu-**nnar**	sǫgu-**nnar**	elli-**nnar**	auga-**ns**	hjarta-**ns**
Pl *nom*	bogar-**nir**	tungur-**nar**	sǫgur-**nar**		augu-**n**	hjǫrtu-**n**
acc	boga-**na**	tungur-**nar**	sǫgur-**nar**		augu-**n**	hjǫrtu-**n**
dat	bogu-**num**	tungu-**num**	sǫgu-**num**		augu-**num**	hjǫrtu-**num**
gen	boga-**nna**	tunga-**nna**	sagna-**nna**		augna-**nna**	hjartna-**nna**

ADJECTIVES: Strong

	Masc					Endings
Sg *nom*	stór-**r**	lang-**r**	vitr	heil-**l**	lítil-**l**	-r*
acc	stór-**an**	lang-**an**	vitr-**an**	heil-**an**	litl-**an**	-an
dat	stór-**um**	lǫng-**um**	vitr-**um**	heil-**um**	litl-**um**	-um
gen	stór-**s**	lang-**s**	vitr-**s**	heil-**s**	lítil-**s**	-s
Pl *nom*	stór-**ir**	lang-**ir**	vitr-**ir**	heil-**ir**	litl-**ir**	-ir
acc	stór-**a**	lang-**a**	vitr-**a**	heil-**a**	litl-**a**	-a
dat	stór-**um**	lǫng-**um**	vitr-**um**	heil-**um**	litl-**um**	-um
gen	stór-**ra**	lang-**ra**	vitr-**a**	heil-**la**	lítil-**la**	-ra*

* With modifications, see Section 2.1.

ADJECTIVES: Strong (cont.)

	Fem					Endings
Sg *nom*	stór	lǫng	vitr	heil	lítil	(ǫ)–
acc	stór-**a**	lang-**a**	vitr-**a**	heil-**a**	litl-**a**	-a
dat	stór-**ri**	lang-**ri**	vitr-**i**	heil-**li**	lítil-**li**	-ri*
gen	stór-**rar**	lang-**rar**	vitr-**ar**	heil-**lar**	lítil-**lar**	-rar*
Pl *nom*	stór-**ar**	lang-**ar**	vitr-**ar**	heil-**ar**	litl-**ar**	-ar
acc	stór-**ar**	lang-**ar**	vitr-**ar**	heil-**ar**	litl-**ar**	-ar
dat	stór-**um**	lǫng-**um**	vitr-**um**	heil-**um**	litl-**um**	-um
gen	stór-**ra**	lang-**ra**	vitr-**a**	heil-**la**	lítil-**la**	-a

	Neut					Endings
Sg *nom*	stór-**t**	lang-**t**	vitr-**t**	heil-**t**	líti-**t**	-t
acc	stór-**t**	lang-**t**	vitr-**t**	heil-**t**	líti-**t**	-t
dat	stór-**u**	lǫng-**u**	vitr-**u**	heil-**u**	litl-**u**	-u
gen	stór-**s**	lang-**s**	vitr-**s**	heil-**s**	lítil-**s**	-s
Pl *nom*	stór	lǫng	vitr	heil	lítil	(ǫ)–
acc	stór	lǫng	vitr	heil	lítil	(ǫ)–
dat	stór-**um**	lǫng-**um**	vitr-**um**	heil-**um**	litl-**um**	-um
gen	stór-**ra**	lang-**ra**	vitr-**a**	heil-**la**	lítil-**la**	-a

Possessive Adjectives

Singular	**minn**			**þinn**			**sinn**		
	Masc	**Fem**	**Neut**	**Masc**	**Fem**	**Neut**	**Masc**	**Fem**	**Neut**
Sg *nom*	minn	mín	mitt	þinn	þín	þitt	sinn	sín	sitt
acc	minn	mína	mitt	þinn	þína	þitt	sinn	sína	sitt
dat	mínum	minni	mínu	þínum	þinni	þínu	sínum	sinni	sínu
gen	míns	minnar	míns	þíns	þinnar	þíns	síns	sinnar	síns
Pl *nom*	mínir	mínar	mín	þínir	þínar	þín	sínir	sínar	sín
acc	mína	mínar	mín	þína	þínar	þín	sína	sínar	sín
dat	→	mínum	←	→	þínum	←	→	sínum	←
gen	→	minna	←	→	þinna	←	→	sinna	←

Dual	**okkarr**			**ykkarr**		
	Masc	**Fem**	**Neut**	**Masc**	**Fem**	**Neut**
Sg *nom*	okkarr	okkur	okkart	ykkarr	ykkur	ykkart
acc	okkarn	okkra	okkart	ykkarn	ykkra	ykkart
dat	okkrum	okkarri	okkru	ykkrum	ykkarri	ykkru
gen	okkars	okkarrar	okkars	ykkars	ykkarrar	ykkars
Pl *nom*	okkrir	okkrar	okkur	ykkrir	ykkrar	ykkur
acc	okkra	okkrar	okkur	ykkra	ykkrar	ykkur
dat	→	okkrum	←	→	ykkrum	←
gen	→	okkarra	←	→	ykkarra	←

* With modifications, see Section 2.1.

Plural		**várr**			**yð(v)arr**	
	Masc	**Fem**	**Neut**	**Masc**	**Fem**	**Neut**
***Sg** nom*	várr	vár	várt	yð(v)arr	yður	yð(v)art
acc	várn	vára	várt	yð(v)arn	yðra	yð(v)art
dat	várum	várri	váru	yðrum	yð(v)arri	yðru
gen	várs	várrar	várs	yð(v)ars	yð(v)arrar	yð(v)ars
***Pl** nom*	várir	várar	vár	yðrir	yðrar	yður
acc	vára	várar	vár	yðra	yðrar	yður
dat	→	várum	←	→	yðrum	←
gen	→	várra	←	→	yð(v)arra	←

ADJECTIVES: Weak

	Masc		**Fem**		**Neut**		Endings		
***Sg** nom*	stór-**i**	lang-**i**	stór-**a**	lang-**a**	stór-**a**	lang-**a**	-i	-a	-a
acc	stór-**a**	lang-**a**	stór-**u**	lǫng-**u**	stór-**a**	lang-**a**	-a	-u	-a
dat	stór-**a**	lang-**a**	stór-**u**	lǫng-**u**	stór-**a**	lang-**a**	-a	-u	-a
gen	stór-**a**	lang-**a**	stór-**u**	lǫng-**u**	stór-**a**	lang-**a**	-a	-u	-a
***Pl** nom*	stór-**u**	lǫng-**u**	stór-**u**	lǫng-**u**	stór-**u**	lǫng-**u**	→	-u	←
acc	stór-**u**	lǫng-**u**	stór-**u**	lǫng-**u**	stór-**u**	lǫng-**u**	→	-u	←
dat	stór-**um**	lǫng-**um**	stór-**um**	lǫng-**um**	stór-**um**	lǫng-**um**	→	-um	←
gen	stór-**u**	lǫng-**u**	stór-**u**	lǫng-**u**	stór-**u**	lǫng-**u**	→	-u	←

ADJECTIVES: Comparative

	Masc	**Fem**	**Neut**	**Masc**	**Fem**	**Neut**	Endings		
***Sg** nom*	arm-**ar-i**	arm-**ar-i**	arm-**ar-a**	yng-**r-i**	yng-**r-i**	yng-**r-a**	-i	-i	-a
acc	arm-**ar-a**	arm-**ar-i**	arm-**ar-a**	yng-**r-a**	yng-**r-i**	yng-**r-a**	-a	-i	-a
dat	arm-**ar-a**	arm-**ar-i**	arm-**ar-a**	yng-**r-a**	yng-**r-i**	yng-**r-a**	-a	-i	-a
gen	arm-**ar-a**	arm-**ar-i**	arm-**ar-a**	yng-**r-a**	yng-**r-i**	yng-**r-a**	-a	-i	-a
***Pl** nom*	→	arm-**ar-i**	←	→	yng-**r-i**	←	→	-i	←
acc	→	arm-**ar-i**	←	→	yng-**r-i**	←	→	-i	←
dat	→	ǫrm-**ur-um**	←	→	yng-**r-um**	←	→	-um	←
gen	→	arm-**ar-i**	←	→	yng-**r-i**	←	→	-i	←

ADJECTIVES: Superlative

Strong (Regular strong endings)

	Masc	**Fem**	**Neut**	**Masc**	**Fem**	**Neut**
***Sg** nom*	arm-**ast-r**	ǫrm-**ust**	arm-**ast**	yng-**st-r**	yng-**st**	yng-**st**
acc	arm-**ast-an**	arm-**ast-a**	arm-**ast**	yng-**st-an**	yng-**st-a**	yng-**st**
dat	ǫrm-**ust-um**	arm-**ast-ri**	ǫrm-**ust-u**	yng-**st-um**	yng-**st-ri**	yng-**st-u**
gen	arm-**ast-s**	arm-**ast-rar**	arm-**ast-s**	yng-**st-s**	yng-**st-rar**	yng-**st-s**
***Pl** nom*	arm-**ast-ir**	arm-**ast-ar**	ǫrm-**ust**	yng-**st-ir**	yng-**r-i**	yng-**st**
acc	arm-**ast-a**	arm-**ast-ar**	ǫrm-**ust**	yng-**st-a**	yng-**r-i**	yng-**st**
dat	→	ǫrm-**ust-um**	←	→	yng-**st-um**	←
gen	→	arm-**ast-ra**	←	→	yng-**st-ra**	←

ADJECTIVES: Superlative (cont.)

Weak (Regular weak endings)

	Masc	Fem	Neut	Masc	Fem	Neut
Sg *nom*	arm-**ast-i**	arm-**ast-a**	arm-**ast-a**	yng-**st-i**	yng-**st-a**	yng-**st-a**
acc	arm-**ast-a**	ǫrm-**ust-u**	arm-**ast-a**	yng-**st-a**	yng-**st-u**	yng-**st-a**
dat	arm-**ast-a**	ǫrm-**ust-u**	arm-**ast-a**	yng-**st-a**	yng-**st-u**	yng-**st-a**
gen	arm-**ast-a**	ǫrm-**ust-u**	arm-**ast-a**	yng-**st-a**	yng-**st-u**	yng-**st-a**
Pl *nom*	→	ǫrm-**ust-u**	←	→	yng-**st-u**	←
acc	→	ǫrm-**ust-u**	←	→	yng-**st-u**	←
dat	→	ǫrm-**ust-um**	←	→	yng-**st-um**	←
gen	→	ǫrm-**ust-u**	←	→	yng-**st-u**	←

PRONOUNS: Personal

	1st	2nd	3rd Masc	Fem	Neut	Refl
Sg *nom*	ek	þú	han-**n**	hon	þat	
acc	mik	þik	han-**n**	han-**a**	þat	sik
dat	mér	þér	hon-**um**	hen-**ni**	því	sér
gen	mín	þín	han-**s**	hen-**nar**	þess	sín
Du *nom*	vit	(þ)it				
acc	okkr	ykkr				sik
dat	okkr	ykkr				sér
gen	okkar	ykkar				sín
Pl *nom*	vér	(þ)ér	þei-**r**	þæ-**r**	þau	
acc	oss	yðr	þá	þæ-**r**	þau	sik
dat	oss	yðr	→	þei-**m**	←	sér
gen	vár	yð(v)ar	→	þei(r)-**ra**	←	sín

PRONOUNS: Demonstrative

	Masc	Fem	Neut	Masc	Fem	Neut
Sg *nom*	sá	sú	þat	þessi/sjá	þessi/sjá	þetta
acc	þan-**n**	þá	þat	þenna	þessa	þetta
dat	þei-**m**	þei(r)-**ri**	því	þess-**um**	þessa-**ri**	þessu
gen	þess	þei(r)-**rar**	þess	þessa	þessa-**rar**	þessa
Pl *nom*	þei-**r**	þæ-**r**	þau	þess-**ir**	þess-**ar**	þessi
acc	þá	þæ-**r**	þau	þess-**a**	þess-**ar**	þessi
dat	→	þei-**m**	←	→	þess-**um**	←
gen	→	þei(r)-**ra**	←	→	þessa-**ra**	←

PRONOUNS: Interrogative, Indefinite, etc.

Interrogative

	Masc	Fem	Neut	Masc	Fem	Neut
				(Regular strong adj. endings)		
Sg *nom*	hver-**r**	hver	hver-**t**/hvat	hvár-**r**	hvár	hvár-**t**
acc	hver-**n**	hver**j**-**a**	hver-**t**/hvat	hvár-**n**	hvár-**a**	hvár-**t**
dat	hver**j**-**um**	hver-**ri**	hver**j**-**u**	hvár-**um**	hvár-**ri**	hvár-**u**
gen	hver-**s**	hver-**rar**	hver-**s**	hvár-**s**	hvár-**rar**	hvár-**s**
Pl *nom*	hver-**ir**	hver**j**-**ar**	hver	hvár-**ir**	hvár-**ar**	hvár
acc	hver**j**-**a**	hver**j**-**ar**	hver	hvár-**a**	hvár-**ar**	hvár
dat	→	hver**j**-**um**	←	→	hvár-**um**	←
gen	→	hver-**ra**	←	→	hvár-**ra**	←

Indefinite

	Masc	Fem	Neut	Masc	Fem	Neut
				(Regular strong adj. endings)		
Sg *nom*	nǫkkur-**r**	nǫkkur	nǫkku-**t**	ein-**n**	ein	ei-**tt**
acc	nǫkkur-**n**	nǫkkur-**a**	nǫkku-**t**	ein-**n**	ein-**a**	ei-**tt**
dat	nǫkkur-**um**	nǫkkur-**ri**	nǫkkur-**u**	ein-**um**	ein-**ni**	ein-**u**
gen	nǫkkur-**s**	nǫkkur-**rar**	nǫkkur-**s**	ein-**s**	ein-**nar**	ein-**s**
Pl *nom*	nǫkkur-**ir**	nǫkkur-**ar**	nǫkkur	ein-**ir**	ein-**ar**	ein
acc	nǫkkur-**a**	nǫkkur-**ar**	nǫkkur	ein-**a**	ein-**ar**	ein
dat	→	nǫkkur-**um**	←	→	ein-**um**	←
gen	→	nǫkkur-**ra**	←	→	ein-**na**	←

	Masc	Fem	Neut
Pl *nom*	báð-**ir**	báð-**ar**	bæð-**i**
acc	báð-**a**	báð-**ar**	bæð-**i**
dat	→	báð-**um**	←
gen	→	be-**ggja**	←

Negative

	Masc	Fem	Neut
Sg *nom*	engi	engi	ekki
acc	eng-**an**	eng-**a**	ekki
dat	eng-**um**	eng-**ri**	eng-**u**
gen	engi-**s**/enski-**s**	eng-**ra**	engi-**s**/enski-**s**
Pl *nom*	eng-**ir**	eng-**ar**	engi
acc	eng-**ir**	eng-**ar**	engi
dat	→	eng-**um**	←
gen	→	eng-**um**	←

NUMERALS

(For *einn* 'one', see Indefinite Pronouns)

	Masc	Fem	Neut	Masc	Fem	Neut	Masc	Fem	Neut
nom	tvei-**r**	tvæ-**r**	tvau	þrí-**r**	þrj-**ár**	þrj-**ú**	fjór-**ir**	fjór-**ar**	fjǫg-**ur**
acc	tvá	tvæ-**r**	tvau	þrj-**á**	þrj-**ár**	þrj-**ú**	fjór-**a**	fjór-**ar**	fjǫg-**ur**
dat	→	tvei-**m**(**r**)	←	→	þri-**m**(**r**)	←	→	fjór-**um**	←
gen	→	tve-**ggja**	←	→	þri-**ggja**	←	→	fjǫgur-**ra**	←

VERBS: Weak

Indicative

Pres	lofa	tala	lifa	flytja	kveðja	Endings
1sg	lof-**a**	tal-**a**	lif-**i**	flyt	kveð	(-a/i)–
2sg	lof-**a-r**	tal-**a-r**	lif-**i-r**	flyt-**r**	kveð-**r**	(-a/i)-r*
3sg	lof-**a-r**	tal-**a-r**	lif-**i-r**	flyt-**r**	kveð-**r**	(-a/i)-r*
1pl	lof-**um**	tǫl-**um**	lif-**um**	flyt**j-um**	kveð**j-um**	-um
2pl	lof-**ið**	tal-**ið**	lif-**ið**	flyt-**ið**	kveð-**ið**	-ið
3pl	lof-**a**	tal-**a**	lif-**a**	flyt**j-a**	kveð**j-a**	-a
Past	(-að-)	(-að-)	(-ð-)	(flutt-)	(kvadd-)	
1sg	lof-**að-a**	tal-**að-a**	lif-**ð-a**	fl**ut-t-a**	kv**ad-d-a**	-að/ð†-a
2sg	lof-**að-ir**	tal-**að-ir**	lif-**ð-ir**	fl**ut-t-ir**	kv**ad-d-ir**	-að/ð†-ir
3sg	lof-**að-i**	tal-**að-i**	lif-**ð-i**	fl**ut-t-i**	kv**ad-d-i**	-að/ð†-i
1pl	lof-**uð-um**	tǫl-**uð-um**	lif-**ð-um**	fl**ut-t-um**	kv**ǫd-d-um**	-að/ð†-um
2pl	lof-**uð-uð**	tǫl-**uð-uð**	lif-**ð-uð**	fl**ut-t-uð**	kv**ǫd-d-uð**	-að/ð†-uð
3pl	lof-**uð-u**	tǫl-**uð-u**	lif-**ð-u**	fl**ut-t-u**	kv**ǫd-d-u**	-að/ð†-u

Subjunctive

Pres						
1sg	lof-**a**	tal-**a**	lif-**a**	flyt**j-a**	kveð**j-a**	-a
2sg	lof-**ir**	tal-**ir**	lif-**ir**	flyt-**ir**	kveð-**ir**	-ir
3sg	lof-**i**	tal-**i**	lif-**i**	flyt-**i**	kveð-**i**	-i
1pl	lof-**im**	tal-**im**	lif-**im**	flyt-**im**	kveð-**im**	-im
2pl	lof-**ið**	tal-**ið**	lif-**ið**	flyt-**ið**	kveð-**ið**	-ið
3pl	lof-**i**	tal-**i**	lif-**i**	flyt-**i**	kveð-**i**	-i
Past	(-að-)	(-að-)	(-ð-)	(flutt-)	(kvadd-)	
1sg	lof-**að-a**	tal-**að-a**	lif-**ð-a**	fl**yt-t-a**	kv**ed-d-a**	-að/(i)ð†-a
2sg	lof-**að-ir**	tal-**að-ir**	lif-**ð-ir**	fl**yt-t-ir**	kv**ed-d-ir**	-að/(i)ð†-ir
3sg	lof-**að-i**	tal-**að-i**	lif-**ð-i**	fl**yt-t-i**	kv**ed-d-i**	-að/(i)ð†-i
1pl	lof-**að-im**	tal-**að-im**	lif-**ð-im**	fl**yt-t-im**	kv**ed-d-im**	-að/(i)ð†-im
2pl	lof-**að-ið**	tal-**að-ið**	lif-**ð-ið**	fl**yt-t-ið**	kv**ed-d-ið**	-að/(i)ð†-ið
3pl	lof-**að-i**	tal-**að-i**	lif-**ð-i**	fl**yt-t-i**	kv**ed-d-i**	-að/(i)ð†-i

Imperative

	lof-a	tal-a	lif	flyt	kveð	-a/–

Participles

Pres	lof-**andi**	tal-**andi**	lif-**andi**	flyt**j-andi**	kveð**j-andi**	(See below)
Past	(-að-)	(-að-)	(-ð-)	(flutt-)	(kvadd-)	
m	lof-**að-r**	tal-**að-r**	lif-**ð-r**	fl**ut-t-r**	kv**ad-d-r**	-að/ð†-
f	lof-**uð**	tǫl-**uð**	lif-**ð**	fl**ut-t**	kv**ǫd-d**	(+ Adj.
n	lof-**a-t**	tal-**a-t**	lif-**t**	fl**ut-t**	kv**at-t**	Endings)

---

* With modifications, see Section 7.7.

† With modifications, see Section 5.4.

VERBS: Weak (cont.)

Indicative			
Pres	**duga**	**vaka**	Endings
1sg	dug-**i**	vak-**i**	-i
2sg	dug-**i-r**	vak-**i-r**	-i-r
3sg	dug-**i-r**	vak-**i-r**	-i-r
1pl	dug-**um**	vǫk-**um**	-um
2pl	dug-**ið**	vak-**ið**	-ið
3pl	dug-**a**	vak-**a**	-a
Past	(-ð-)	(-t-)	
1sg	dug-**ð-a**	vak-**t-a**	-ð*-a
2sg	dug-**ð-ir**	vak-**t-ir**	-ð*-ir
3sg	dug-**ð-i**	vak-**t-i**	-ð*-i
1pl	dug-**ð-um**	vǫk-**t-um**	-ð*-um
2pl	dug-**ð-uð**	vǫk-**t-uð**	-ð*-uð
3pl	dug-**ð-u**	vǫk-**t-u**	-ð*-u
Subjunctive			
Pres			
1sg	dug-**a**	vak-**a**	-a
2sg	dug-**ir**	vak-**ir**	-ir
3sg	dug-**i**	vak-**i**	-i
1pl	dug-**im**	vak-**im**	-im
2pl	dug-**ið**	vak-**ið**	-ið
3pl	dug-**i**	vak-**i**	-i
Past	(-ð-)	(-t-)	
1sg	dyg-**ð-a**	vek-**t-a**	(i)-ð*-a
2sg	dyg-**ð-ir**	vek-**t-ir**	(i)-ð*-ir
3sg	dyg-**ð-i**	vek-**t-i**	(i)-ð*-i
1pl	dyg-**ð-im**	vek-**t-im**	(i)-ð*-im
2pl	dyg-**ð-ið**	vek-**t-ið**	(i)-ð*-ið
3pl	dyg-**ð-i**	vek-**t-i**	(i)-ð*-i
Imperative			
	dug(-**i**)	vak(-**i**)	(-i)
Participles			
Pres	dug-**andi**	vak-**andi**	(See below)
Past			
m	[þol-**ð-r**]	vak-**t-r**	(-a)ð*-
f	[þol-**ð**]	vǫk-**t**	(+ Adj.
n	dug-**a-t**	vak-**a-t**	Endings)

VERBS: Strong

Indicative		
Pres	**renna**	**rísa**
1sg	renn	rís
2sg	renn-**r**	rís-**s**
3sg	renn-**r**	rís-**s**
1pl	renn-**um**	rís-**um**
2pl	renn-**ið**	rís-**ið**
3pl	renn-**a**	rís-**a**
Past	(rann, runnu)	(reis, risu)
1sg	rann	reis
2sg	rann-**t**	reis-**t**
3sg	rann	reis
1pl	runn-**um**	ris-**um**
2pl	runn-**uð**	ris-**uð**
3pl	runn-**u**	ris-**u**
Subjunctive		
Pres		
1sg	renn-**a**	rís-**a**
2sg	renn-**ir**	rís-**ir**
3sg	renn-**i**	rís-**i**
1pl	renn-**im**	rís-**im**
2pl	renn-**ið**	rís-**ið**
3pl	renn-**i**	rís-**i**
Past	(runnu)	(risu)
1sg	rynn-**a**	ris-**a**
2sg	rynn-**ir**	ris-**ir**
3sg	rynn-**i**	ris-**i**
1pl	rynn-**i**	ris-**im**
2pl	rynn-**ið**	ris-**ið**
3pl	rynn-**i**	ris-**i**
Imperative		
	renn	rís
Participles		
Pres	renn-**andi**	rís-**andi**
Past	(runnit)	(risit)
m	runn-**inn**	ris-**inn**
f	runn-**in**	ris-**in**
n	runn-**it**	ris-**it**

* With modifications, see Section 5.4.

bjóða	fara	gefa	bera	láta	hlaupa	Endings
býð	fer	gef	ber	læt	hleyp	–
býð-r	fer-r	gef-r	ber-r	læt-r	hleyp-r	-r*
býð-r	fer-r	gef-r	ber-r	læt-r	hleyp-r	-r*
bjóð-um	fǫr-um	gef-um	ber-um	lát-um	hlaup-um	-um
bjóð-ið	far-ið	gef-ið	ber-ið	lát-ið	hlaup-ið	-ið
bjóð-a	far-a	gef-a	ber-a	lát-a	hlaup-a	-a
(bauð, buðu)	(fór, fóru)	(gaf, gáfu)	(bar, báru)	(lét, létu)	(hljóp, hljópu)	
bauð	fór	gaf	bar	lét	hljóp	–
baut-t	fór-t	gaf-t	bar-t	léz-t	hljóp-t	-t
bauð	fór	gaf	bar	lét	hljóp	–
buð-um	fór-um	gáf-um	bár-um	lét-um	hljóp-um	-um
buð-uð	fór-uð	gáf-uð	bár-uð	lét-uð	hljóp-uð	-uð
buð-u	fór-u	gáf-u	bár-u	lét-u	hljóp-u	-u
bjóð-a	far-a	gef-a	ber-a	lát-a	hlaup-a	-a
bjóð-ir	far-ir	gef-ir	ber-ir	lát-ir	hlaup-ir	-ir
bjóð-i	far-i	gef-i	ber-i	lát-i	hlaup-i	-i
bjóð-im	far-im	gef-im	ber-im	lát-im	hlaup-im	-im
bjóð-ið	far-ið	gef-ið	ber-ið	lát-ið	hlaup-ið	-ið
bjóð-i	far-i	gef-i	ber-i	lát-i	hlaup-i	-i
(buðu)	(fóru)	(gáfu)	(báru)	(létu)	(hljópu)	
byð-a	fœr-a	gæf-a	bær-a	lét-a	hlyp-a	(i)-a
byð-ir	fœr-ir	gæf-ir	bær-ir	lét-ir	hlyp-ir	(i)-ir
byð-i	fœr-i	gæf-i	bær-i	lét-i	hlyp-i	(i)-i
byð-im	fœr-im	gæf-im	bær-im	lét-im	hlyp-im	(i)-im
byð-ið	fœr-ið	gæf-ið	bær-ið	lét-ið	hlyp-ið	(i)-ið
byð-i	fœr-i	gæf-i	bær-i	lét-i	hlyp-i	(i)-i
bjóð	far	gef	ber	lát	hlaup	–
bjóð-andi	far-andi	gef-andi	ber-andi	lát-andi	hlaup-andi	(See below)
(boðit)	(farit)	(gefit)	(borit)	(látit)	(hlaupit)	
boð-inn	far-inn	gef-inn	bor-inn	lát-inn	hlaup-inn	(Like Article)
boð-in	far-in	gef-in	bor-in	lát-in	hlaup-in	
boð-it	far-it	gef-it	bor-it	lát-it	hlaup-it	

* With modifications, see Section 7.7.

VERBS: Preterite-Present

Indicative

Pres	**mega**	**munu**	**skulu**	**eiga**	**kná**
1sg	má	mun	skal	**á**	kná
2sg	má-**tt**	mun-**t**	skal-**t**	**á-tt**	kná-**tt**
3sg	má	mun	skal	**á**	kná
1pl	meg-**um**	mun-**um**	skul-**um**	eig-**um**	kneg-**um**
2pl	meg-**uð**	mun-**uð**	skul-**uð**	eig-**uð**	kneg-**uð**
3pl	meg-**u**	mun-**u**	skul-**u**	eig-**u**	kneg-**u**
Past	(mátt-)	(mund-)	(skyld-)	(átt-)	(knátt-)
1sg	má-**tt-a**	mun-**d-a**	skyl-**d-a**	á-**tt-a**	kná-**tt-a**
2sg	má-**tt-ir**	mun-**d-ir**	skyl-**d-ir**	á-**tt-ir**	kná-**tt-ir**
3sg	má-**tt-i**	mun-**d-i**	skyl-**d-i**	á-**tt-i**	kná-**tt-i**
1pl	má-**tt-um**	mun-**d-um**	skyl-**d-um**	á-**tt-um**	kná-**tt-um**
2pl	má-**tt-uð**	mun-**d-uð**	skyl-**d-uð**	á-**tt-uð**	kná-**tt-uð**
3pl	má-**tt-u**	mun-**d-u**	skyl-**d-u**	á-**tt-u**	kná-**tt-u**

Subjunctive

Pres	**mega**	**munu**	**skulu**	**eiga**	**kná**
1sg	meg-**a**	mun-**a**/myn-**a**	skyl-**a**	eig-**a**	kneg-**a**
2sg	meg-**ir**	mun-**ir**/myn-**ir**	skyl-**ir**	eig-**ir**	kneg-**ir**
3sg	meg-**i**	mun-**i**/myn-**i**	skyl-**i**	eig-**i**	kneg-**i**
1pl	meg-**im**	mun-**im**/myn-**im**	skyl-**im**	eig-**im**	kneg-**im**
2pl	meg-**ið**	mun-**ið**/myn-**ið**	skyl-**ið**	eig-**ið**	kneg-**ið**
3pl	meg-**i**	mun-**i**/myn-**i**	skyl-**i**	eig-**i**	kneg-**i**
Past	(mátt-)	(mund-)	(skyld-)	(átt-)	(knátt-)
1sg	mæ-**tt-a**	myn-**d-a**	skyl-**d-a**	**æ-tt-a**	knæ-**tt-a**
2sg	mæ-**tt-ir**	myn-**d-ir**	skyl-**d-ir**	**æ-tt-ir**	knæ-**tt-ir**
3sg	mæ-**tt-i**	myn-**d-i**	skyl-**d-i**	**æ-tt-i**	knæ-**tt-i**
1pl	mæ-**tt-im**	myn-**d-im**	skyl-**d-im**	**æ-tt-im**	knæ-**tt-im**
2pl	mæ-**tt-ið**	myn-**d-ið**	skyl-**d-ið**	**æ-tt-ið**	knæ-**tt-ið**
3pl	mæ-**tt-i**	myn-**d-i**	skyl-**d-i**	**æ-tt-i**	knæ-**tt-i**

Imperative

	mega	**munu**	**skulu**	**eiga**	**kná**
				eig	

Participles

	mega	**munu**	**skulu**	**eiga**	**kná**
Pres	meg-**andi**			eig-**andi**	
Past	má-**tt**			á-**tt**	

Pret. Infinitive

	mega	**munu**	**skulu**	**eiga**	**kná**
		mun-**d**-u	skyl-**d**-u		kná-**tt-u**

kunna	**muna**	**unna**	**vita**	**þurfa**	Endings
k**a**nn	m**a**n	**a**nn	v**ei**t	þ**a**rf	–
k**a**nn-**t**	m**a**n-**t**	**a**nn-**t**	v**eiz**-**t**	þ**a**rf-**t**	-t
k**a**nn	m**a**n	**a**nn	v**ei**t	þ**a**rf	–
kunn-**um**	mun-**um**	unn-**um**	vit-**um**	þurf **um**	-um
kunn-**uð**	mun-**ið**	unn-**uð**	vit-**uð**	þurf-**uð**	-uð
kunn-**u**	mun-**a**	unn-**u**	vit-**u**	þurf-**u**	-u
(kunn-)	(mund-)	(unn-)	(viss-)	(þurft-)	
kunn-**a**	mun-**d**-**a**	unn-**a**	vi**s**-**s**-**a**	þurf-**t**-**a**	-ð*-a
kunn-**ir**	mun-**d**-**ir**	unn-**ir**	vi**s**-**s**-**ir**	þurf-**t**-**ir**	-ð*-ir
kunn-**i**	mun-**d**-**i**	unn-**i**	vi**s**-**s**-**i**	þurf-**t**-**i**	-ð*-i
kunn-**um**	mun-**d**-**um**	unn-**um**	vi**s**-**s**-**um**	þurf-**t**-**um**	-ð*-um
kunn-**uð**	mun-**d**-**ið**	unn-**uð**	vi**s**-**s**-**uð**	þurf-**t**-**uð**	-ð*-uð
kunn-**u**	mun-**d**-**a**	unn-**u**	vi**s**-**s**-**u**	þurf-**t**-**u**	-ð*-u
kunn-**a**	mun-**a**	unn-**a**	vit-**a**	þurf-**a**	-a
kunn-**ir**	mun-**ir**	unn-**ir**	vit-**ir**	þurf-**ir**	-ir
kunn-**i**	mun-**i**	unn-**i**	vit-**i**	þurf-**i**	-i
kunn-**im**	mun-**im**	unn-**im**	vit-**im**	þurf-**im**	-im
kunn-**ið**	mun-**ið**	unn-**ið**	vit-**ið**	þurf-**ið**	-ið
kunn-**i**	mun-**i**	unn-**i**	vit-**i**	þurf-**i**	-i
(kunn-)	(mund-)	(unn-)	(viss-)	(þurft-)	
k**y**nn-**a**	m**y**n-**d**-**a**	**y**nn-**a**	vi**s**-**s**-**a**	þ**y**rf-**t**-**a**	(i)-ð*-a
k**y**nn-**ir**	m**y**n-**d**-**ir**	**y**nn-**ir**	vi**s**-**s**-**ir**	þ**y**rf-**t**-**ir**	(i)-ð*-ir
k**y**nn-**i**	m**y**n-**d**-**i**	**y**nn-**i**	vi**s**-**s**-**i**	þ**y**rf-**t**-**i**	(i)-ð*-i
k**y**nn-**im**	m**y**n-**d**-**im**	**y**nn-**im**	vi**s**-**s**-**im**	þ**y**rf-**t**-**im**	(i)-ð*-im
k**y**nn-**ið**	m**y**n-**d**-**ið**	**y**nn-**ið**	vi**s**-**s**-**ið**	þ**y**rf-**t**-**ið**	(i)-ð*-ið
k**y**nn-**i**	m**y**n-**d**-**i**	**y**nn-**i**	vi**s**-**s**-**i**	þ**y**rf-**t**-**i**	(i)-ð*-i
kunn	mun	unn	vit		–
kunn-**andi**	mun-**andi**	unn-**andi**	vit-**andi**	þurf-**andi**	(See below)
kunn-**a**-**t**	mun-**a**-**t**	unn(-**a**)-**t**	vit-**a**-**t**	þurf-**t**	(-a)-t
					-ð*-u

* With modifications, see Sections 5.4, 15.3.

VERBS: Reflexive

Indicative

	Weak			Strong	Endings
Pres	**kallask**	**sýnask**	**gleðjask**	**farask**	wk | str
1sg	kǫll-**umk**	sýn-**umk**	gleð**j-umk**	fer-**umk**	-umk
2sg	kall-**a-sk**	sýn-**i-sk**	gle-**zk**	fer-**sk**	-sk*
3sg	kall-**a-sk**	sýn-**i-sk**	gle-**zk**	fer-**sk**	-sk*
1pl	kǫll-**um(s)k**	sýn-**um(s)k**	gleð**j-um(s)k**	fǫr-**um(s)k**	-um(s)k
2pl	kall-**izk**	sýn-**izk**	gleð-**izk**	far-**izk**	-izk
3pl	kall-**ask**	sýn-**ask**	gleð**j-ask**	far-**ask**	-ask
Past	(-að-)	(-d-)	(gladd-)		
1sg	kǫll-**uð-umk**	sýn-**d-umk**	gl**ǫd-d-umk**	fór-**umk**	-umk
2sg	kall-**að-isk**	sýn-**d-isk**	gl**ad-d-isk**	fór-**zk**	-isk | -zk
3sg	kall-**að-isk**	sýn-**d-isk**	gl**ad-d-isk**	fór-**sk**	-isk | -sk*
1pl	kǫll-**uð-um(s)k**	sýn-**d-um(s)k**	gl**ǫd-d-um(s)k**	fór-**um(s)k**	-um(s)k
2pl	kǫll-**uð-uzk**	sýn-**d-uzk**	gl**ǫd-d-uzk**	fór-**uzk**	-uzk
3pl	kǫll-**uð-usk**	sýn-**d-usk**	gl**ǫd-d-usk**	fór-**usk**	-usk

Subjunctive

Pres					
1sg	kǫll-**umk**	sýn-**umk**	gleð**j-umk**	fǫr-**umk**	-umk
2sg	kall-**isk**	sýn-**isk**	gleð-**isk**	far-**isk**	-isk
3sg	kall-**isk**	sýn-**isk**	gleð-**isk**	far-**isk**	-isk
1pl	kall-**im(s)k**	sýn-**im(s)k**	gleð-**im(s)k**	far-**im(s)k**	-im(s)k
2pl	kall-**izk**	sýn-**izk**	gleð-**izk**	far-**izk**	-izk
3pl	kall-**isk**	sýn-**isk**	gleð-**isk**	far-**isk**	-isk
Past	(-að-)	(-d-)	(gladd-)		
1sg	kǫll-**uð-umk**	sýn-**d-umk**	gl**ed-d-umk**	fœr-**umk**	(i)-umk
2sg	kall-**að-isk**	sýn-**d-isk**	gl**ed-d-isk**	fœr-**isk**	(i)-isk
3sg	kall-**að-isk**	sýn-**d-isk**	gl**ed-d-isk**	fœr-**isk**	(i)-isk
1pl	kall-**að-im(s)k**	sýn-**d-im(s)k**	gl**ed-d-im(s)k**	fœr-**im(s)k**	(i)-im(s)k
2pl	kall-**að-izk**	sýn-**d-izk**	gl**ed-d-izk**	fœr-**izk**	(i)-izk
3pl	kall-**að-isk**	sýn-**d-isk**	gl**ed-d-isk**	fœr-**isk**	(i)-isk

Imperative

	kall-**a-sk**	sýn-**sk**	gle-**zk**	far-**sk**	-sk*

Participles

Pres	kall-**andi-sk**	sýn-**andi-sk**	gleð**j-andi-sk**	far-**andi-sk**	-sk
	(-að-)	(-d-)	(gladd-)		
Past	kall-**a-zk**	sýn-**zk**	gl**a-zk**	far-**izk**	-zk | -izk

* Dental consonant + *-sk* = *-zk*, see Section 10.4.

VERBS: Irregular

vera **'be'**

	Indicative	Subjunctive
Pres		
1sg	em	sé
2sg	er-**t**	sé-**r**
3sg	er	sé
1pl	er-**um**	sé-**m**
2pl	er-**uð**	sé-**ð**
3pl	er-**u**	sé
Past		
1sg	var	vær-**a**
2sg	var-**t**	vær-**ir**
3sg	var	vær-**i**
1pl	vár-**um**	vær-**im**
2pl	vár-**uð**	vær-**ið**
3pl	vár-**u**	vær **i**

Imperative

Sg	ver
Pl	ver-**ið**

Participles

Past	ver-**it**

hafa **'have'**

	Indicative	Subjunctive
Pres		
1sg	h**e**f-(**i**)	haf-**a**
2sg	h**e**f-(**i**)**r**	haf-**ir**
3sg	h**e**f-(**i**)**r**	haf-**i**
1pl	h**ǫ**f-**um**	haf-**im**
2pl	haf-**ið**	haf-**ið**
3pl	haf-**a**	haf-**i**
Past		
1sg	haf-**ð-a**	h**e**f-**ð-a**
2sg	haf-**ð-ir**	h**e**f-**ð-ir**
3sg	haf-**ð-i**	h**e**f-**ð-i**
1pl	h**ǫ**f-**ð-um**	h**e**f-**ð-im**
2pl	h**ǫ**f-**ð-uð**	h**e**f-**ð-ið**
3pl	h**ǫ**f-**ð-u**	h**e**f-**ð-i**

Imperative

	haf

Participles

Pres	haf-**andi**
Past	
m	haf-**ð-r**
f	h**ǫ**f-**ð**
n	haf-**t**

VERBS: Present Participle Declension

	Masc	Fem	Neut	Endings (Like Comp. Adj.)		
Sg *nom*	verð-**and-i**	verð-**and-i**	verð-**and-a**	-i	-i	-a
acc	verð-**and-a**	verð-**and-i**	verð-**and-a**	-a	-i	-a
dat	verð-**and-a**	verð-**and-i**	verð-**and-a**	-a	-i	-a
gen	verð-**and-a**	verð-**and-i**	verð-**and-a**	-a	-i	-a
Pl *nom*	→	verð-**and-i**	←	→	-i	←
acc	→	verð-**and-i**	←	→	-i	←
dat	→	verð-**ǫnd-um**	←	→	-um	←
gen	→	verð-**and-i**	←	→	-i	←

Appendix 3
Vocabulary of Words and Phrases

This vocabulary is a complete listing of words and significant phrases in the lessons, exercises, and readings. Words are alphabetized employing the following conventions.

- *ð* is listed with *d*.
- *þ, æ, œ, ǫ, ø* come at the end of the alphabet in that order.
- Short vowels and long vowels are treated as separate letters. Words beginning with a short (unaccented) vowel are alphabetized ahead of words beginning with a long (accented) vowel. The same rule applies to short and long vowels within a word. For example, *austr* comes before *á*, and *farmaðr* comes before *fá*.

a, á, b, d, ð, e, é, f, g, h, i, í, j, k, l, m, n, o, ó,
p, r, s, t, u, ú, v, x, y, ý, z, þ, æ, œ, ǫ(ö), ø

Principal parts of verbs are listed as follows:

- Weak verbs:
  infinitive (dental suffix or past-tense stem)
- Strong verbs:
  infinitive (3sg. pres.; 3sg. past, 3pl. past; neut. ppart.)
- Preterite-present verbs:
  infinitive (3sg. pres, 3pl. pres.; 3sg past; neut. ppart. or pret. inf.)

Where phrases and idioms are listed, the Icelandic convention of using the pronouns **einnhverr** 'somebody' [sb] and **eitthvat** 'something' [sth] has been adopted to indicate which case the object of a verb or preposition takes, and to distinguish whether the object is a person or thing.

[e-n] (**einhvern**) =somebody [sb] *acc*
[e-t] (**eitthvat**) =something [sth] *acc*
[e-m] (**einhverjum**) =(for) [sb] *dat*
[e-u] (**einhverju**) =(for) [sth] *dat*
[e-s] (**einhvers**) =(of) [sb] or [sth] *gen*

Examples:

fala [e-t] af [e-m] offer to buy [sth] from [sb]
firra [e-n] [e-u] deprive [sb] of [sth]
mæla [e-t] við [e-n] say [sth] to [sb]
segja [e-m] frá [e-m] tell, inform [sb] about [sb]
segja [e-m] til [e-s] tell, inform [sb] where [sth/sb] is to be found

A

Aðalból *n* Adalbol (*place name*)
Aðalsteinn *m* Athelstane (*personal name*)
Aðils *m* Adils (*personal name*)
aðrar *adj, see* **annarr**
af *prep* [*w dat*] off, out of, from; of; with; in regard to, concerning; on account of, by reason of; **skjóta af** shoot with
af *adv* off, away; **verða af** come about, appear
afarkostir *m pl* hard terms
afl *n* strength; **sterkr at afli** strong
aka (ekr; ók, óku; ekit) *vb* drive
aldar, **aldir** *f, see* **ǫld**
aldr *m* age, life; **á ungum aldri** young, of a young age
aldri *adv* never
Alfǫðr *m* 'All-Father', a name of Odin
allmikill *adj* very great
allr (*f* ǫll, *n* allt) *adj/pron* all, entire, whole; **um alla hluti** in all respects; **alls konar** of every kind, of all kinds; **allra helzt** especially; **at ǫllu** in all respects
allvaldr *m* sovereign, king
alskipaðr *adj* fully manned
alt *adv* all the way
alvara *f* earnestness, seriousness
alþýða *f* all the people, the majority of people, the public, the common people
Andvari *m* Andvari ('Vigilance') (*personal name*), dwarf whose gold is used to pay Otr's wergild
annarr (*f* ǫnnur, *n* annat; *acc m* annan, *f* aðra, *dat m* ǫðrum, *n* ǫðru; *pl m* aðrir, etc.; *see* 13.3) *adj* other, another; second; **annarr... annarr...** *indef pron* the one... the other...; **at ǫðrum kosti** otherwise
aptr *adv* back
arfr *m* inheritance
Arinbjǫrn *m* Arinbjorn (*personal name*)
armr (*f* ǫrm, *n* armt) *adj* wretched, vile, wicked; poor, unfortunate
Arnarstakkr *m* 'Eagle's Haystack', a mountain in the south of Iceland (*place name*)
Arnarstakksheiðr *f* Heath of Arnarstakkr (*place name*)
askr *m* ash (tree)
at *prep* [*w dat*] at, to; with respect to; for, as; **auðigr at fé** wealthy; **kærr at** fond of; **sterkr at afli** strong; **vera/verða at sætt** constitute a settlement or agreement
at *adv* **berask at** happen; **gaman sé at** it is amusing
at *conj* that; so that
at *inf marker* to
auðigr *adj* wealthy; **auðigr at fé** wealthy
Auðhumla *f* Audhumla (*mythological name*, the primeval cow)
Auðr *f* Aud (*personal name*)
auga *n* eye
auka (eykr; jók, jóku; aukit) *vb* increase
Aurland *n* Aurland (*place name*)
ausa (eyss; jós, jósu/jusu; ausit) *vb* sprinkle, pour
austr *adv* east
austanverðr *adj* eastern

Á

á *prep* [*w acc*] on, onto, into (*motion*); with respect to; [*w dat*] on, at, in (*location*); **á dǫgum** in the days; **á einu hverju sumri** one summer; **á himni** in heaven; **á lífi** alive; **á ungum aldri** young; **fegrð á hár (líki)** beauty of hair (body); **kveða á** fix, determine
á *adv* **á brott** away; **hversu lízk þér á** how do you like
á (*gen* ár; *pl* ár, *dat* ám, *gen* á) *f* river
á *vb, see* **eiga**
áðr *adv* before, already; *conj* before
ágætr (*superl* ágætastr) *adj* excellent, outstanding
Álfheimr *m* 'Land of the Elves' (*place name*)
álfr *m* elf
Álfr *m* Alf ('Elf') (*personal name*)
álit *n* appearance, countenance; **fagr**

álitum beautiful (in appearance), handsome
ár *n* year
Ásgerðr *f* Asgerd (*personal name*)
áss (*dat* æsi/ás, *gen* áss/ásar; *pl* æsir, *acc* ásu/æsi) *m* god; **Æsir** *pl* one of the two major groups of gods
át *vb, see* **eta**
átján *num* eighteen
átt, átti *vb, see* **eiga**
átta *num* eight

B

bað *vb, see* **biðja**
bak *n* back
Baldr *m* Baldr (*mythological name*)
bani *m* death
banna (-að-) *vb* forbid, prohibit; **banna jarðir at byggja ok vinna** forbid lands to be rented and worked
bar *vb, see* **bera**
bardagi *m* battle
barðisk *vb, see* **berja**
barn (*pl* bǫrn) *n* child
barsk, báru *vb, see* **bera**
batt *vb, see* **binda**
bauð *vb, see* **bjóða**
baugr (*dat* baug(i)) *m* ring
bazk *vb, see* **biðja**
báðir (*f* báðar, *n* bæði, *gen* beggja) *adj/pron dual* both
báru *vb, see* **bera**
beðit *vb, see* **biðja**
beiða (-dd-) *vb* [*w gen*] ask; *refl* **beiðask** request for oneself
bein *n* bone
beinlauss *adj* boneless
bekkr (*dat* bekk, *gen* -jar; *pl* -ir) *m* bench
belgr (*dat* belg, *gen* -s/jar; *pl* -ir) *m* pelt, skin of an animal (taken off whole); skin-bag; bellows
bera (berr; bar, báru; borit) *vb* carry, bear; **bera saman** collect, gather together; **bera út á** carry out into; **bera vápn á [e-n]** raise weapons against [sb]; **vel viti borinn** intelligent, endowed with good sense; *refl* **berask at** happen
berg *n* rock, boulder
berja (barð-) *vb* beat, strike, smite; *refl* **berjask** fight
betr *comp adv* better (*see* **vel**)
betri *comp adj* better (*see* **góðr**)
bezt *superl adv* best (*see* **vel**)
beztr *superl adj* best (*see* **góðr**)
biðja (biðr; bað, báðu; beðit) *vb* ask, request, bid; [*w gen*] ask for, request; **biðja konu** ask for a woman in marriage; *refl* **biðjask undan** be evasive
Bifrǫst *f* the rainbow bridge to heaven
bik *n* pitch
bil *n* moment
binda (bindr; batt, bundu; bundit) *vb* bind, tie, tie up
Bjarnardóttir *f* daughter of Bjorn
bjartr *adj* bright, radiant
bjó *vb, see* **búa**
bjóða (býðr; bauð, buðu; boðit) *vb* [*w acc of person, dat of thing*] offer
bjósk *vb, see* **búa**
Bjǫrgyn *m* Bergen, Norway (*place name*)
bjǫrn (*dat* birni, *gen* bjarnar; *pl* birnir, *acc* bjǫrnu; *see* 11.5, 17.6) *m* bear
Bjǫrn (*dat* Birni, *gen* Bjarnar; *see* 11.5) *m* Bjorn ('Bear') (*personal name*)
blása (blæss; blés, blésu; blásit) *vb* blow
blóð *n* blood
blót *n* sacrifice
blunda (-að) *vb* shut the eyes, doze
boð *n* bidding, command; message
bogi *m* bow; **kom á boga Einars miðjan** struck the middle of Einars bow
bogmaðr *m* archer
borg (*gen* -ar; *pl* -ir) *f* stronghold, fortification; town
Borg *f* Borg (*place name*)
Borgarfjǫrðr *m* 'Borg's Fjord', a fjord in Western Iceland (*place name*)
borinn *ppart, see* **bera**
botn (*gen* botns; *pl* botnar) *m* bottom; head of a bay, lake, dale, etc.
bók (*pl* bœkr) *f* book
ból *n* lair
bóndi *see* **búandi**

bónorð *n* request, petition; **hefja upp bónorð** propose marriage
brann *vb, see* **brenna**
brast *vb, see* **bresta**
braut *var of* **brot(t)**
brá *f* eyelash
brá, **brásk** *vb, see* **bregða**
brátt *adv* quickly
Brávǫllr *m* Bravoll, a plain in Sweden (*place name*)
bregða (bregðr; brá, brugðu; brugðit) *vb* [*w dat*] cause to move; thrust (a weapon); alter, change; *refl* **bregðask** change oneself into another shape
Breiðablik *n* Breidablik ('Broad Gleam') (*mythological place name*)
brenna (brennr; brann, brunnu; brunnit) *vb* burn
bresta (brestr; brast, brustu; brostit) *vb* break
brestr (*pl* -ir) *m* break, crash; **eigi mun svá mikill brestr orðinn** such a great break is not likely to have occurred
brjósk *n* cartilage
brjóta (brýtr; braut, brutu; brotit) *vb* break
brot(t) *adv* **á brott** away (*motion*); **í brot(t)** away (*motion*)
brottu *adv* **í brottu** away (*location*)
bróðir (*acc/dat/gen* bróður; *pl* brœðr, *dat* brœðr, *gen* brœðra; *see* 9.5, 14.8) *m* brother
bróðurgjǫld *n pl* ransom, wergild (blood money) for a brother
brók (*pl* brœkr) *f* pants-leg; breeches
brunnr *m* well
brúarsporðr *m* bridge-head
brúðlaup *n* wedding; **gera brúðlaup til** marry
brynja *f* coat of mail
Brynjólfr *m* Brynjolf (*personal name*)
brýtr *vb, see* **brjóta**
brœðr, **brœðra** *m pl, see* **bróðir**
bundit *ppart, see* **binda**
Buri *m* Buri (*personal name*)
búa (býr; bjó, bjoggu; búit) *vb* live (in a place), dwell; *refl* **búask** prepare (oneself); **búask til** prepare (oneself) for; **undir at búa** to bear up under
búandi (*also* **bóndi**) (*pl* búendr) *m* farmer; head of a household
búð (*pl* -ir) *f* tent, booth
bygð *f* home, settlement, abode
byggja (bygð-) *vb* inhabit, dwell; rent, let out
byrðr *f* burden, load
byrr (*gen* -jar; *pl* -ir) *m* fair wind; **[e-m] gefr vel byri** *impers* [sb] gets fair winds
býr, **býsk** *vb, see* **búa**
bǫrn *n pl, see* **barn**
bæði *adv* both
bœkr *f pl, see* **bók**
bœr (*dat* bœ, *gen* bœjar; *pl* bœir) *m* farm, farmstead; farmhouse
bœta (-tt-) *vb* to better, improve; **bœta til um** improve
bǫl (-v-) *n* trouble, misfortune, 'bale'
bǫlvasmiðr *m* trouble-smith, forger of misfortune

D

dagr *m* day; **á dǫgum** in the days (of); **þann dag** on that day
dalr (*dat* dal(i)) *m* valley, dale
Danmǫrk (*dat* Danmǫrku) *f* Denmark
dauðr (*n* dautt) *adj* dead
deyja (deyr; dó, dóu; dáit) *vb* die
deila *f* dispute
djúpr *adj* deep
dóttir (*acc/dat/gen* dóttur; *pl* dœtr, *dat* dœtrum, *gen* dœtra; *see* 9.5, 14.8) *f* daughter
draga (dregr; dró, drógu; dregit) *vb* pull, draw; **draga fyrir** draw beyond; **draga saman** assemble
drakk *vb, see* **drekka**
drap *vb, see* **drepa**
draup *vb, see* **drjúpa**
drápu *vb, see* **drepa**
dregr *vb, see* **draga**
drekka (drekkr; drakk, drukku; drukkit) *vb* drink
drepa (drepr; drap, drápu; drepit) *vb* kill; [*w dat*] put
drjúpa (drýpr; draup, drupu; dropit) *vb* drip

dró *vb, see* **draga**
dvelja (dvalð-) *vb* delay, defer; *refl* **dveljask** stay
dvergr *m* dwarf
dýr *n* animal, beast
dældarmaðr *m* gentle, easy man
dœgr *n* a half day (twelve hours of day or night); a full day of 24 hours; **fjǫgurra (fimm) dœgra haf**, a sail of four (five) days; **sjau dœgra sigling** a sail of seven days
dœl *f* dale, hollow
dǫgum *m, see* **dagr**
Døkkálfr *m* 'Dark-Elf'
døkkr (-v-) *adj* dark

E

eða *conj* or
Edda *f* Edda (*literary work*); **Snorra Edda** 'Snorri's Edda', *The Prose Edda* written by Snorri Sturluson
ef *conj* if
efla (-d-) *vb* make, perform
egg (-j-) *f* edge
eggja (-að-) *vb* egg on, urge, incite
Egill *m* Egil (*personal name*)
eiga (á, eigu; átti; átt) *vb* own, possess; be married to, have (relatives); **eiga eptir** leave behind; **sem hon átti ætt til** which was characteristic for her family
eigi *adv* not, no
Einarr *m* Einar (*personal name*)
einn (*f* ein, *n* eitt) *num* one; **einn hverr** one, a certain; **á einu hverju sumri** one summer; (*n* **eitt**) one thing, the same thing
einvaldskonungr *m* sole ruler, monarch
Eiríkr *m* Eirik (*personal name*)
eitt *num* (*n*), *see* **einn**
ek (*acc* mik, *dat* mér, *gen* mín; *see* 3.6) *pron* I
ekki *indef pron* (*n*), *see* **engi**; *as adv* not
eldask (-ld-) *refl vb* grow old
eldr *m* fire
Elfráðr *m* Alfred (*personal name*)
Ella *m* Ælla, King of Northumbria (*personal name*)
elli *f* old age
ellifu *num* eleven
ellri *comp adj* older (*see* **gamall**)
ellstr *superl adj* oldest (*see* **gamall**)
elska (-að-) *vb* love; be fond of
em *vb, see* **vera**
en *conj* but; and (on the other hand)
en *conj* than
endi *m* end
engi (*f* engi, *n* ekki; *gen m/n* enskis) *indef pron* no one, not one, no; (*pl*) none; (*after neg*) any; (*n* **ekki**) nothing
England *n* England
enn *adv* still, yet
enskis *indef pron, see* **engi**
eptir *prep* [*w acc*] after (*time*); [*w dat*] after, along with; according to; **þar eptir** accordingly; **eiga eptir** leave behind; **spyrja eptir** ask about
eptir *adv* behind, left over
er *rel pron/adv* when; where; who, which, that; *conj* when; since; **þar er** where; **þá er** when
er, **ert**, **erum** *vb, see* **vera**
Erlingr *m* Erling (*personal name*)
es = **er**
eta (etr; át, átu; etit) *vb* eat
etja (att-) *vb* [*w dat*] incite, egg on
ey (*dat* ey/eyju, *gen* -jar; *pl* -jar) *f* island
eyða (-dd-) *vb* lay waste; spend up, squander; *refl* **eyðask** be squandered, come to naught
Eylimi *m* Eylimi (*personal name*); legendary king, father of Hjordis
eyra *n* ear
Eymundr *m* Eymund (*personal name*)
Eysteinn *m* Eystein (*personal name*)

F

faðir (*acc/dat/gen* fǫður; *pl* feðr, *dat* feðrum, *gen* feðra; *see* 9.5, 14.8) *m* father
fagna (-að-) *vb* [*w dat*] welcome
fagr (*f* fǫgr, *n* fagrt; *comp* fegri, *superl* fegrstr) *adj* beautiful, fair, fine; **fagr álitum** beautiful (in appearance), handsome

falla (fellr; fell/féll, fellu/féllu; fallit) *vb* fall
fannsk *vb, see* **finna**
fara (ferr; fór, fóru; farit) *vb* go, travel; fare; **var farinn** had travelled; **fara með fíflsku** commit folly; *refl* **farask** go (of events), turn out; perish
farar *f pl, see* **fǫr**
farmaðr *m* traveller, sea-farer
fá (fær; fekk, fengu; fengit) *vb* get; [*w gen*] marry; **fá sér liðs** gather a band of men, get support
Fáfnir *m* Fafnir (*personal name*); son of Hreidmar who turns himself into a dragon
fár *adj* few
feðgar *m pl* father and son(s)
feginn *adj* happy, glad, pleased
fegrð *f* beauty; **fegrð á hár (líki)** beauty of hair (body)
fegri *comp adj* more beautiful (*see* **fagr**)
fegrstr *superl adj* fairest, most beautiful (*see* **fagr**); **fegrst talaðr** most eloquent
fekk *vb, see* **fá**
fell *n* mountain
fell, **fellr** *vb, see* **falla**
ferð (*pl* -ir) *f* trip, journey
fé (*gen* fjár; *pl gen* fjá) *n* property, wealth, money; cattle; **auðigr at fé** wealthy
fimm *num* five
fimmtán *num* fifteen
fingr *m* finger
finna (finnr; fann, fundu; fundit) *vb* find; *refl* **finnask** appear; **finnask á** appear; **þá er honum fannsk mikit um** whom he liked very much
Finnr *m* Finn (*personal name*)
finnskr *adj* Finnish
Firðir *m pl* the Fjords (*place name*)
fiskr *m* fish
fíflska *f* folly, foolishness; **fara með fíflsku** commit folly
fjórir (*f* fjórar, *n* fjǫgur, *all gen* fjǫgurra; *see* 14.1) *num* four
fjórtán *num* fourteen
fjǫgur, **fjǫgurra** *num, see* **fjórir**
fjǫldi *m* multitude
fjǫlkunnigr *adj* skilled in magic, 'much knowing'
fjǫlmenni *n* crowd
fjǫlmennr *adj* populous, with many people, well attended
fjǫr (-v-) *n* life
fjǫrðr (*dat* firði, *gen* fjarðar; *pl* firðir, *acc* fjǫrðu, *gen* fjarða; *see* 11.5, 17.6) *m* fjord
Fjǫrðu, **Fjǫrðum** *m pl, see* **Firðir**
fjǫrlausn *f* ransom for one's life
fjǫrsegi *m* heart ('life-muscle')
flá (flær; fló, flógu; flegit) *vb* flay, strip
fleiri *comp adj* more (*see* **margr**)
flestr *comp adj* most (*see* **margr**)
flytja (flutt-) *vb* convey, carry; deliver (an address), recite; **flytja til eyrna [e-m]** convey to the ears of [sb], inform [sb]
flýja (-ð-) to flee
formáli *m* 'fore-speech', foretelling
fors (*pl* -ar) *m* waterfall
fólk *n* people
fór, **fóru** *vb, see* **fara**
fóstbróðir *m* foster-brother
fóstr (*gen* -rs) *n* fostering, fosterage
fóstri *m* foster-father
fram *adv* forward, forth; **ganga vel fram** fight valiantly; **um fram** in addition
frauð *n* froth, juice (of roasted meat)
frá *prep* [*w dat*] from; about; **segja frá** relate, tell about
frá *adv* away, off; **ofan frá** below
fránn *adj* gleaming, flashing
Freyr *m* Frey (*mythological name*, one of the Vanir)
Freysgoði *m* 'Frey's Chief' (*nickname*)
frétt (*pl* -ir) *f* news
Frigg *f* Frigg, wife of Odin (*mythological name*)
fríðastr *superl adj, see* **fríðr**
fríðr (*n* frítt) *adj* beautiful, handsome, fine; **fríðr sýnum** fine in appearance
frjósa (frýss; fraus, frusu; frosit) *vb* freeze
frægr *adj* famous
frœkn (*also* **frœkinn**) *adj* bold, daring, valiant
fugl *m* bird
fuglsrǫdd *f* bird's voice, speech of birds
fullr *adj* full
fullsteiktr *ppart* fully roasted (*from*

steikja)
fundr (*gen* -ar; *pl* -ir) *m* meeting; audience
funi *m* flame
furða *f* wonder, marvel
fylking *f* battle array, the ranks of an army; battalion
fylla (-d-) *vb* fill
fyrir *prep* [*w acc*] before, in front of (*motion*); for, because of; instead of; [*w dat*] before, in front of (*location*); at the head of (leading); with; for, by; because of; **fyrir ... sakar** on account of, because of; **fyrir sér** of oneself; **fyrir sik** for oneself, on one's own behalf; **fyrir strauminum** with the current; **fyrir útan** [*w acc*] outside; out beyond; **fyrir því, at** because; **draga fyrir** draw beyond; **ráða fyrir** rule over
fyrr *adv* before, earlier; **fyrr en** *conj* before
fyrri *comp adj* former
fyrst *superl adv* first, earliest
fyrstr *superl adj* first, foremost
fœða (-dd-) *vb* feed
fǫður *m, see* **faðir**
fǫr (*pl* farar) *f* journey

G

gaf *vb, see* **gefa**
gagn (*pl* gǫgn) *n* advantage, benefit, produce, revenue
gamall (*acc* gamlan, *f* gǫmul, *n* gamalt; *comp* ellri, *superl* ellstr) *adj* old
gaman *n* fun, amusement, pleasure; **gera gaman** entertain; **at gaman sé at** that it is amusing
ganga (gengr; gekk, gengu; gengit) *vb* go, walk; **ganga af** leave off, be finished with; **ganga at [e-m]** attack [sb]; **ganga á hǫnd [e-m]** submit to [sb], go into [sb]'s service, become [sb]'s retainer; **ganga fyrir** go before; **ganga til** approach, go up to a thing; **ganga vel fram** fight valiantly; **ganga yfir [e-n]** befall, happen to [sb]
Gangleri *m* Gangleri (*personal name*)
garðr *m* fence, wall
gefa (gefr; gaf, gáfu; gefit) *vb* give
gegnum *adv* through; (*also* **í gegnum**) *prep* [*w acc*] through
geirr *m* spear
gekk, **gengir**, **gengit**, **gengr** *vb, see* **ganga**
gera (-ð-) *vb* make, do, build; **gera brúðlaup til** marry; **gera gaman** entertain; *refl* **gerask** become
geta (getr; gat, gátu; getit) *vb* get; [*w gen*] guess; **geta at eiga** get in marriage, marry; **geta til** suppose, surmise
Gimlé *n* Gimle (*place name*)
Gísli *m* Gisli (*personal name*)
gjald *n* (*usu in pl* gjǫld) tribute; payment; reward; compensation; wergild (blood money)
glepja (glapð-) *vb* confuse, confound
Glitnir *m* Glitnir (*place name*)
Gnitaheiðr (*gen* -ar) *f* Gnitaheath (*place name*), where Fafnir, as a dragon, lies upon great wealth
goð *n* god, one of the pagan gods
goðagremi *f* wrath of the gods
goði *m* chief
goðkunnigr *adj* related to the gods
goðorð *n* chieftainship, rank and authority of a **goði**
góðr (*n* gott; *comp* betri, *superl* beztr) *adj* good; **góðr af** proud of
góðhestr *m* good (riding) horse
grafa (grefr; gróf, grófu; grafit) *vb* dig
Gramr *m* Gram (*mythological name*), name of Sigurd the Dragon Slayer's sword
granahár *n* whisker
Grani *m* Grani (*mythological name*), Sigurd the Dragon-Slayer's horse
gras *n* grass, plant, herb
gráliga *adv* maliciously
gráta (grætr; grét, grétu; grátit) *vb* cry
greiða (-dd-) *vb* pay
gremi *f* wrath, anger
griðarof *n pl* breach of the peace, trucebreaking
grimmr *adj* grim, fierce, savage
grjót *n* stones (*collective*), rubble
Grjótgarðr *m* Grjotgard ('Stone-Fence') (*personal name*)
gróf *vb, see* **grafa**
Grœnland *n* Greenland

grœnn *adj* green
grǫf (*gen* grafar; *pl* grafir/grafar) *f* pit, ditch
grǫn (*gen* granar; *pl* granar) *f* lip
gull *n* gold
gullbaugr (*dat* gullbaug(i)) *m* gold ring
Gunnarr *m* Gunnar (*personal name*)
Gunnlaugr *m* Gunnlaug (*personal name*)
gǫfugligr *adj* magnificent
gǫfugr *adj* noble
gøgnum *var of* **gegnum**
gǫrla *adv* fully, quite
gǫrr (-v-) *adj* done; **at svá gǫrvu** thus, this being the case, as things stood
gørt *var of* **gert** *ppart, see* **gera**
gørviligstr *superl adj, see* **gørviligr**
gørviligr *adj* accomplished, capable, enterprising

H

haf (*pl* hǫf) *n* sea; **fjǫgurra (fimm) dœgra haf**, a sail of four (five) days
hafa (hef(i)r, -ð-) *vb* have; hold, keep; take; **hafa [e-m] heim með sér** bring [sb] home with oneself; **nǫkkut hafask at** undertake ('have at') something
hafnar, **hafnir** *f, see* **hǫfn**
hafsbotn (*gen* -botns; *pl* -botnar) *m* gulf; the Arctic Ocean (*place name*)
halda (heldr; helt, heldu; haldit) *vb* [*w acc/dat*] hold, hold fast; hold on to, keep, retain; direct, set on a course; *refl* **haldask** hold true, remain valid, stand
hamrammr *adj* fierce, furious in battle (*lit.* 'shape-mighty'; used of warriors who 'changed shape', i.e., went berserk)
hana *pron, see* **hon**
hann (*acc* hann, *dat* honum, *gen* hans; *pl* þeir; *see* 5.1) *pron* he
hans *poss pron* his
Haraldr *m* Harald (*personal name*)
harðr (*f* hǫrð, *n* hart) *adj* hard
harðdrœgr *adj* hard to handle
Haukadalr (*dat* Haukadal(i)) *m* 'Hawks' Dale' (*place name*)
haust *n* fall
Hákon (*gen* -ar) *m* Hakon (*personal name*)
hálfa *f* region, part
hár *n* hair
hár *adj* tall, high; loud
Hár *m* Har ('High') (*mythological name*, pseudonym of Odin)
hárfagr *adj* fair-haired
hásæti *n* high-seat, throne
hátt *adv* loudly
Hávarðr *m* Havard (*personal name*)
hefði, **hefi**, **hefir**, **hefr** *vb, see* **hafa**
hefja (hefr; hóf, hófu; hafit) *vb* raise; begin; **hefja upp bónorð** propose marriage
hefna (-d-) *vb* avenge
heiðr (*pl* -ar) *f* heath
heill *adj* healthy, well, 'hale'; whole
heim *adv* (to) home (*motion*)
heima *adv* at home (*location*)
heima *m, see* **heimr**
heimamaðr *m* servant, man belonging to a household
heimr *m* home, dwelling; land, region of the world; the world; **kringla heimsins** the globe, earth; **of alla heima** over the whole world
heita (heitir; hét, hétu; heitit) *vb* be named, be called; promise
heldi, **heldr**, **heldu** *vb, see* **halda**
Helgi *m* Helgi ('Holy') (*personal name*)
helgistaðr *m* holy place
helmingr *m* half; **skipta í helminga** divide into two equal portions
helzk *vb, see* **halda**
helzt *superl adv* especially; **allra helzt** especially
hendi *f, see* **hǫnd**
hennar *poss pron* her, hers
herkonungr *m* warrior-king
herr (*gen* -jar; *pl* -jar) *m* army, host
herra *m* master, lord
hersaga *f* war-tidings (*see also* **herr**, **saga**)
hersir *m* local chieftain
hersǫgu *f, see* **hersaga**
hestaat *n* horse fight
hestavít *n* horse fight
hestr *m* horse, stallion
heyra (-ð-) *vb* hear

hégómi *m* insincerity
hér *adv* here
hét *vb, see* **heita**
Hildigunnr *f* Hildigunn (*personal name*)
Himinbjǫrg *n pl* 'Heaven Mountains' (*place name*)
himinn *m* heaven; **á himni** in heaven
hinn *art, var of* **inn**
hinn *pron* this (the other)
hitta (-tt-) *vb* meet; *refl* **hittask** meet one another
hjarta (*pl* hjǫrtu, *gen* hjartna) *n* heart
hjá *prep* [*w dat*] with, by, beside
hjartablóð *n* heart's blood
hjálmr *m* helmet
Hjálprekr *m* Hjalprek (*personal name*), a legendary king
hjó *vb, see* **hǫggva**
Hjǫrdís *f* Hjordis (*personal name*); mother of Sigurd
Hjǫrleifr *m* Hjorleif (*personal name*)
hjǫrtr (*dat* hirti, *gen* hjartar; *pl* hirtir, *acc* hjǫrtu; *see* 11.5, 17.6) *m* deer, stag, hart
Hjǫrtr (*dat* Hirti, *gen* Hjartar; *see* 11.5) *m* Hjort ('Deer') (*personal name*)
hlaup *n* leap, jump
hlaupa (hleypr; hljóp, hljópu; hlaupit) *vb* run
Hliðskjálf *f* name of Odin's throne
Hlíðarendi *m* Hlidarendi, a farm in southern Iceland (*place name*)
hlíf (*pl* -ar) *f* cover, protection (esp. of a shield or armor)
hluti *m* part
hlutr (*dat* hlut, *gen* -ar; *pl* -ir) *m* part; **um alla hluti** in all respects
hlýða (-dd-) [*w dat*] *vb* listen to; **hlýða til** listen to
hlæja (hlær; hló, hlógu; hlegit) *vb* laugh
hof *n* temple
Hof *n* Hof ('Temple') (*place name*)
Hofsland *n* the Hof estate
hon (*acc* hana, *dat* henni, *gen* hennar; *pl* þær; *see* 5.1) *pron* she
honum *pron, see* **hann**
horfa (-ð-) *vb* look, (turn so as to) look on; **horfa á** look at; **horfask til** be in prospect
horn *n* horn
Horn *n* Horn, farm in Southeastern Iceland, one of the first settlements in Iceland (*place name*)
hóf *vb, see* **hefja**
hófsmaðr *m* man of moderation and restraint
hógværr *adj* gentle, quiet
Hrafn *m* Hrafn ('Raven') (*personal name*)
Hrafnkell *m* Hrafnkel (*personal name*)
hraustr *adj* bold
Hreiðmarr *m* Hreidmar (*mythological name*), father of Otr, Fafnir, and Regin
hrím *n* hoar-frost, rime
hrímsteinn *m* rime-stone
hringr *m* ring
hross *n* horse, mare
Hrotti *m* Hrotti (*mythological name*), name of a sword
Hróaldr *m* Hroald (*personal name*)
Hróðgeirr *m* Hrodgeir (*personal name*)
hrósa (-að-) *vb* [*w dat*] boast (of)
hræða (-dd-) *vb* [*w acc*] frighten; *refl* **hræðask** be frightened; **hræðask [e-t]** be afraid of [sth]
hugði *vb, see* **hyggja**
hugr (*dat* hug(i), *gen* -ar; *pl* -ir) *m* mind; mood; courage; **vera í hug [e-m]** be in [sb]'s mind
hulði, huldr *vb, see* **hylja**
hundrað (*pl* hundruð) *n* hundred
hús *n* house
hvar *int adv* where
hvarf *n* disappearance
Hvarf *n* 'Disappearance', Cape Farewell in Greenland (*place name*)
hvass (*f* hvǫss, *n* hvas(s)t) *adj* sharp, keen
hvat *n int pron* what; *rel pron* what, that which (*see* **hverr**)
hvárr *int pron* who, which (of two); *indef pron* each (of two)
hvárrtveggja *indef pron* each (of two)
hvárt *conj* whether
hverr (*n* hvat; -j-) *int pron* who, what, which; **af hverju** why, for what reason; *indef pron* each, any(one), every(one); **einn hverr** one, a

certain
hversu *adv* how; **hversu lízk þér á** how do you like
hvert *adv* to where
hvetja (hvatt-) *vb* whet, sharpen
hvé *adv* how, to what extent
hví *adv* why, for what reason (*n dat of* **hvat**)
hvítr *adj* white
Hvítserkr *m* Hvitserk ('White-Shirt') (*personal name*)
hyggja (hugð-) *vb* think; **hyggja at** pay attention to, consider
hylja (huld/hulð-) *vb* hide, cover
Hœnir *m* Hœnir (*mythological name*), one of the Æsir
hǫf *n pl, see* **haf**
hǫfðingi *m* leader
hǫfðu *vb, see* **hafa**
hǫfn (*gen* hafnar; *pl* hafnir) *f* harbor
hǫfuð *n* head
hǫfuðsbani *m* death, destruction
hǫfuðstaðr *m* capital, chief place
hǫgg (-v-) *n* stroke, blow
hǫggva (høggr; hjó, hjoggu; hǫgg(v)it) *vb* strike, hack, hew
hǫnd (*dat* hendi, *gen* handar; *pl* hendr) *f* hand; **ganga á hǫnd [e-m]** submit to [sb], go into [sb]'s service, become [sb]'s retainer; **ór hendi þér** out of your hand; **selja í hendr** turn over; **taka hǫndum** take hold of, seize with the hands
Hǫrðakonungr *m* king of Hǫrðaland (in Western Norway)

I

igða *f* nuthatch (species of bird)
illa (*comp* verr, *superl* verst) *adv* badly, 'ill'
illr (*comp* verri, *superl* verstr) *adj* bad, evil, 'ill'
Ingi *m* Ingi (*personal name*)
Ingibjǫrg *f* Ingibjorg (*personal name*)
inn (*f* in, *n* it) *art* the
inn *adv* in (*motion*); **inn í** into
innlenzkr *adj* native
it *art* (*n*), *see* **inn**

Í

í *prep* [*w acc*] in, into (*motion*); [*w dat*] in, within; at (*location*); **í þann tíma** at that time
Írland *n* Ireland
Ísland *n* Iceland
íslenzkr *adj* Icelandic
Ívarr *m* Ivar (*personal name*)
íþrótt (*pl* -ir) *f* skill, feat, accomplishment

J

jafna (-að-) *vb* compare, liken; **jafna til** compare with, liken to
jafningi (*pl* -jar) *m* equal, match
jalda *f poet* mare
jarl *m* earl
Játvarðr *m* Edward (*personal name*)
Jórsalaland *n* 'Jerusaem's Land', Israel (*place name*)
Jǫlduhlaup *n* 'Mare's Leap', Slyne Head in Ireland (*place name*)
jǫrð (*dat* -u) *f* earth
jǫtunn *m* giant
Jǫtunheimar *m pl* Land of Giants

K

kalla (-að-) *vb* call, name
kanna (-að-) *vb* search, explore
kannt *vb, see* **kunna**
kapalhestr *m* packhorse
kapítuli *m* chapter
kappi *m* hero, great fighter
kasta (-að-) *vb* [*w dat*] throw, cast; **kasta boganum** throw the bow
kastali *m* castle
kaupa (keypt-) *vb* buy
kemr *vb, see* **koma**
kjósa (kýss; kaus/kǫri, kusu/kuru, kosit/kørit) *vb* choose
Kerlingardalsá *f* 'River of the Valley

of the Old Woman' (*place name*)
klauf *vb, see* **kljúfa**
kljúfa (klýfr; klauf, klufu; klofit) *vb* split, cleave
klyf (*pl* -jar) *f* pack (for a horse)
klæði *n* cloth; garment, clothing
knǫrr (*dat* knerri, *gen* knarrar; *pl* knerrir, *acc* knǫrru, *gen* knarra) *m* ship; merchant vessel
Kolskeggr *m* Kolskegg (*personal name*)
koma (kemr; kom, kómu; komit) *vb* come; *refl* **komask** reach, arrive; **koma at** arrive; **koma á** strike; **koma upp** come about, happen; **komask undan** escape
komsk *vb, see* **koma**
kona (*pl gen* kvenna) *f* woman, wife; **biðja konu** ask for a woman in marriage
konar *gen sg of obs* ***konr** *m* kind, sort; **alls konar** of every kind, of all kinds
konungr *m* king
konungsson *m* prince
kostr (*gen* -ar; *pl* -ir) *m* choice, alternative; **at ǫðrum kosti** otherwise
kómu *vb, see* **koma**
krapparúm *n* bow-room (on a ship)
kringla *f* disk, circle, orb; **kringla heimsins** the globe, earth
kunna (kann, kunnu; kunni; kunnat) *vb* know, understand; be able
kunnigr *adj* known; knowing, skilled in magic
kvað *vb, see* **kveða**
kvaddi *vb, see* **kveðja**
kváðu, kváðusk *vb, see* **kveða**
kveða (kveðr; kvað, kváðu; kveðit) *vb* say; **kveða á** fix, determine; *refl* **kveðask** say of oneself [*w inf*]
kveðja (kvadd-) *vb* greet
kveld *n* evening
Kveld-Úlfr *m* Kveld-Ulf ('Evening-Wolf') (*personal name*)
kvikvendi *n pl* living creatures, animals, beasts
Kvígandafell *n* 'Heifer Mountain' (*place name*)
kyrr *adj* still, quiet
kýr (*acc/dat* kú, *gen* kýr; *pl nom/acc* kýr, *dat* kúm, *gen* kúa) *f* cow
kǫllum *vb, see* **kalla**
kærr *adj* dear; **kærr at** fond of
kœmi *vb, see* **koma**

L

lagabrot *n* lawbreaking; **lagabrot landsréttar** breaking the law of the land
lagði, lagðisk *vb, see* **leggja**
lagðr *m* tuft (of wool or hair)
lagt *vb, see* **leggja**
land (*pl* lǫnd) *n* land
landnám *n* settlement, 'land taking'
Landnámabók *f* Book of Settlements
landsréttr *m* law of the land; **lagabrot landsréttar** breaking the law of the land
Langanes *n* Langanes ('Long Headland'), peninsula in Northeast Iceland (*place name*)
langfeðgar *m pl* forefathers, ancestors (through the father's line)
langr *adj* long
langt *adv* far
lausn (*gen* -ar; *pl* -ir) *f* ransom
lauss *adj* free
laust *n adj, see* **lauss**
laust *vb, see* **ljósta**
lax (*gen* lax; *pl* laxar) *m* salmon
lá *vb, see* **liggja**
láta (lætr; lét, létu; látit) *vb* let, allow; put, place, set; [*w inf*] have something done; **láta fram** let go, yield, hand over; *refl* **látask** declare (of oneself)
leggja (lagð-) *vb* lay, place; set, fix, arrange; [*w dat*] stab, thrust; **leggja [e-t] á [e-n]** impose, lay [sth] upon [sb]; **leggja [e-u] í gegnum [e-n]** thrust [sth] through [sb]; **leggja til (orð)** say; **leggja við** accuse of, declare guilty of or subject to; *refl* **leggjask** lay oneself, lie down; **leggjask at sofa** go to sleep
leggr (*gen* -jar; *pl* -ir) *m* leg, limb; hollow bone (of arm and leg)
leið (*pl* -ir) *f* way; path, road
leit *vb, see* **líta**
leita (-að-) *vb* [*w gen*] seek, search for

lemja (lamd-) *vb* beat, thrash
lendr *adj* 'landed', having lands; **lendr maðr** 'landed man' (Norw *lendmann*), a Norwegian nobleman whose lands and income were granted by the king
lengi *adv* long, a long time
lengja (-d-) *vb* lengthen
lengra *comp adv* farther
lét, **lézk** *vb*, *see* **láta**
lið *n* troop, force, band of armed supporters; aid, assistance; **fá sér liðs** gather a band of men, get support
liðfœrr *adj* able-bodied
lifa (-ð-) *vb* live; **lifa við** live on, feed on
liggja (liggr; lá, lágu, legit) *vb* lie
litlu *adv* a little (*dat sg neut of* **lítill**); **litlu síðar** a little later
líf *n* life; **á lífi** alive
líki *n* form, shape, likeness; body
líkligr *adj* likely, probable; **sem líkligt er** as might be expected
líknsamr *adj* gracious, merciful
líta (lítr; leit, litu; litit) *vb* look; **líta á** look at, consider; **hversu lízk þér á** how do you like
lítill (*f* lítil, *n* lítit; *acc m* litlan, *f* litla, *dat m* litlum, *n* litlu; *pl* litlir, etc.; *comp* minni, *superl* minnstr) *adj* little, small
lítt (*comp* minnr, *superl* minnst) *adv* little
Ljósálfr *m* 'Light-Elf'
ljóss *adj* light, fair; clear
ljósta (lýstr; laust, lustu; lostit) *vb* strike, hit
loðbrók *f* 'Hairy Breeches' (*nickname*)
lofa (-að-) *vb* praise
Loki *m* Loki (*mythological name*), the trickster god, one of the Æsir
lokit *ppart*, *see* **lúka**
lunga *n* lung
lúka (lýkr; lauk, luku; lokit) *vb* [*w dat*] end, finish
lýsa (-t-) *vb* shine
lǫg *n pl* law(s)
lǫgmaðr *m* lawman, lawyer

M

maðr (*acc* mann, *dat* manni, *gen* manns; *pl nom/acc* menn, *dat* mǫnnum, *gen* manna; *see* 2.6) *m* man; person, human being
Magnús *m* Magnus (*personal name*)
man *vb*, *see* **muna**
mann, **manna**, **manns** *m*, *see* **maðr**
mannfólk *n* mankind, humanity
mannvænn *adj* promising
margr (*f* mǫrg, *n* mar(g)t; *comp* fleiri, *superl* flestr) *adj* [*w sg*] many a (in collective sense); [*w pl*] many
marka (-að-) *vb* notice; infer
má *vb*, *see* **mega**
mál *n* speech, language; case, matter, affair
málmr *m* ore; metal
mátt, **mátti** *vb*, *see* **mega**
með *prep* [*w acc*] with (bringing, carrying along, or forcing); [*w dat*] with (accompanying or being together); along; with, by, using; between; **upp með** up along
meðan *conj* while
mega (má, megu; mátti; mátt) *vb* be able, be allowed; **vera má þat** maybe
mein *n* hurt, harm; **verða [e-m] at meini** cause [sb] harm
meir(r) *comp adv* more (*see* **mjǫk**)
meiri *comp adj* greater (*see* **mikill**)
menn *m pl*, *see* **maðr**
mest *superl adv* most (*see* **mjǫk**); **sem mest** as much as possible
mestr *superl adj* greatest; most (*see* **mikill**)
metnaðarmaðr *m* man of ambition
mey, **meyjar** *f*, *see* **mær**
mér *pron*, *see* **ek** (*see also* 3.6)
miðla (-að-) *vb* share
miðr (-j-) *adj* middle; **boga Einars miðjan** to the middle of Einars bow
mik *pron*, *see* **ek** (*see also* 3.6)
mikill (*f* mikil, *n* mikit, *acc m* mikinn; *comp* meiri, *superl* mestr) *adj* big, large, great; much; (of rivers) swollen, running high; **mikill fyrir sér** strong, powerful, mighty
mikit *adv* much (*see* **mikill**)
miklu *adv* [*w comp*] much (*n dat sg of* **mikill**)

milli *prep* [*w gen*] between; **standa milli** impede
minn (*f* mín, *n* mitt; *acc m* minn, *f* mína, *dat m* mínum, *n* mínu, *gen m/n* míns; *pl m* mínir, *f* mínar, *n* mín, *acc m* mína, *dat* mínum; *see* 16.4) *poss adj* my, mine
minni *comp adj* littler, smaller, lesser (*see* **lítill**)
minnr *comp adv* less (*see* **lítt**)
minnst *superl adv* least (*see* **lítt**)
minnstr *superl adj* littlest, smallest, least (*see* **lítill**)
mín *pron*, *see* **ek** (*see also* 3.6)
mjólk *f* milk
mjólk-á *f* milk-stream, river of milk
mjǫk (*comp* meir(r), *superl* mest) *adv* much, greatly, very; almost
móðir (*acc/dat/gen* móður; *pl* mœðr, *dat* mœðr, *gen* mœðra; *see* 9.5, 14.8) *f* mother
móti *prep* [*w dat*] toward, against
muna (man, muna; mundi; munat) *vb* remember
munnr *m* mouth
munu (mun, munu; mundi; *pret inf* mundu) *vb* will, shall (*future*), be likely
mylja (muld-) *vb* crush to pieces
myndi *vb*, *see* **munu**
mæla (-t-) *vb* say, speak; **mæla við** say to, speak to
mær (*acc* mey, *dat* meyju, *gen* meyjar; *pl nom/acc* meyjar, *dat* meyjum, *gen* meyja) *f* girl, maiden
mǫgr (*dat* megi, *gen* magar; *pl* megir, *acc* mǫgu) *m* boy, youth

N

nafn (*pl* nǫfn) *n* name
nam *vb*, *see* **nema**
nauð *f* need
nauðgjald *n* forced payment
ná (-ð-) *vb* [*w dat*] reach, attain
nábúi *m* neighbor
nám *n* acquisition, occupation; **land-nám** land-taking, settlement
nátt *var of* **nótt**
náttstaðr *m* night-quarters, lodging for the night
nefna (-d-) *vb* name, call; mention by name
neinn (= **né einn**) (*n* neitt) *indef pron* no, not one; [*w neg*] (not ...) any
neitt *indef pron*, *see* **neinn**
nema *conj* but (that); (= **né**) nor
nema (nemr; nam, námu; numit) *vb* take; **nema á brott** abduct
nes (-j-) *n* headland, peninsula
neyta (-tt-) *vb* [*w gen*] use, make use of
né *conj* nor
niðr *adv* down; **setja niðr** settle (a dispute)
niðri *adv* down (in)
nítján *num* nineteen
níu *num* nine
Njáll *m* Njal (*personal name*)
norðanverðr *adj* northern
norðr *adv* north
norðrhálfa *f* northern region
norn *f* Norn
Nóregr *m* Norway
nótt (*gen* nætr; *pl* nætr) *f* night
nú *adv* now
nær *prep* [*w dat*] near
nær *adv* near, nearly
nær *conj* when
næst *adv* next (following); **því næst** then, next, thereupon
nǫkkurr (*f* nǫkkur, *n* nǫkkut) *indef pron* some, someone; one, a certain; (*n*) something
nǫkkut *n adj as adv* somewhat, in some degree (*see* **nǫkkurr**); **nǫkkut hafask at** undertake ('have at') something; **vera nǫkkut við** be somehow connected with
Nǫrvasund *n pl* the Straits of Gibraltar (*place name*)
Nǫrvi *m* Norvi (*personal name*)

O

oddr *m* point
of *adv* too
of *prep* [*w acc/dat*] over (*distance*); for, during (*time*)

ofan *adv* down, from above; **ofan frá** below
ok *conj* and (in addition); as
okkarr *poss adj* our (two); **okkrum mundi þykkja** it would seem to us
okkr *pron, see* **vit** (*see also* 16.3)
opt *adv* often
orð *n* word
orðinn *ppart, see* **verða**
ormr *m* snake, serpent
ormslíki *n* form of a snake
ormstunga *f* 'Serpent's Tongue' (*nickname*)
orrosta *f* battle
oss *pron, see* **vér** (*see also* 3.6)
otr (*gen* -rs; *pl* -rar) *m* otter
Otr *m* Otr (*mythological name*), Otter, son of Hreidmar
otrbelgr *m* otter skin
otrgjǫld *n pl* otter's ransom, wergild (blood money) for a dead otter
oxi (*pl* øxn) *m* ox

Ó

ó- (*also* **ú-**) *pref* un-, in-
Óðinn *m* Odin (*mythological name*), chief god of the Æsir
ójafnaðr (*gen* -ar) *m* injustice; unfairness
ójafnaðarmaðr *m* unjust man, quarrelsome and overbearing, difficult to deal with
Óláfr *m* Olaf (*personal name*)
ólíkligr *adj* unlikely
ólíkr *adj* unlike, different; **ólíkr sýnum** different in appearance; **ólíkari reyndum** more different in reality
ór (*also* **úr**) *prep* [*w dat*] out of, from; **ór hendi þér** out of your hands
óráð *n* evil plan, ill-advised plan
óreyndr *adj* unproved
ósáttr *adj* unreconciled, at odds
ótiginn *adj* not noble (of family), of common descent
óttask (-að-) *refl vb* fear
óvinr (*gen* -ar; *pl* -ir) *m* enemy
óœðri *comp adj* lower

P

penningr *m* penny, coin

R

Ragnarr *m* Ragnar (*personal name*)
rak *vb, see* **reka**
Randalín *f* Randalin (*personal name*)
rangr (*f* rǫng) *adj* wrong; crooked
rann *vb, see* **renna**
rauðavíkingr *m* 'red' viking, a particularly fierce and violent viking
rauðr *adj* red
ráð *n* counsel, advice, plan; match, marriage; **synja ráðs** refuse a proposal of marriage; **taka til ráða** adopt a plan
ráða (ræðr; réð, réðu; ráðit) *vb* [*w dat*] advise, counsel; decide, determine; control, rule, govern; prevail in; **ráða fyrir** rule over; **ráða um við [e-n]** consult with [sb]; **þá er eigi ráðit** then there is no help for
Refill *m* Refil (*mythological name*), name of a sword
Refr *m* Ref ('Fox') (*personal name*)
Reginn *m* Regin (*mythological name*), son of Hreidmar and foster-father of Sigurd
reið *vb, see* **ríða**
reiði *f* anger
reiðr (*n* reitt) *adj* angry, wrathful
reka (rekr; rak, ráku; rekit) *vb* be carried along, drift; **reka fyrir strauminum** drift with the current
renna (rennr; rann, runnu; runnit) *vb* run, flow
Reykjanes *n* Reykjanes ('Smoky Headland'), peninsula in Southwest Iceland (*place name*)
reykr (*gen* -jar; *pl* -ir) *m* smoke, steam
reyna (-d-) *vb* try, prove; experience; **reyna með** put to the test
reynd *f* experience; **reyndum** in reality
réð *vb, see* **ráða**
rétt *adv* straight (*see* **réttr**)

réttlátr *adj* just
réttr *adj* straight; right, just
ríða (ríðr; reið, riðu; riðit) *vb* ride, go on horseback; **ríða leið sína** ride on his way
ríkr *adj* powerful, mighty
ríki (-j-) *n* realm, kingdom; power; **setja til ríkis** put in power
rísa (ríss, reis, risu, risit) *vb* rise
róg *f* stife, discord
rógmálmr *m* metal of strife
runnu *vb, see* **renna**
rýrr *adj* thin
ræðr *vb, see* **ráða**
rǫdd (*gen* raddar; *pl* raddir) *f* voice
Rǫgnvaldr *m* Rognvald (*personal name*)

S

saga *f* story
sagði, **sagt** *vb, see* **segja**
salr (*gen* -ar; *pl* -ir) *m* room, hall
saltr *adj* salt(y)
saman *adv* together; **bera saman** collect, gather together
samr *adj* same
sá (*f* sú, *n* þat; *acc* þann, *dat* þeim, *gen* þess; *pl* þeir; *see* 12.1) *dem pron/adj* that (one)
sá *vb, see* **sjá**
sár *n* wound
sátu *vb, see* **sitja**
segi *m* slice, strip, shred
segja (sagð-) *vb* say, tell; **segja frá** relate, tell about; **segja til** tell, inform of
seinþreyttr *adj* slow to stir up; **seinþreyttr til vandræða** slow to be drawn into a quarrel
selagnúpr *m* 'Seal-Cliff' (*nickname*)
selja (-d-) *vb* deliver, hand over; **selja í hendr** turn over (to)
sem *rel pron* who, which, that; *conj* as; [*w subjunct*] as if; **sem mest** as much as possible; **þar sem** there where
senda (-nd-) *vb* send
serkr (*gen* -s/jar; *pl* -ir, *gen* -ja) *m* shirt
setja (-tt-) *vb* set, put, place; **setja [e-n] fyrir** order [sb] to keep watch; **setja niðr** settle (a dispute); **setja til ríkis** put in power; *refl* **setjask** settle oneself, sit down
sex *num* six; **sex tigir** *num* [*w gen*] sixty
sextán *num* sixteen
sé *vb, see* **vera** (*see also* 16.2)
sér *refl pron, see* **sik**
sér *vb, see* **sjá**
sigla (-d-) *vb* sail
sigling (*pl* -ar) *f* sailing; voyage by sail; **sjau dœgra sigling** a sail of seven days
sigra (-að-) *vb* conquer, vanquish, be victorious, overcome; *refl* **sigrask** gain victory
Sigríðr *f* Sigrid (*personal name*)
sigrsæll *adj* victorious
sigrumsk *vb, see* **sigra**
Sigmundr (*gen* -ar) *m* Sigmund (*personal name*); son of Volsung and father of Sigurd
Sigurðr (*gen* -ar) *m* Sigurd (*personal name*); legendary hero who slays Fafnir the dragon
sik (*dat* sér, *gen* sín) *refl pron* him-/her-/it-/oneself, themselves
silfr *n* silver
sinn *n* a time, instance
sinn (*f* sín, *n* sitt; *acc m* sinn, *f* sína, *dat m* sínum, *n* sínu, *gen m/n* síns; *pl m* sínir, *f* sínar, *n* sín, *acc m* sína, *dat* sínum; *see* 14.3) *refl poss adj* his, her, its, their (own)
sitja (sitr; sat, sátu; setit) *vb* sit
sitt *refl poss adj* (*n*), *see* **sinn** (*see also* 14.3)
síð *adv* late
síðan *adv* then, later, afterwards, after that
síðar *comp adv* later (*see* **síð**)
síðr *comp adv* less; **þótt ek ætla þat síðr mun vera** although I think that is less likely
sín, **sína**, **síns**, **sínum** *refl poss adj, see* **sinn** (*see also* 14.3)
sín *refl pron, see* **sik**
Sírekssstaðir *m pl* Sireksstadir ('Sirek's Farmstead') (*place name*)
sjau *num* seven; **sjau tigir** *num* [*w gen*] seventy

sjautján *num* seventeen
sjá (sér; sá, sá; sét) *vb* see
sjálfr *adj* self, him-/her-/it-/oneself, themselves
sjóða (sýðr; sauð, suðu; soðit) *vb* boil, 'seethe'
sjón *f* sight, eyesight
sjóni *m* 'The Seer' (*nickname*)
sjónlítill *adj* having poor eyesight
skal *vb, see* **skulu**
Skalla-Grímr *m* Skalla-Grim (*personal name*)
skammr (*f* skǫmm, *n* skam(m)t; *comp* skem(m)ri, *superl* skem(m)str) *adj* short, brief
skapa (-að-) *vb* shape, form
skarpr *adj* sharp
skaut *vb, see* **skjóta**
skáld *n* poet, 'skald'
Skáldskaparmál *n pl* 'Poetic Diction', the second section of *The Prose Edda*
skáldskapr (*gen* -ar; *pl* -ir) *m* poetry, 'skaldship'
skemmstr *superl adj, see* **skammr**
skemmtiliga *adv* entertainingly
skildi *m, see* **skjǫldr**
skilja (-d-) *vb* part, divide, separate; discern, understand; *refl* **skiljask** part
skilnaðr *m* parting
skip *n* ship
skipakostr *m* naval force
skipta (-pt-) *vb* [*w dat*] divide, share; **skipta í helminga** divide into two equal portions
skína (skínn; skein, skinu; skinit) *vb* shine
skírr *adj* pure
skírskota (-að-) *vb* refer to, appeal to; **þat skírskota ek undir þik** I call you to witness
skjóta (skýtr; skaut, skutu; skotit) *vb* shoot; **skjóta af** shoot with
skjǫldr (*dat* skildi, *gen* skjaldar; *pl* skildir, *acc* skjǫldu, *gen* skjalda; *see* 11.5, 17.6) *m* shield
skotit *ppart, see* **skjóta**
skógr (*gen* -ar; *pl* -ar) *m* forest, woods
skór (*dat* skó, *gen* skós; *pl* skúar, *acc/gen* skúa, *dat* skóm) *m* shoe
skreið *vb, see* **skríða**
skríða (skríðr; skreið, skriðu; skriðit) *vb* crawl, creep
Skuld *f* Skuld ('Debt'), one of the Norns
skulu (skal, skulu; skyldi; *pret inf* skyldu) *vb* shall (necessity); must
skúa *m, see* **skór**
skúta *f* small boat, skiff
skyldi, **skyldu** *vb, see* **skulu**
skǫmm *f* shame
sleikja (-t-) *vb* lick
slíkr *adj* such
smár *adj* small
smiðr *m* smith
smíða (-að-) *vb* work in wood or metals, make, build
smyrja (smurð-) *vb* anoint, 'smear'
smæri *comp adj* smaller (*see* **smár**)
snemma (*also* **snimma**) (*comp* snemr, *superl* snemst) *adv* early, soon
Snorri *m* Snorri (*personal name*); Snorri Sturluson, author of *The Prose Edda*
snúa (snýr; snøri/sneri; snúit) *vb* turn; *refl* **snúask** turn oneself
snær (*gen* snævar/snæfar) *m* snow
Snæfellsnes *n* Snæfellsnes ('Snow Mountain's Headland'), peninsula in Western Iceland (*place name*)
sofa (sefr; svaf, sváfu; sofit) *vb* sleep
Sogn *n* Sogn, area in Western Norway (*place name*)
Sólundir *pl* Solundir, islands off Sogn in Western Norway (*place name*)
sonargjǫld *n pl* ransom, wergild (blood money) for a son
sonr (*dat* syni, *gen* sonar; *pl* synir, *acc* syni/sonu; *see* 3.4, 14.4) *m* son
sól *f* sun
spakr *adj* wise
spekingr *m* wise man, sage
speni *m* teat
spilla (-t-) *vb* [*w dat*] spoil, destroy
spillir *m* spoiler; **spillir bauga** *poet* generous lord, spoiler (= distributor) of rings
spjót *n* spear
spyrja (spurð-) *vb* ask; **spyrja eptir** ask about
spýja (spýr; spjó, spjó; spúit) *vb* spew
staddr *adj* present; located
staðr (*gen* -ar; *pl* -ir) *m* place; stead,

parcel of land
Staðr (*gen* -ar) *m* Stad, a peninsula in Western Norway (*place name*)
stakkr *m* haystack
standa (stendr; stóð, stóðu; staðit) *vb* stand, be located; **standa milli** impede; **standa við** withstand
stangarhǫgg *n* Staff-Struck (*nick-name*)
Starkaðr *m* Starkad (*personal name*)
steði (-ja) *m* anvil
steðr *f pl, see* **stoð**
steig *vb, see* **stíga**
steikja (-t/ð-) *vb* roast
Steinarr *m* Steinar (*personal name*)
Steinbjǫrn *m* Steinbjorn ('Stone-Bear') (*personal name*)
steinn *m* stone; stone dwelling, cave
sterkr *adj* strong; **sterkr at afli** strong
stilla (-lt-) *vb* restrain, calm, still
stilltr *adj* calm, composed
stíga (stígr; steig/sté, stigu; stigit) *vb* step (up); **stíga á bak** mount on horseback
stoð (*pl* steðr) *f* pillar
stokkinn *ppart* spattered, stained (*esp* with blood) (*from* **støkkva**)
stokkr *m* stock of an anvil
stóð, **stóðu** *vb, see* **standa**
stóll *m* chair
stólpi *m* post
stórlyndr *adj* magnanimous
stórr *adj* big, great, important
stórráðr *adj* ambitious
stórskip *n* large ship
straumr *m* stream, current
stund (*dat* -u; *pl* -ir) *f* length of time, a while
stundum *adv* sometimes (*dat pl of* **stund**); **stundum... stundum...** sometimes... at other times...
Sturlubók *f* 'Sturla's Book', version of the **Landámabók** made by Sturla Thordarson
stýra (-ð-) *vb* [*w dat*] steer; rule, govern
støkkva (støkkr; stǫkk, stukku; stokkit) *vb* spring, burst, leap; be sprinkled, spattered
stǫng (*gen* stangar; *pl* stangir/stengr) *f* pole, staff
suðr (*gen* suðrs) *n* the south; *adv* southward
sumar (*dat* sumri) *n* summer
sumr *adj* some
sundr (*also* **í sundr**) *adv* apart, asunder
sunna *f* sun
sunnan *adv* from the south
sunnanverðr *adj* southern; **á sunnanverðum enda** on the southern end
Sunnudalr (*dat* Sunnudal(i)) *m* Sunnudal ('Sun Dale') (*place name*)
sú (*acc* þá, *dat* þeiri, *gen* þeirar; *pl* þær; *see* 12.1) *dem pron/adj* (*f*), that (one) (*see* **sá**)
Súrr *m* Sur (*personal name*)
Svalbarði *m* Svalbard ('Cold Coast'), archipelago in the Arctic Ocean (*place name*)
svalr *adj* cool, fresh
svara (-að-) *vb* answer, reply
svardagi *m* oath
Svartálfar *m pl* black elves
Svartálfheimr *m* world of the black elves
svartr (*f* svǫrt, *n* svart) *adj* black
svá *adv* so, thus, in this way; such; **svá ... at** so ... that; **ok svá** and also
sváfu *vb, see* **sofa**
sveigja (-ð-) *vb* bend; **sveigja at** deal with harshly
svelgja (svelgr; svalg, sulgu; sólgit) *vb* swallow
sveinn *m* boy, lad
sveiti *m* sweat; blood
sverð *n* sword
sverðsegg (-j-) *f* sword's edge
sverja (svarð-) *vb* swear
svipta (-pt-) *vb* [*w dat*] sweep, pull quickly
Svíakonungr *m* king of the Swedes
Svíar *m pl* Swedes
Svíþjóð *f* Sweden
svíkja (svíkr; sveik, sviku; svikit) *vb* betray
svǫrt *adj, see* **svartr**
syngja (*older* **syngva**) (syngr; sǫng, sungu; sungit) *vb* sing
syni, **synir** *m, see* **sonr**
synja (-að-) *vb* [*w gen*] refuse, deny
systir (*acc/dat/gen* systur; *pl* systr,

dat systrum, *gen* systra; *see* 9.5, 14.8) *f* sister
sýn (*pl* -ir) *f* sign, vision, appearance; **ólíkr sýnum** different in appearance; **fegri sýnum** more beautiful (in appearance)
sýna (-d-) *vb* show; *refl* **sýnask** [*w dat*] appear, seem (*impers*); **sýnisk mér** it seems to me
sæti *n* seat
sætt *f* settlement, agreement, reconciliation; **vera/verða at sætt** constitute a settlement or agreement
sættask (-tt-) *refl vb* become reconciled
sœkja (sótt-) *vb* seek; **sœkja sǫkum** prosecute
sœnskr *adj* Swedish
sǫgðu *vb, see* **segja**
sǫðull *m* saddle
sǫgu *f, see* **saga**
sǫk (*gen* sakar; *pl* sakar/sakir) *f* reason, cause, sake; prosecution, lawsuit; **sǫk til [e-s]** reason for [sth], cause of [sth]; **fyrir ... sakar** on account of, because of
sǫkkva (søkkr; sǫkk, sukku; sokkit) *vb* sink

T

taka (tekr; tók, tóku; tekit) *vb* take, catch, seize; reach, stretch forth, touch; receive (a person); begin; *refl* **takask** begin, happen; **taka af** take away, remove from; **taka á** touch; **taka hǫndum** take hold of, seize with the hands; **taka í sundr** cut in two; **taka til ráða** adopt a plan; **taka [e-m] vel** receive [sb] well; **taka við** receive; **taka undir sik** take charge of
tala (-að-) *vb* speak; **fegrst talaðr** most eloquent
Tálknafjǫrðr *m* name of a fjord in NW Iceland
tekit *ppart, see* **taka**
temja (tamd-) *vb* tame
tiginn *adj* noble (of family)
tigr (*gen* -ar; *pl nom* -ir, *acc* -u) *m* ten, group of ten; **sex tigir** *num* [*w gen*] sixty; **sjau tigir** *num* [*w gen*] seventy; **þrír tigir** *num* [*w gen*] thirty
til *prep* [*w gen*] to, until; for; with respect to, for the sake of; **til þess** the reason for this; **til þess at** to, in order to; **til þess er** until; **búask til** prepare for; **gera brúðlaup til** marry; **jafna til** compare with; **sem hon átti ætt til** which was characteristic for her family
til *adv* **vera til** to exist, be at hand; **bœta til um** improve; **ganga til** approach, go up to a thing; **leggja til (orð)** say
tíðendi *n pl* news, tidings; **er þetta var tíðenda** when this happened
tími *m* time; **þenna tíma** at this time; **í þann tíma** at that time
tíu *num* ten
topt *n* toft, site of a house; foundation or bare walls, ruins of a house
Toptavǫllr *m* Toptavoll ('Field of Ruined Walls') (*place name*)
tók, tóksk, tóku *vb, see* **taka**
tólf *num* twelve
trúa (-ð-) *vb* [*w dat*] trust
Tryggvi *m* Tryggvi (*personal name*)
tunga *f* tongue
tuttugu *num* twenty
tveir (*f* tvær, *n* tvau; *acc m* tvá, *all dat* tveim(r), *all gen* tveggja; *see* 14.1) *num* two
tyggja (tyggr; tǫggr, tuggu; tuggit) *vb* chew
tylft (*pl* -ir) *f* dozen, group of twelve; a half day's sail
tæla (-d-) *vb* betray; entice, entrap
tœki *vb, see* **taka**

U

ull (*dat* ullu) *f* wool
ullarlagðr *m* tuft of wool
um *prep* [*w acc*] around, about, in regard to; during, in (*time*); **um alla hluti** in all respects; **um fram** in addition; **um várit** in the spring; **bœta til um** improve
umhverfis *adv* around, round about

undan *adv* away; **biðjask undan** be evasive; **komask undan** escape
undir *prep* [*w acc/dat*] under
ungmenni *n* young people, children
ungr *adj* young; **á ungum aldri** young
unna (ann, unnu; unni; unnat) *vb* [*w dat of person, gen of thing*] grant, allow; [*w dat*] love
upp *adv* up (*motion*), upwards; **upp með** up along; **koma upp** come about, happen
Uppsalir *m pl* Uppsala ('Upper Halls'), a town in Sweden (*place name*)
Urðarbrunnr *m* 'Urd's Well' (*place name*)
urðarmaðr *m* outlaw; **gera at urðarmanni** to outlaw
Urðr *f* Urd ('Fate'), one of the Norns (*see* **verða**)
urðu *vb, see* **verða**

Ú

ú- *pref, see* **ó-**
úlfr *m* wolf
úr *prep, see* **ór**
út *adv* out (*motion*), outwards
útan *adv* from without, from outside; **fyrir útan** [*w acc*] outside; out beyond
úti *adv* outside (*location*)
útlenzkr *adj* foreign
útsjár *m* ocean

V

Valaskjálf *f* 'Vali's Seat' (*place name*)
valda (veldr; olli, ollu; valdit) *vb* [*w dat*] wield, rule over; cause
valði *vb, see* **velja**
vandliga *adv* carefully
vandræði *n pl* trouble, difficulty
var *vb, see* **vera**
varð *vb, see* **verða**
varr *adj* aware; **verða varr við [e-t]** become aware of [sth]
vaskligr *adj* brave, bold
vaskr *adj* brave, valiant
vatn (*pl* vǫtn) *n* water
vágskorinn *adj* indented (cut) with bays
ván (*pl* -ir) *f* hope; expectation, prospect
vándr (*n* vánt) *adj* bad, wretched
vápn *n* weapon; **bera vápn á [e-n]** raise weapons against [sb]
Vápnafjǫrðr *m* Vápnafjord ('Weapon's Fjord') (*place name*)
vár *n* spring; **um várit** in the spring
vár *pron, see* **vér** (*see also* 3.6)
várr *poss adj* our
váru *vb, see* **vera**
veggr (*gen* -jar/s; *pl* -ir) *m* wall
vegr *m* way, path, road
veiða (-dd-) *vb* catch; hunt
veiðr (*acc/dat* veiði, *gen* veiðar; *pl* veiðar) *f* catch
veikr *adj* weak
veit *vb, see* **vita**
veitt *ppart, see* **veiða**
veizla *f* feast, party
vekja (vakt-) *vb* wake
vel (*comp* betr, *superl* bezt) *adv* well, very, very much; **vel viti borinn** intelligent, endowed with good sense
veld *vb, see* **valda**
velja (valð-) *vb* choose, select
venja (vanð-/vand-) *vb* accustom, train
vera (er; var, váru; verit) *vb* be; **vera nǫkkut við** be somehow connected with; **vera til** exist, be at hand; **[e-t] er/var at** it is/was [sth]
verða (verðr; varð, urðu; orðit) *vb* become; happen, come to pass; **verða af** come about, appear; **verða [e-m] at meini** cause [sb] harm; **verða varr við [e-t]** become aware of [sth]; **eigi mun svá mikill brestr orðinn** such a great break is not likely to have occurred
Verðandi *f* Verdandi ('Becoming', *pres part of* **verða**), one of the Norns
verit *ppart, see* **vera**
verr *comp adv* worse (*see* **illa**)
verri *comp adj* worse (*see* **illr**)
verst *superl adv* worst (*see* **illa**)
verstr *superl adj* worst (*see* **illr**)
vestr *n* the west; *adv* west, westwards
vetr (*gen* vetrar; *pl* vetr) *m* winter; year (*in reckoning time*); **um vetrinn**

during the winter
Vé *m* Ve, brother of Odin (*mythological name*)
vér (*acc/dat* oss, *gen* vár; *see* 3.6) *pron* we (*pl*)
Vésteinn *m* Vestein (*personal name*)
við *prep* [*w acc*] with, to; at, by, close to; according to, after; **lifa við** live on, feed on; **mæla við** say to, speak to; **taka við** receive; **vera nǫkkut við** be somehow connected with
viðr (*dat* við(i)) *m* tree
vilja (vill; vildi; viljat; *pret inf* vildu) *vb* want, wish, will
vinátta *f* friendship
vinna (vinnr; vann, unnu; unnit) *vb* gain, win; work, perform, do; till, cultivate (land)
vinr (*gen* -ar; *pl* -ir) *m* friend
vinsæll *adj* popular, blessed with friends
virðask (-rð-) *refl vb* [*w dat*] seem, think (*impers*); **mér virðisk** it seems to me
vist (*gen* -ar; *pl* -ir) *f* food, provisions
vit (*acc/dat* okkr, *gen* okkar; *see* 16.3) *pron* we (two)
vit *n* good sense, wit, intelligence; **vel viti borinn** intelligent, endowed with good sense
vita (veit, vitu; vissi; vitat) *vb* know
vitja (-að-) *vb* visit
vitr (*gen* vitrs) *adj* wise
vígja (-ð-) *vb* ordain, consecrate
víking *f* sea-raiding; **vera í víking** be engaged in sea-raiding
víkingr *m* a viking, sea-raider
Vílir *m* Vili, brother of Odin (*mythological name*)
víss *adj* certain, sure
vænn *adj* fine, handsome, beautiful
væri *vb, see* **vera** (*see also* 16.2)
vættr (*dat* vætti, *gen* vættar, *pl* vættir) *f* creature, being; **ekki vætta** nothing at all
vǫllr (*dat* velli, *gen* vallar; *pl* vellir, *acc* vǫllu, *gen* valla; *see* 11.5, 17.6) *m* field
Vǫlsungr *m* Volsung (*personal name*); father of Sigmund
vǫxtr (*dat* vexti, *gen* vaxtar; *pl* vextir, *acc* vǫxtu, *gen* vaxta; *see* 11.5, 17.6) *m* size, stature; **mikill vexti** big, great in stature

Y

yðar *pron, see* **þér** (*see also* 3.6)
yðarr *poss adj* your (*pl*)
yðr *pron, see* **þér** (*see also* 3.6)
yfir *prep* [*w acc/dat*] over, above; **konungr yfir** king of
yfirkonungr *m* supreme king
yfirlit *n* look, personal appearance
yfirmaðr *m* leader, chieftain
Yggdrasill *m* the tree of life
Ymir *m* Ymir (*mythological name*, the first giant)
Ynglingar *m pl* line of early Swedish kings
Yngvarr *m* Yngvar (*personal name*)
yrði *vb, see* **verða**

Þ

þak *n* roof
þangat *adv* (to) there, thither; **þangat til** to there
þann *dem pron/adj, see* **sá** (*see also* 12.1)
þar *adv* there; **þar eptir** thereafter, accordingly; **þar sem** there where
þat (*dat* því, *gen* þess; *pl* þau; *see* 5.1) *pron* (*n*) it
þat (*dat* því, *gen* þess; *pl* þau; *see* 12.1) *dem pron/adj* (*n*) that (one) (*see* **sá**)
þau (*dat* þeim, *gen* þeira; *see* 5.1) *pron* they (*n and mixed*)
þau (*dat* þeim, *gen* þeira) *dem pron/adj* those (*n*) (*see* **þat** *and* **þeir**; *see also* 12.1)
þá *pron, see* **þeir** (*see also* 5.1)
þá *dem pron/adj, see* **sú** *and* **þeir** (*see also* 12.1)
þá *adv* then; **þá er** *conj* when
þáttr (*dat* þætti) *m* short story, tale
þegar *adv* at once, immediately; *conj* as soon as
þegnskapr (*gen* -ar) *m* generosity, open-handedness
þeim *pron, see* **þeir** (*see also* 5.1)

þeim *dem pron/adj, see* **sá** *and* **þeir** (*see also* 12.1)
þeir (*f* þær, *n* þau; *acc* þá, *dat* þeim, *gen* þeira; *see* 5.1) *pron* they (*m*)
þeir (*f* þær, *n* þau; *acc* þá, *dat* þeim, *gen* þeira) *dem pron/adj* those (*m*) (*see* **sá**; *see also* 12.1)
þeira *pron, see* **þeir** (*see also* 5.1)
þeira *poss pron* their, theirs
þeira *dem pron/adj, see* **þeir** (*see also* 12.1)
þeirar, **þeiri** *dem pron/adj, see* **sú** (*see also* 12.1)
þekja (þakð-) *vb* cover, thatch
þenna *dem pron/adj, see* **þessi** (*see also* 12.1)
þess *dem pron/adj, see* **sá** *and* **þat** (*see also* 12.1)
þessi (*f* þessi, *n* þetta; *see* 12.1) *dem pron/adj* this (one); **þenna tíma** at this time
þetta *dem pron/adj, see* **þessi** (*see also* 12.1)
þér (*acc/dat* yðr, *gen* yð(v)ar; *see* 3.6) *pron* you (*pl*)
þér *pron, see* **þú** (*see also* 3.6)
þiggja (þiggr; þá, þágu; þegit) *vb* accept
þik *pron, see* **þú** (*see also* 3.6)
þing *n* assembly
þingbrekka *f* slope on which assembly meetings were held
þingheimr *m* the attendance (those in attendance) at a **þing**
þinn (*f* þín, *n* þitt; *acc m* þinn, *f* þína, *dat m* þínum, *n* þínu, *gen m/n* þíns; *pl m* þínir, *f* þínar, *n* þín, *acc m* þína, *dat* þínum; *see* 16.4) *poss adj* your (*sg*)
þit (*acc/dat* ykkr, *gen* ykkar; *see* 16.3) *pron* we (two)
þín *pron, see* **þú** (*see also* 3.6)
Þjóð *f* Thjod ('People') (*place name*, modern province of Thy in Jutland, Denmark)
þora (-ð-) *vb* dare
Þorgeirr *m* Thorgeir (*personal name*)
Þorgerðr *f* Thorgerd (*personal name*)
Þorgils *m* Thorgils (*personal name*)
Þorgrímr *m* Thorgrim (*personal name*)
Þorkell *m* Thorkel (*personal name*)
Þormóðr *m* Thormod (*personal name*)
þorp *n* village, hamlet
Þorsteinn *m* Thorstein (*personal name*)
þó *adv* yet, though, nevertheless
Þóra *f* Thora (*personal name*)
Þórarinn *m* Thorarin (*personal name*)
Þórbjǫrn *m* Thorbjorn (*personal name*)
Þórdís *f* Thordis (*personal name*)
Þórðr *m* Thord (*personal name*)
Þórir *m* Thorir (*personal name*)
Þórólfr *m* Thorolf (*personal name*)
þótt (= **þó at**) *conj* [*w subjunct*] although, even though
þótti *vb, see* **þykkja**
þrettán *num* thirteen
þriði *ord num* third
þrír (*f* þrjár, *n* þrjú; *acc m* þrjá, *all dat* þrim(r)/þrem(r), *all gen* þriggja; *see* 14.1) *num* three; **þrír tigir** *num* [*w gen*] thirty
þrǫngr *adj* narrow
þurfa (þarf, þurfu; þurfti; þurft) *vb* [*w gen*] need, have need of
þú (acc þik, *dat* þér, *gen* þín; *see* 3.6) *pron* you (*sg*); **ór hendi þér** out of your hands
því *pron, see* **þat** (*see also* 5.1)
því *dem pron/adj, see* **þat** (*see also* 12.1)
því *conj* because (*n dat of* **þat**); **(fyrir) því at** because
þykkja (þótt-) *vb* [*w dat*] seem (*impers*); **Ásum þótti ørvænt hans heim** the gods gave up hope of his returning home; **okkrum mundi þykkja** it would seem to us
þysja (þust-) *vb* rush
þær (*dat* þeim, *gen* þeira; *see* 5.1) *pron* they (*f*)
þær (*dat* þeim, *gen* þeira) *dem pron/adj* those (*f*) (*see* **sú** *and* **þeir**; *see also* 12.1)
þœtti *vb, see* **þykkja**
þǫkðu *vb, see* **þekja**

Æ

Æsa *f* Æsa (*personal name*)
Æsir *pl of* **Áss**
æti *vb, see* **eta**
ætla (-að-) *vb* think, intend; agree

ætt (*pl* -ir) *f* family; **sem hon átti ætt til** which was characteristic for her family

ætti *vb*, *see* **eiga**

ævi *f* time, lifetime, age

Œ

œðri *comp adj* higher

œgir (*gen* -is) *m* one who frightens

œgishjálmr *m* helmet of dread

œrinn *adj* sufficient, enough

œska *f* youth, childhood

œxla (-t-) *vb* multiply, increase

Ǫ

ǫðru, **ǫðrum** *adj*, *see* **annarr**

ǫflugr *adj* strong, powerful

ǫld (*gen* aldar; *pl* aldir) *f* age

ǫll, **ǫllu**, **ǫllum** *adj*, *see* **allr**

Ǫlvir *m* Olvir (*personal name*)

ǫnnur *adj*, *see* **annarr**

Ǫnundr *m* Onund (*personal name*)

ǫr (-v-) *f* arrow

ǫrn (*dat* erni, *gen* arnar; *pl* ernir, *acc* ǫrnu, *gen* arna; *see* 11.5, 17.6) *m* eagle

ørvænt *adj* past hope; **Ásum þótti ørvænt hans heim** the gods gave up hope of his returning home

øxn *m*, *see* **oxi**

Øxna-Þórir *m* Thorir 'of the Oxen' (*personal name*)

FURTHER SUGGESTED READINGS
OLD NORSE - OLD ICELANDIC LANGUAGE, RUNES, SOCIETY, AND CULTURE...

THE VIKING LANGUAGE SERIES

A modern introduction to Old Norse language, runes, Icelandic sagas, Viking history and literature. Perfect for the modern classroom, online teaching, and the self-learner.

Viking Language 1: Learn Old Norse, Runes and Icelandic Sagas (2nd Edition) is a new introduction to Old Norse, Icelandic sagas, and runes. Everything from beginner to advanced in one book: graded lessons, vocabulary, grammar exercises, pronunciation, and extensive maps. Includes sections on Viking history, literature, and myth. Innovative word-frequency method greatly speeds learning and Modern Icelandic has changed little from Old Norse; students are well on the way to mastering Modern Icelandic. EBOOK AVAILABLE.

Viking Language 2: The Old Norse Reader is a treasure trove of Scandinavian lore, immersing the learner in a wide variety of Old Norse sources and runes. *The Reader* offers a large vocabulary, chapters on Eddic and skaldic poetry, and a full reference grammar: the latter can be invaluable while learning to read sagas. It includes complete sagas, runic inscriptions, myths, creation stories, legends, with Eddic poems about Scandinavian gods, monster-slayers, dwarves, giants, and warrior kings and Valkyries.

PRONUNCIATION ALBUMS

Audio Lessons 1-8, Audio Lessons 9-15

Two MP3 albums teach the pronunciation of saga passages and runes in *Viking Language 1*. The pronunciation is a slightly archaic Modern Icelandic as used in the saga and language courses at the University of Iceland. Both albums are available on Amazon and iTunes for download and purchase. **Check out free sample lessons at oldnorse.org.**

FURTHER OLD NORSE RESOURCES FROM JULES WILLIAM PRESS...

Old Norse–Old Icelandic: Concise Introduction to the Language of the Sagas answers the need for a modern method to learn the language of the sagas. This new primer requires no previous language knowledge, and the beginner quickly starts reading original passages from Icelandic sagas, mythological texts, and sources about the Viking Age. Designed for quick learning on one's own or in class, the lessons supply all necessary grammar, exercises, and vocabulary.

Supplementary Exercises for Old Norse - Old Icelandic complements *Old Norse-Old Icelandic: Concise Introduction to the Language of the Sagas* by providing additional exercises and vocabulary activties. Together, these two books make the sagas accessible for anyone learning Old Norse and the Viking Age.

AUCH IN DEUTSCH ERHÄLTLICH

(Also Available in German)

Altnordisch 1: Die Sprache der Wikinger, Runen und isländischen Sagas gliedert sich in fünfzehn inhaltlich aufeinander aufbauende Lektionen bestehend aus altnordischen Textpassagen, Runen, Grammatikbaukästen, Übungen, Karten. Das Buch enthält ein vollständiges Wörterverzeichnis, eine Kurzgrammatik sowie Hinweise zur (rekonstruierten) Aussprache.

The Viking Language Series is available as paperbacks and ebooks on Amazon (UK, US, DE, FR, IT, ES, JP, CA) and for booksellers on Ingram.

Free Answer Key and Audio Pronunciation Samples:
www.oldnorse.org.

JWP Jules William Press
juleswilliampress.com

OTHER WORKS BY JESSE BYOCK

Viking Age Iceland combines anthropology, archaeology, and history offering crucial insights into the Icelandic sagas and the inner workings of a feuding society with intriguing proto-democratic tendencies. Unusual for Western Europe, Iceland had no king, no foreign policy, no defence forces, and no great lords. It should have been a utopia, yet its sagas are dominated by blood feud and killings. Reasons for this, argues Jesse Byock, lie in the cultural codes and processes of conflict within the island's social order and the Viking world.

Feud in the Icelandic Saga explores conflicts at the core of the Old Icelandic sagas. Jesse Byock shows how the dominant concern of medieval Icelandic society was the channeling of violence into accepted patterns of feud and the regulation of conflict, processes that are reflected in the family and the *Sturlunga* sagas. This comprehensive study of narrative structure and the control of violence explores the sagas as revealing expressions of medieval social thought.

Printed in Great Britain
by Amazon

54248482R00111